WESTMAR COLLEGE

The Eckardts are members of the executive committee of Zachor: The Holocaust Resource Center and have participated in numerous national and international conferences on the Holocaust. In 1979 they were consultants to the President's Commission on the Holocaust, accompanying that body on a study mission to Poland, the Soviet Union, Denmark, and Israel. The Eckardts currently are members of the Department of Religion Studies at Lehigh University, Bethlehem, Pennsylvania.

W9-CES-830

LONG
NIGHT'S
JOURNEY
INTO DAY

LONG NIGHT'S JOURNEY INTO DAY

LIFE AND FAITH AFTER THE HOLOCAUST

A. ROY ECKARDT *with*
ALICE L. ECKARDT
Lehigh University

Wayne State University Press
Detroit, 1982

BT
93
.E25

Copyright © 1982 by Wayne State
University Press, Detroit, Michigan
48202. All rights are reserved. No
part of this book may be reproduced
without formal permission.

**Library of Congress Cataloging in
Publication Data**

Eckardt, A. Roy (Arthur Roy), 1918–
   Long night's journey into day.

   Bibliography: p.
   Includes index.
   1. Holocaust (Christian theology)
I. Eckardt, Alice.   II. Title.
BT93.E25   261.2'6   81-14788
ISBN 0-8143-1692-1   AACR2

Grateful acknowledgment is made to
the John M. Dorsey Publishing Fund
for assistance in the publication of
this volume.

The quotation from Elie Wiesel,
"Ominous Signs and Unspeakable
Thoughts," is © 1974 by The New
York Times Company. Reprinted by
permission. Quotations from *After
Auschwitz* by Richard L. Rubenstein,
Copyright © 1966 by The Bobbs-
Merrill Company, Inc. Reprinted by
permission of the publisher, The
Bobbs-Merrill Company, Inc.,
Indianapolis, Indiana.

101661

FOR ALECK
WHO HELPED ARREST THE
CANCER

ELLEN!
WHERE ARE THE CHILDREN?

Ilse Aichinger

CONTENTS

FOREWORD BY ROBERT McAFEE
BROWN   9

PREFACE   13

PERSONAL ACKNOWLEDGMENTS   15

1   RETURN TO THE KINGDOM OF
NIGHT   17

2   REMEMBERING   27

3   SINGULARITY   41

4   DANGERS AND OPPORTUNITIES   66

5   BETWEEN SERVITUDE AND
FREEDOM   82

6   LIBERATION   111

7   TURN TO THE KINGDOM OF DAY   139

NOTES   151

SELECTED BIBLIOGRAPHY   171

INDEX   196

FOREWORD

The Holocaust is everybody's problem. It is, self-evidently, a problem for Jews, suggesting that being God's people may be a curse rather than a blessing; it is a problem for Christians, whose abysmal historical record of antisemitism was a significant factor in Hitler's creation of the so-called Final Solution; it is a problem for Germans, under whose aegis and culture the genocide of six million Jews was sponsored and often enthusiastically endorsed; and it is a problem for all of us, since humankind in general was knowledgeable and often complicit in acts that almost succeeded in wiping out an entire people.

Correction: the Holocaust is everybody's mystery. "Problem" is not quite the word. In distinguishing between problems and mysteries in *The Philosophy of Existence*, Gabriel Marcel suggested that a problem is in principle soluable: there is an answer, and once we find it we have disposed of the problem. It does not continue to haunt us. We can forget it and move on to other things. Mysteries, on the other hand, can be lived within, can be explored and probed and examined. But we do not arrive at answers or explanations. We do not dispose of mysteries. They continue to haunt us. We cannot forget them and move on to other things. Sometimes they are mysteries of great hope and promise that enlighten us even if we cannot look directly at their source of light. And sometimes, as in the case of the Holocaust, they are mysteries of iniquity, of evil so deep and so dark that they seem impenetrable. We are not permitted, for that reason, to ignore them. If we seek to do so, we let iniquity triumph once more by depriving us of lessons we could have learned in order to forestall repetitions.

That is why the imagery of the Eckardts' title, *Long Night's Journey into Day*, is much more than a clever reversal of Eugene O'Neill's. Most of the book is about a nocturnal journey. Only fleetingly does day begin to dawn at the end. And that is as it should be. Any vision of dawn from such a night will turn out to be premature, a false dawn. Daylight here will not come automatically, as physical daylight comes to us. The psychic, even spiritual, daylight toward which this book points can be had only by hard effort, painful confrontation, and the shedding

9

of much intellectual and spiritual clothing we had thought would keep us warm in the night but actually was insulating us from the truth.

So this book is an act of remembering. Remembering has always been an important human exercise, but in relation to the Holocaust it assumes central importance. It has always been important to remember the Holocaust as response to that stern imperative on the monument at Treblinka: *Never Again*. But two new factors make the imperative even sterner. One is that before long all the eyewitnesses will be gone, and our remembrance needs further tutoring by theirs. The other is the emergence of a type of remembering that tells us to forget, that says it never happened, that says the Holocaust was a hoax, that says it was a plot orchestrated by Jews to gain world sympathy for the state of Israel. Such claims do not deserve the dignity of attention or rebuttal, and yet they exist, and they employ powerful weapons: they feed on the implicit antisemitism always lurking just below the surface of any culture; and they feed the insecurities of those who want very much to believe there never was a Holocaust—for if there never was a Holocaust, then we are not so bad after all, we did not do all those things we do not want to believe we did, and dignity is restored to the human venture.

Unfortunately for those who want a guilt-free humanity, and for the Jews who were the victims, the Holocaust did occur, and its immoral enormities are probably even greater than we yet know about. Only by remembering, then, can we avert a repetition. As the Baal Shem Tov said, in words inscribed at Yad Vashem, the Holocaust memorial in Jerusalem, "To forget is to prolong the exile; to remember is the beginning of redemption."

So this book, once again, is an exercise of memory. It cuts through many of the shields with which we protect ourselves from remembering, and (even more painful surgery) it forces us to reexamine the moral and theological postures from which we do our remembering. Constant reminders of the uniqueness of the events shatter our previous assessments. (Who would have thought that there were comparative and superlative forms of the notion of "uniqueness," as the Eckardts demonstrate early in this book?) And once for all (let us hope), this book shows that the Holocaust was not simply one further instance of the enormity of evil, but an event absolutely without parallel. Let it be forever registered on the human consciousness that Jews were killed not for *doing* what they did but for *being* who they were. Their "crime," punishable by death, was having the wrong grandparents. Refinement: one wrong grandparent sufficed.

The early part of the book is a universal dialogue with all people, whoever they are, about human responsibility and about craven attempts to evade it. No one can evade either the overt indictments or the overt challenges to learn from the past for the sake of the future. With the Eckardts we enter at least the outer precincts of night, as the only way we can ever be permitted to make our way back toward the day. The latter part is a particular dialogue within the Christian community. This is important not only because Christian history played so cooperatively into Hitler's hands, but because Christians were, with a few magnificent exceptions, complicit in the Nazi destruction of the Jews. And in spite of whatever difficulties Hannah Arendt's phrase "the banality of evil" may pose (especially for some Jews), it does serve as a pointer to Christians today not to diminish the enormity of what was done to Jews back then. It enhances the recognition that it was done by people frighteningly like us, who could probably do it again. We Christians have a special responsibility in girding ourselves to see that our own past history is not repeated, either by individuals or by institutions purporting to preach and witness in the name of Christ.

Since a dialogue is not meant to be a monologue, I respond to the Eckardts' book at two points where I hope the intramural Christian dialogue will continue.

First, this volume contains an extensive analysis of Jürgen Moltmann's theology after the Holocaust. While acknowledging the personal integrity of his attempt, the Eckardts find little else to commend. I see it as one of Moltmann's great virtues (theological as well as personal) that he continually moves away from safe areas and out onto controversial frontiers. He has done the same thing in relation to Latin American liberation theology, where he has been similarly challenged. Now it is not exactly a widespread characteristic of German theologians to leave their safe theological fortresses, and while Moltmann is not to be exempted from critical analysis, I hope that those dealing with Christian-Jewish questions, and also those dealing with liberation concerns, can see him more as a struggling comrade-in-arms than as one suspect within the ranks. It is those closest to us who usually receive our most vigorous pummeling, since we had expected them to come all the way toward us. Moltmann has surely been in the vanguard of the venturesome, and one must express gratitude for his rendering himself vulnerable in ways he could easily avoid if he wished to define his task by the time-honored rules of the academy.

My second demurrer has to do with part of the theological reconstruction to which the Eckardts call us. I affirm with them that any theology after the Holocaust that is going to have integrity must put up for grabs most, if not all, of what it previously held, and my own writing has centered on this theme for several years, not least because, having been confronted by the world of Elie Wiesel, I can never return to the world of my previous habitation. Some earlier Christian convictions are irretrievable in a post-Holocaust era, such as classical Christian notions of divine omnipotence and many conventional Christian ways of trying to establish clear equations between virtue and reward, sinfulness and punishment. Other convictions will need radical recasting, and among those I would place most interpretations of the Resurrection. In whatever way that event is to be a signal of hope, it is certainly the mark par excellence of what it means to call one's self a Christian. I cannot let go of the Resurrection claim to the degree the Eckardts seem to think we must, and I take issue with some of the implications they draw from the interpretation of Wolfhart Pannenberg, since I refuse to be bound by his interpretation in the first place. Much more is "salvageable" when one does not have to operate from within his particular view of what Christians are entitled to affirm or deny.

This is not the place to pursue such a discussion, and I note it partly in the hope that the writers of the present volume will be encouraged at the spectacle of pressing a fellow traveler on the "long night's journey into day" to fresh activity, and in the hope that their readers will be encouraged to pursue their own dialogues, either with the authors or with one another.

Robert McAfee Brown
Professor of Theology and Ethics
Pacific School of Religion

PREFACE

This study was initiated through a humanities fellowship from the Rockefeller Foundation, and we would like to express our appreciation to the foundation and to Lehigh University for aid and support. Our major research was undertaken at the University of Tübingen, the Center of Holocaust Research at Yad Vashem, and the Division of Holocaust Studies of the Institute of Contemporary Jewry at the Hebrew University. We have returned several times to Europe and Israel for additional research, and we have also participated in a number of national and international conferences on the Holocaust and on Christian-Jewish relations. In several European countries and in Israel we have conducted a number of oral history sessions with scholars, literary figures, psychiatrists, religious officials, and lay persons. In addition, written inquiries have been directed to respondents in different lands, within and outside the churches. In the summer of 1979, we were consultants to the President's Commission on the Holocaust, taking part in a fact-finding and study mission to Poland, the Soviet Union, Denmark, and Israel. All in all, our study and reflection have extended over a period of six years.

The "we" used throughout this book is not a literary device, but signifies joint endeavor. Alice L. Eckardt of the Department of Religion Studies, Lehigh University, has served as research associate and administrator of the undertaking, has contributed many ideas to it, and has done some of the writing.

In addition to library and other research, a congeries of personal experiences forms much of the background of this book. To mention a few of these: visits to the Anne Frank House in Amsterdam; pilgrimages to the sites of a number of concentration and death camps; a journey with a pastor from Reutlingen, West Germany, to an interfaith gathering in Strasbourg arranged by the secretary-general of the Jewish consistory of the Lower Rhine; a visit behind the Wall with the family of a theologian resident in East Berlin; a letter from an East German scholar stating that he would never collaborate in a project funded by "that capitalist Rockefeller Foundation"; encounters with distinguished literary personages and artists such

13

as Hermann G. Adler, Yehuda Bacon, Abel J. Herzberg, Abba Kovner, and Manès Sperber; participation in a long and vibrant session with members of L'Amitié Judéo-Chrétienne, Paris; and a journey with a Jewish friend to a small Polish village to meet the family that had hidden him, his brother, and his mother, at deadly risk.

We have used materials from some of our public addresses in this volume, along with a number of our journal articles listed in the Bibliography. We presented joint lectures before the Graduate Colloquium of the Institutum Judaicum, University of Tübingen, and in Jerusalem on two occasions, the one a public meeting sponsored by several Christian and Jewish ecumenical agencies and by the Hebrew University, and the other a private meeting of the Rainbow Group. One of us lectured on our subject at Yad Vashem and the other presented the 1978 Hugh Th. Miller Lectures at Christian Theological Seminary, Indianapolis. We have adapted these materials for present purposes.

This book is much more than the effort of just two people, even though we bear, of course, the only accountability for its contents and point of view. To list all the persons who have aided our work is impossible. We express gratitude to all. However, it would be immoral not to identify the individuals named in the Personal Acknowledgments. Beyond these, special thanks are tendered to Professor Gerhard Schulz and the Seminar für Zeitgeschichte, University of Tübingen, as also to Dr. Sherwyn T. Carr, editor at the Wayne State University Press, whose contribution to this work is as commanding as it is propitious. With typical competency and good cheer, Elizabeth MacAdam typed the original manuscript.

Without his knowing it at all, Elie Wiesel helped us to keep going.

The book remembers Captain Aleck C. Gaylor, U.S. Army (Ret.), friend of almost sixty years, who was gravely wounded in Germany during the invasion of Europe. The dedication is also a reminder that the Nazi destruction of the Jews was finally stopped by people and bullets and bombs, and not by such professorial strivings as this volume.

14

PERSONAL ACKNOWLEDGMENTS

The following are singled out either for the specific aid and counsel they gave us, or for contributing to the book's apperceptive mass, or both.

DENMARK

Anker Gjerding, Finn Henning Lauridsen

FRANCE

Bernhard Blumenkranz, Roger Braun, Bernard Dupuy, Marie-Thérèse Hoch, Edmond Jacob, Bertrand Joseph, Léon Poliakov, Roland de Pury, Åke Skoog, Manès Sperber

GREAT BRITAIN

Hermann G. Adler, Caesar C. Aronsfeld, Lionel Blue, Albert H. Friedlander, Charlotte Klein, H. David Leuner, Jonathan Magonet, Dov Marmur, Gerald Noel, Dorothy and James Parkes, Peter Schneider, Ulrich E. Simon

ISRAEL

Adina Achron, Ora Alcalay, Yitzhak Arad, Yehuda Bacon, Shalmi Barmor, Avraham Zvie Bar-On, Yehuda Bauer, Eliezer Berkovits, Clara Gini, Israel Gutman, Cynthia Haft, Gertrude and Rudolf Kallner, Hilel Klein, Abba Kovner, Avital Levy, Bernard Resnikoff, Livia Rothkirchen, Chaim Schatzker, Pesach Schindler, Coos J. Schoneveld, Verena V. Wahlen, Heinrich Zvi Winnik

15

THE NETHERLANDS

Yehuda Aschkenasy, Jan Bastiaans, Hendrik Berkhof, Rudolf Boon, Samuel Gerssen, Abel J. Herzberg, Louis de Jong, David Lilienthal, Cornelis A. Rijk, Avraham Soetendorp, Willem Zuidema

NORTH AMERICA

Robert McAfee Brown, Joel Colton, Yaffa Eliach, Robert Everett, Rose and Emil Fackenheim, Eva Fleischner, Blu and Irving Greenberg, Raul Hilberg, Claire Huchet-Bishop, David Hyatt, Josephine Z. Knopp, Nora Levin, Franklin H. Littell, Donald W. McEvoy, John T. Pawlikowski, Donald L. Ritter, Alvin H. Rosenfeld, Michael Ryan, Roger Simon, Diana and Eli Zborowski

NORWAY

Leo Eitinger, Oskar Mendelsohn, Magne Saebø

WEST GERMANY

Ulrike Berger, Otto Betz, Armin Boyens, Volkmer Deile, Wolfgang Gerlach, Dietrich Goldschmidt, Franz von Hammerstein, Kristen Hausen, Martin Hengel, Ruth and Heinz Kremers, Hans Küng, Pinchas Lapide, N. Peter Levinson, Pnina Navè Levinson, Friedrich-Wilhelm Marquardt, Reinhold Mayer, Jürgen Moltmann, Frederick B. Norris, Peter von der Osten-Sacken, Dieterich Pfisterer, Elisabeth and Rudolf Pfisterer, Wolfgang Pöhlmann, Rolf Rendtorff, Eleonore Schmeissner, Dieter Schoeneich, Carola and Klaus Scholder, Linda and Dieter Splinter, Martin Stöhr, Hans Stroh, Volker von Törne, Rudolf Weckerling

1

RETURN TO
THE KINGDOM
OF NIGHT

Had the Jew Jesus of Nazareth lived in the "right" time and "right" place, he would have been dispatched to a gas chamber. Many of the Nazi executions of Jews were carried out by believing Christians. When these two truths are put together, as, incredibly, they must be, the rationale of this book begins to express itself. We seek here to deal, in selected ways, with the contemporary impact and meaning of the Holocaust. Our approach is moral, philosophical, and theological.[1]

Can the Holocaust event ever be explained? Perhaps it is not explainable. A few singular persons have brought that event to the fore. Were it not for the work of individuals such as Elie Wiesel, the Holocaust would occupy a much lesser place in today's social conscience. Psychohistorically speaking, the passing of a full generation since the Nazi years has afforded a certain distancing that is important for scholars as a requisite to creative reflection and that has led a growing number of Christian and Jewish thinkers to grapple publicly with the subject. The concern of the Jewish community, generally considered, is quite transparent in its origins: the Holocaust is the most horrendous event in the long history of this people. Jewish thought and life have been shaken to the foundations. On the Christian side (from which the present writers speak), it is more and more acknowledged that what Jules Isaac called the "teaching of contempt" for Jews and Judaism helped make the Holocaust possible and perhaps even inevitable.[2] If only for this reason, the Holocaust is as much a Christian event as a Jewish one.

The vastness of the subject of the Holocaust and its aftermath, its many impalpable elements, and its severely controversial aspects make for a measure of pluralism and tentativeness within any effort to grapple with it. The pluralistic and provisional character of our understanding of the event is linked as well to the differing kinds of questions that analysts come to raise. Insofar as these parties involve themselves in problems of causation and social conditioning, they will consult sociohistorical and psychohistorical sources. Others, concerned with questions of meaning and value, will turn to literary creations and to philosophic and theological materials. Yet the lines are always crossing, for the latter sources are inevitably influenced by given social milieux, just as the former sources are conditioned by existential and moral experience. This means that to set one type of approach qualitatively above the other is not convincing.

DIE ENDLÖSUNG

Uri Zvi Greenberg's accounting in the prose poem "To the Mound of Corpses in the Snow" is an epitome of our subject. An SS officer demands that the narrator's father, an old man, remove his clothes. Never before had the holy man stood entirely naked even before his own eyes. When the officer saw that his victim still persisted in wearing underclothes, socks, and skull-cap, the brute struck him and he fell. "He gave a groan that was like the finishing of a last prayer, after which there is no more prayer, only a clouded sky, a heap of corpses, and a live officer." The blood from the saintly father's face turned the snow red. . . .[3]

Let us consider how the concept "Holocaust" is to be understood.[4] We resort to German phraseology for the sake of grappling, as though from inside Nazi demonry itself, with the eschatological and salvational nature of the *Judenvernichtung,* the total annihilation of Jews. The German Nazis determined upon *die Endlösung der Judenfrage* ("the Final Solution of the question of Jews"). This formulation was put forth officially on 20 January 1942 at a conference at Gross-Wannsee, although the actual decision was probably made earlier.[5] The Wannsee dictum was the logical consummation of, or it merely gave expression to, a resolve whose roots are traceable to 1919, when Adolf

Hitler declared that his ultimate objective was "the removal of the Jews altogether."

According to the minutes of the Wannsee Conference, the 11 million Jews of all Europe were marked for death.[6] Yet it is misleading to comprehend the Holocaust solely within the *Aktion* of simple killing.

The Endlösung means that everything is permitted now, any and every method is to be utilized in the struggle—indeed, in the *enjoying* of the struggle[7]—to obliterate the single pestilence that is destroying the entire world: the Jew. The German Nazis taught that the Jew is the *Untermensch*, the contaminator from below. Accordingly, his name is to be taken away; he does not deserve a name. He is only a number tattooed into his flesh.

The Endlösung is the competitive "race of the dead" at Treblinka and elsewhere, a physiological competition that makes one man's survival absolutely dependent upon the next man's extinction. For the "race of the dead" decreed which prisoners would be murdered and which ones "spared."

At the heart of the Endlösung is the utilization of Jews as officially selected agents for reviling and torturing their fellow Jews. The Jew is turned into the accomplice of his executioners. Thus, the Endlösung is ultimate degradation. It is the attempted dehumanization of the Jew, but also the torture process that makes this possible. The Endlösung is total mental, physical, and spiritual breakdown. It is the ontic separation of children and parents, wives and husbands. Child, parent, wife, husband—all these are enforced witnesses to the suffering and annihilation of their loved ones.

The chronology of what Jan Bastiaans calls "das perfide System" was: declare the Jew to be the *Untermensch;* then do everything to make him this, thereby vindicating your major premise; and only then, kill him. In this respect, the Endlösung had nothing to do with the specific advent of death, for the ultimate shamefulness lay in staying alive. Objectively speaking, death was transfigured into a form of mercy. Death became salvation—although, of course, the manner of death incarnated the dehumanization and was the mirror image of the terror. It is often said that the nightmares of the captives were more frightening than their encounter with death.

Speaking of life in the Vilna ghetto, Abba Kovner (who

helped lead the uprising there) attests that the most appalling thing was not death, but to be defiled to the depths of one's soul every hour of the day. But perhaps the ultimate in attempted dehumanization was the German Nazi effort to obliterate the Jews and Jewishness from all human memory. At the same time, we are not allowed to forget the complicity of those people and nations other than the persecutors themselves. There is much truth in Elie Wiesel's judgment that the victims suffered more "from the indifference of the onlookers than from the brutality of the executioner." Cynthia Haft writes that the futility of the agony is contained in the words "et ils savaient que vous ne pleureriez pas" ("and they knew that you would not weep").[8]

Again, the Endlösung reached out even to those who gave the appearance of surviving it. Many could not endure the shock of "liberation." They died. For vast numbers of those who lived, the years after release were as dreadful as, or worse than, the horror of the camps. Most sadly, some no longer retained the strength that human beings are required to muster if they are to be happy.[9] Thus, to be freed was, in many cases, not to be freed. How could these people adapt to a life that they had lost? Many lacked the power to retrieve their former world, a fight that would demand enormous inner resources. Even those with some strength left found that the old world was gone. Their loved ones and friends, their homes and their countries: all had been destroyed.

But the starkness of the horror of the Endlösung is not fully brought out until its official character is realized: the Final Solution was the official action of a great modern state.

Most of the Jews of Europe were simply trapped people; there was nothing they could do to elude a certain fate. Some, of course, were led to collaborate with the enemy, under a variety of those impulses that capture any human being who, facing persecution and annihilation, seeks desperately to escape. Yet collaborationism was relatively rare. It is of course the case that in the days and hours before death many victims had been brought to that terrible state which allowed no psychic possibility save "consent" to destruction. (The quotation marks signify the truth that these persons were in fact beyond compliance/noncompliance.)

We do not complete the correct usage of the term "Holocaust" until we include the fact of Jewish resistance to the German Nazi program.

The resistance was at once spiritual, moral, and physical. In Jerusalem the institution called Yad Vashem bears the official title "Martyrs' and Heroes' Memorial Authority."[10] Who is a martyr? Who is a hero? Among the greatest of these were the mothers and fathers who sought to comfort their children in the final moments before shared death. Many were the Jews who went to their destruction in quiet dignity. It is said that in their final hours, numbers of the pious ones danced and sang in celebration of their God—a protestation of faith in defiance of agents of antifaith. Nor can we overlook the massive effort to serve life, to maintain normality, even in the ghettos and concentration and death camps. Schools and literary clubs were organized; plays, lectures, and concerts were arranged; child care and charitable activities were fostered.

A number of Jews and Jewish communities engaged in physical and armed struggle against the foe. The Warsaw ghetto uprising is well known, the first armed revolt of any people within occupied Europe. There was a resistance movement even in Auschwitz.[11] There was an uprising at Treblinka, which, with outbreaks elsewhere, was inspired by the Warsaw revolt. The Treblinka revolt is even more unbelievable than that in Warsaw, because a murder center was the scene, and, at least indirectly, the aim of destroying Treblinka was achieved.[12] In at least one known though exceptional case, an entire Jewish village rose as a single person against the Germans: Tuchin (Tuczyn) in the Ukraine, with a population of some three thousand. About two-thirds of them escaped to the forests, although many of these were later delivered up by Ukrainian peasants. The Germans offered safety to any Jews who would return, and some three hundred foolishly accepted the offer. They were promptly shot in the Jewish cemetery. A few of the escapees got through and joined the Russian partisans.[13]

These and the many other acts of resistance refute the misleading and immoral stereotype that the Jews of Europe simply went as sheep to the slaughter.[14] In this resistance the kingdom of night was confronted by the kingdom of day.

Our understanding of the concept "Holocaust" itself poses

momentous questions. For example, what is the relation of the Holocaust to different "holocausts," to other acts of mass human destruction? This Holocaust, whose weight we have taken upon ourselves—in what ways is it a singular event? Such questions will exercise us throughout these pages.

There is the valley of the shadow of death. And there is the Endlösung, that much deeper valley of historical dehumanization, terror, agony, and final murder of the Jew only because he is a Jew. Yet there is also the historic resistance of the Jew to the war against him. A single light burns: the German Nazi campaign to dehumanize the Jewish people was a total failure. Jewry as a whole refused to fall to the level of the *Untermensch*. Only those who became the real *Untermenschen* did that: the enemies of the Jews.

DILEMMAS OF THE SCHOLAR

A student of the Holocaust and its aftermath may exhibit a form of detached, clinical objectivity.[15] In contrast, there is the approach of a participant, *un homme engagé*, an interpreter who insists that detachment is the adversary of human obligation. Along which path are we to make our journey? Or is it possible to travel both roads? It may be useful to include an autobiographical note, not for personal reasons, but because it bears upon the methodological and moral dilemmas that pervade our subject.

It was in an intellectual-experiential way that we came to the particular issue of the Holocaust, its meaning and its consequences. This occurred after we had attended for a number of years to the historical, ideational, and moral relationships between Christianity and Judaism, between Christians and Jews. Although it is the case that a beginning study in the latter general realm was prepared back in the immediate post-Holocaust time (1945–47), the effort was not primarily a response to the Nazi Endlösung, even though it did deal somewhat with that reality and sought to grapple with antisemitism, especially Christian theological antisemitism.[16] The bare truth is that we did not come to the subject of the Holocaust, nor earlier to that of Christian-Jewish relations, through any traumatic personal

22

encounters within or even outside the Europe of 1933–45. Rather, it was the anti-Jewish problematic within Christian teaching and the history of Christianity that finally led us, perhaps inexorably, to take up the Holocaust.

The last thing we should ever imply is that personal participation in, or victimization by, the Endlösung makes the survivor incapable of comprehending and of placing the evil within a broad and deep frame of reference. On the contrary, such direct confrontation may be of crucial aid in the achieving of a theory of the event, in the highest and most practical sense of that term. Jacob Robinson points out that the judgments of some authors are weakened by the fact that they never experienced the Holocaust (or any other mass disaster). Many writers did not even follow closely the development of the Endlösung.[17] By contrast, many who suffered in the Holocaust but who somehow managed or were enabled to survive it have attained, especially with the distancing years, a kind of creative objectivity in their very descriptions and assessments of Nazism.

Wherein, then, lies the relevance of our own accounting? There is the danger that the Holocaust will be appropriated only as a nightmare, a horrible episode that erupted within a brief span of years as part of a special ideological development or political tragedy or whim of an insane man, a nightmare from which we have long since awakened. There is the temptation to reduce the Endlösung to an aberration, a kind of cultural-moral mutation. In consequence, any comprehension of the event as the logical and even inevitable climax of a lengthy and indestructible ethos-tradition and Christian theological obsessiveness is readily lost. Against this eventuality, we must root ourselves in the fateful past—a possibility that has only of late gained a foothold within scholarly circles, and within and beyond the churches. We seek for the grace that may derive from a certain historical perspective, from a kind of distancing that is at the same time nearness. Captivation by and concern for the centuries-long story of antisemitism, and particularly the antisemitism that is fatefully linked to one's own religious tradition, may serve to contribute to at least three consequences: it will aid us in avoiding a facile approach; it will help to foster a concerned objectivity; and it may offset a little the personal condition of having passed the Holocaust years at a protected distance.

Those who contend that one must have been a part of the horror in order to write of it face the difficulty that no written word can equal the experience itself. It is a Holocaust survivor, and not a mere onlooker, who has written: "Perhaps, what we tell about what happened and what really happened have nothing to do one with the other."[18] True, the nonparticipant's writing is at least twice removed from the reality. However, the participant's writing remains once removed. In both cases there is a break with noumenal truth.[19] This is not to disagree that in principle, a qualitative difference obtains between literature that is once removed and writings that are twice removed. To those who say, you must have been within the inferno in order to approach it and write of it, we can only respond, with Cynthia Haft, that "we too want this event, so unique, never to be forgotten, that we too feel obliged to join with them in their efforts to remind others and to bear witness, without in any way violating the sanctity of the subject matter."[20]

We trust that the struggle against false objectivity is carried forward through the elements of personal encounter upon which, in considerable measure, this volume is grounded. There is no way to separate one's acts as a human being from one's work without falling into a certain personality split. The two elements are bound together within the larger category of "calling" (vocatio). Objectivity without commitment contains temptations—most lamentably, those of neutrality and coldness. This condition must be fought. It is a fact that the very study of the Holocaust's aftermath becomes, inevitably, part of that aftermath, part of Existenz. There is objectivity for the sake of truth, and there is subjectivity for the sake of goodness. Truth and goodness are not separable. The objectivization of the Holocaust—that is, the removal of, or the refusal to make, evaluative judgments about the event—constitutes, in effect, a justification of the German Nazi program. We either oppose Nazism or we support it; bystanders, by default, range themselves on the side of the supporters.

A further moral complexity manifests itself. Allusion has been made to the German Nazi device of setting camp inmates in competition for their very survival. We ourselves do not totally escape a related form of evil when we call attention to testimonies of, and accounts about, certain sufferers and not to

24

those of other sufferers. Such representations are inevitably caught up in personal judgment: this piece is "better" than that piece; this reference is "more memorable" than that reference; or, at the least, this one is to be called to public attention and not the other one. In a recent fine study, *The Holocaust and the Literary Imagination*, Lawrence L. Langer regrets having had to omit from consideration such works of unusual distinction as Piotr Rawicz's *Blood From the Sky* and Charlotte Delbo's *None of Us Will Return*. Although the purpose of our book is not the critical assessment of literature of the Holocaust, we are obliged to offer a parallel apology. But does an apology resolve the moral problem? What we do is to honor the memory of some human beings and let the remembrance of others die. Here is a special burden for writers, and particularly those who, like the present analysts, are not survivors. There is the added fact that those who work in Holocaust studies profit, if only in reputation, from human torment.[21]

As long ago as 1969, the novelist Cynthia Ozick declared that the Holocaust had become dangerously literary, dangerously legendary, dangerously trivialized to pity, and the pity to poetry.[22] Ozick was already telling us how embarrassing were the riches in the available literary, documentary, and oral-historical materials representative of our general subject, and it is true that the human proclivity to mythologize the past is universal and sometimes dominating. But we do not believe that pity trivializes the Holocaust, unless or until it becomes the exclusive response. Whether pity is trivialized in poetry, we are not competent to judge. However, the real stumbling block to agreement with Ozick is that writers today are forced into the creation and transmission of literature, legend, pity, and poetry in the very acts of observing and guarding against the dangers in these and other pursuits.

This leads us to one other fundamental dilemma. The problem is tied to the bafflement many have confessed before the *Judenvernichtung*. They ask: how is the unspeakable to be spoken about? We ought to speak of it all right, but how can we ever do so? Again, how are we to engage in scholarly work upon a subject that staggers the mind and stabs the soul: the human effects of *this* crusading-political-technological annihilation of an infinity of children, women, and men? We place the children first in our listing, as a reminder that their destroyers robbed them of human completeness. Woe to those who despise the little ones! (Matt. 18:10). Very largely, this book is nothing more than a sequel to a children's story of a dread kind. In the Holocaust some one and a half million Jewish children were destroyed. Most children were immediately put to death upon reaching the camps. The older and stronger ones were put to work as laborers, usually for about six months. Then they were murdered.

It is sometimes contended that the basic lesson of the Holocaust is that there are no lessons. The Endlösung is too shattering for us to learn anything from it.[23] We do not dishonor such existential skepticism when we point out that the noumenal and ostensibly mysterious character of the event is one thing, while the consequences the event has had and is having within human life and thought are quite something else. The asserted bafflement of some parties itself exemplifies the second of these categories. We allude now to the phenomenal impact of the Holocaust, noting the aptness of the ambiguity in the concept "phenomenal": the word has come to mean "powerful" and "decisive," while also retaining its philosophical connotation of "empirical" and "observable." (Yet in chapter 3 and beyond we dare to approach the noumenal dimension of the Holocaust.)

The imponderability and *mysterium tremendum* of the Final Solution, together with the varying attestations to silence before its unspeakableness, have not prevented the appearance of an incredible amount of materials on the subject.[24] In this respect, a problem shared by all students of the Holocaust and its impact is not so much how to speak of the unspeakable, as how to grapple with such a number of publications, documents, and oral and written testimonies, as at the same time they seek out fresh interpretations and venture ideas of their own. Our challenge, all in all, is one of apprehension, another aptly ambiguous word. The ambiguity in "apprehension"—standing as the word does for both the claimed receiving of truth and a certain anxiety respecting the future, including in the present instance the anxiety of harming human beings through one's research and writing—invests that term with a certain fearful propriety.

2
REMEMBERING

We have introduced our subject and spoken of certain dilemmas that face the analyst. In succeeding pages the challenge of moral obligation will occupy us, as this is interrelated with a continuing quest for understanding. This second chapter is concerned with a fundamental psycho-moral problem.

We consider one facet of the Holocaust's aftermath today, the issue of its remembrance as against its amnestia. "Amnestia" means oblivion, intentional overlooking, the exact opposite of "remembrance." We shall approach this matter through the enigma of responsibility and guilt. Our primary experiential focus will be West Germany.

THE TEMPTATION IN
REMEMBRANCE AND THE
DANGER IN AMNESTIA

Lawrence Langer contends that

the failure of the retrospective imagination to find meaning in history or in the consolations of tragedy dramatizes the absurd position of man as Survivor: the act of recollection, instead of forging links with the past, only widens the exasperatingly impassable gulf between the dead and the living, creating a void which makes new beginnings for the future equally impossible until some way of reconciling the fate of those dead with the present can silence the influence they continue to exert on the living.[1]

The stress upon remembering is not without its problems, its temptations.

What does it mean to remember the Endlösung? Can remembrance somehow contribute to the reconciliation of which Langer speaks? What is the purpose of remembering? Elie Wiesel has spent much of his life expressing such remembrance. Yet he himself has asked, "Remember what? And what for? Does anyone know the answer to this?"[2] What are the virtues, the necessities in remembering? Would it not be better to forget? Again, there is the most vexing question: *how* is the Holocaust to be remembered?

Because of the very nature of the Final Solution, its remembrance tends to open up certain moral and psychological dangers. Death and destruction ever draw unto themselves human fascination. What horror tale can possibly compare to the Holocaust, replete with piercing screams, silent but endless tears, rape, homosexual acts, flowing blood, and rotting corpses? The greater the horror, the greater the opportunity for macabre pleasures. That a pornography of the Holocaust should have long since developed may revolt us, but it can scarcely surprise us.[3]

The suffering of Jews has so impregnated our conscious and unconscious selves that our very study of it, our very attention to it, may well foster a kind of tacit or unconscious consent. Are we possessed of the inner resources and the will to keep the eye of our memory fixed where it belongs, upon the plight of the sufferers? Will not our gaze stray, ever so gradually, ever so imperceptibly, over to the persecutors, with hidden interest and secret sympathy, a sympathy so secret that we do not even confess it to ourselves? Those Nazis were men who rose above all inhibitions, broke all fetters, were prepared to tread down anything and everything that blocked their way. How grand it would be to be enabled to follow one's impulses, and without ever having to make any decisions! The blessed rules of the party render wholly unnecessary every burden of choice, every terror of responsibility. In a word, the superego is annihilated by the id. (The Führer taught that conscience is a Jewish invention.) May not the remembrance of the Holocaust, especially in its obsessional aspects, kindle a clandestine drive to repeat 1933, 1938, 1944? In gazing down into the Abyss, may we not open the abyss within ourselves?

It is on occasion claimed that anti-Jewish attitudes and behavior among some German young people today comprise a
means of getting back at Jews for making them feel guilty.
Jürgen Moltmann of Tübingen once suggested to us that in the
new antisemitism of younger people in Gemany, self-hatred
comes forth, gathering up "the hatred of the fathers." But from
the alternative standpoint mentioned in the preceding paragraph, self-love and self-assertion ought probably be added to
self-hatred. The weight of a guilty past is openly denied or at
least defied.

One member of the American clergy reported to us that
several Christian participants in a visit to the memorial of Yad
Vashem manifested hostility in face of all the remembering.
(Would this hostility have surfaced if guilt were not somehow
being summoned up?) A Roman Catholic priest who served as
an official Israeli guide told us that on one recent occasion some
members of a group of German clergy declined to enter the Yad
Vashem museum exhibit, protesting, "This has nothing to do
with us." If, as we shall be arguing, the Endlösung constitutes
the heritage of antisemitism in its final logic, may not the per-
petuators of Holocaust memories be inadvertently keeping alive
resentments and hatreds? May they not be acting, all unintentionally, in ways that sustain and aggravate *Judenfeindschaft*
("hatred of Jews")? This eventuality becomes a special menace
whenever charges of guilt are brought without proper discrimination and care. At a recent conference in Hamburg on the
Holocaust and the Church Struggle, Caesar C. Aronsfeld of
London objected to a concentration upon guilt and repentance,
contending that when people are forced to prostrate or humble
themselves, they will eventually turn upon the party they identify as making this demand. Nathan Rotenstreich of the Hebrew
University emphasizes that it is not easy to entertain or maintain feelings of guilt; they continually threaten one's pride and
self-righteousness.[4]

In addition, the plaint is often made that concentration
upon the remembrance of the Holocaust is a waste of energy
and has harmful consequences. Such effort only serves to keep
us from helping to resolve the really fateful problems that today
plague mankind and, if they are not solved, will lead to man's
extinction: the food shortage, overpopulation, pollution, waste-

fulness, annihilative weaponry—and, for that matter, genocides, not excepting potential genocidal acts against the Jewish people themselves. Every year, fifty million persons die of starvation, more than eight times the number of Jews that were destroyed by the German Nazis. A kindred attitude derives from a kind of baffled pragmatism. What, after all, can be "done" with the Holocaust? This outlook is exemplified in a statement by the German historian Golo Mann, son of Thomas Mann: "I think of Auschwitz once a week and have done so for thirty years. But you can't expect millions of Germans to don sackcloth and ashes and repent all the time. One likes to forget because what can you do with it?"[5]

If there are psycho-moral dangers in remembering the Holocaust, there are counterdangers in not remembering.

A former resistance fighter living in Israel, a man who advocates full discussion of the Holocaust, emphasized to us the unqualified right of individual survivors and their families to forget, if they so desire.[6] Here is suggested one of the moral complications within public Holocaust observances in Israel, from which, primarily because of the mass media, it is so difficult to escape. However, much depends upon who it is that is counseling forgetfulness, and to whom the counsel is directed. There is all the moral difference in the world between a plea by a Jewish spokesman that his people turn away from the horrors of yesteryear, and the actual pronouncement of the West German chancellor (on the thirtieth anniversary of his people's surrender) that Germans have learned their lesson from the past. One may argue with the first party without necessarily charging him with an ideological taint or hypocrisy, but the issue of self-deception and the deception of others is unavoidably raised with respect to the second party. This latter response is also prompted by a moral reaction to the pervading public viewpoint within today's West Germany that the media ought not dwell any longer upon the Nazi atrocities. The same critical response may be called for against all those whose counsel of forgetting is demonstrably accompanied by insensitivity or by antisemitic attitudes. In a word, there is a licit forgetting and there is a culpable one.

A certain professor in a West German university has sent the Holocaust off to oblivion. That is to say, she simply refuses

to discuss the event and its meaning. "Go talk to the murderers," she has said. "Do not ask us who are Jews. It is their
problem, not ours." Such an effort to obliterate truth is perhaps
understandable, although in this particular case the individual
is not a direct survivor of the persecutions. She early succeeded
in fleeing to Palestine and only much later returned to teach in
West Berlin. (Here may lie part of her problem; very many
authentic survivors are now fully able to speak of their experiences.) This woman gave every evidence of being unable to
face the facts of the Holocaust. Yet as a historical scholar, if not
as a human being, she has no real alternative but to assent to its
actuality. She, can hardly function as a teacher should she fail,
time after time, to deal with student queries on the subject. A
possible outcome of her condition is some kind of splitting of
the personality.

The foregoing case is extreme, but it comprises a relevant
witness to the truth that while the remembrance of the
Endlösung carries psycho-moral dangers, a tacit or advocated
forgetfulness bears equal or greater dangers. Personality
wholeness and psychic health demand a reasonable harmony
among the volitional, affective, and cognitive dimensions of
the self. In a vital sense, this is also true at the collective level.
In the words of Harvey Cox, "psychiatrists remind us that the
loss of a sense of time is a symptom of personal deterior-
ation. . . . The same is true for a civilization. So long as it can
absorb what has happened to it and move confidently toward
what is yet to come its vitality persists." Alienation from the
past induces decline and ultimately death.[7]

The Israeli psychiatrist Hilel Klein stressed to us what he
called "the essential historical continuity of the generations."
When parents have not discussed, or have been unable to discuss, their Holocaust experiences, their offspring have tended
to develop psychiatric problems. For example, the children
very often conclude that they have to be ashamed of their
family history. Discontinuity between the generations com-
pounds the development of fantasies and leads to mental ill-
ness. Klein insists that remembrance is essential to individual
and social health. The truth must be known. It must be known
by all.[8]

One rejoinder to the counselors of amnestia is that avoidance, suppression, and repression are aspirin tablets in the treating of cancer. The disease quickly reasserts itself, and when this occurs, the forms are often as terrible as before. Nor does the passage of years necessarily help. Thus, in what has come to be called the post-concentration-camp syndrome, the longer the lapse of time, the more serious the survivors' symptoms and suffering. A final horror of the German Nazi system is its power to reach beyond the generations it ravished, taking unto itself new victims. It is doing so at this very moment. Where, then, is the moral legitimacy in arguing that the Holocaust belongs to the past and ought to be forgotten?

Jürgen Moltmann has voiced concern that his people have suppressed and repressed their dark history. He says, "German guilt was never given expression, and so it could not be forgiven." In *Die Unfähigkeit zu Trauern* ("The Inability to Mourn"), Alexander and Margarete Mitscherlich have argued, from a depth-psychological perspective, that there has not been a sufficient and repentant working through and out of the guilt of the Third Reich in postwar Germany. The Israeli poet Abba Kovner attests that in accordance with "the way of our forefathers," penitence must take priority over mourning.[9] In the present context, the decisive question is one of penitence and confession rather than that of mourning. The phrasing "inability to mourn" suggests only that certain deaths have occurred that appear to be incapable of inducing proper weeping and sorrow. The alternative concept, "inability to repent," conveys a blockage in penitence respecting transgressions for which men are responsible.

In German writing and discourse of recent years a certain phrase appears again and again: *eine unbewältigte Vergangenheit*, "a past that remains unmastered." (The expression has even become somewhat banal.) Is the German past in fact unredeemed? Or is there legitimacy in speaking of its having been mastered (*die Bewältigung der Vergangenheit*)? Culpability for the Endlösung has sometimes been narrowed down to the reputed insanity of one man (but if Hitler was insane, he could hardly be blameworthy), or to his sane but all-destructive ambitions. Less restrictedly, the blame has been assigned to the relatively small Nazi elite. The moral-historical fault in both these attributions is the ignoring of "the facts of participation by tens of thousands of Germans (and their satellites) in the physical destruction of millions of Jews. . . . Many of them could have avoided this awesome responsibility had they wished so."[10]

We have been using the phrases "German Nazis" and "German Nazi system." The wording is carefully chosen. To speak only of "Nazis" would be to misrepresent the truth of the wider and deeper German condition. But to speak only of "Germans" would mean lack of discrimination and fair-mindedness. Furthermore, the designation "Germans" would not wholly avoid self-idolatry. As the noted Dutch Jewish writer Abel J. Herzberg insists, were we ever to claim that Nazi behavior was exclusively German, we should be pretending that we could never stoop to it ourselves. However, the phrase "German Nazis" is not felicitous from an objective, descriptive standpoint. It fails to convey non-German complicity in the destruction of European Jewry and in abiding antisemitism. When, for example, President Franklin D. Roosevelt was asked, five days after the Nazi pogrom of 9 November 1938, whether American immigration restrictions against Jews would be eased, he replied with a sharp and unqualified no.[11]

The linguistic-moral challenge is how to avoid exculpating guilty parties while at the same time not being unfair. No single expression is sufficiently comprehensive to convey the breadth and depth of complicity in the Endlösung. To resort to such phrasing as "enemies of Jews" would be to fall into abstraction and to obscure responsibility, yet the phrasing "German Nazis" hardly overcomes our predicament. In this phrasing a problem is stated; it is not resolved. We are confronted by a special and overwhelming case of the human mystery of responsibility and guilt.

The English word "responsibility" is ambiguous, denoting both accountability and culpability. From the standpoint of moral philosophy, the entire human condition can be epitomized in and through this ambiguity. If man as man is responsible (*verantwortlich*, "accountable"), when is he also responsible (*strafbar*, "culpable")? Furthermore, the special enigma of collective guilt has always beset moral, philosophical, and theological reflection; it is most doubtful that the analysis before the reader will dispose of the question of social guilt/guiltlessness, of moral responsibility/nonresponsibility. However, we may not forget Dostoevsky's insistence that to deprive man

33

of responsibility for his acts is to lower him to a subhuman level and to rob him of his dignity.

SIX MORAL-HISTORICAL PROPOSITIONS

The responsibility of the German people (*Verantwortlichkeit* and *Strafbarkeit*) for the Holocaust years is a less controversial matter than the question of German guilt allegedly persisting into the post-Holocaust period. We venture upon several comments, in no way as a device for resolving the vexing and profound problem before us, but only as a possible means of living with its afflicting presence. None of us escapes the shattering questions: where are you (Gen. 3:9)? What are you doing with that one space which you now fill? How are you expending your one life? What choices are you making? What decisions are you reaching and following out?

1. *Historical memory must take all available facts into account.*

Exemplification of this proposition is forthcoming from any and every quarter, and certainly as much from anti-German data as from data that are more sympathetic. Yet it is a moral fact that many Germans were victims and not victimizers. Many of them fitted both these categories.

Just east of Tübingen lies the village of Pfrondorf, where we resided while conducting part of our research. There was once a farmhouse on the very spot where we found quarters. In World War II the dwelling was destroyed by an aerial bomb, reportedly with no warning. Were there children in the house? Did they die in the explosion? One could easily call upon much more dramatic and terrible events, such as the firebombing of Dresden. We allude to this particular instance only because the questions about the children kept repeating themselves to us, a fact doubtless occasioned by the personal circumstances. We never were able to secure any pertinent information.

2. *A blighted historical memory is not restored to health so long as its original and fundamental inspirations remain within the body politic.*

It is well known that neo-Nazism has been spreading within West Germany. Scores of our informants in that country have emphasized that a latent, fearsome anti-Jewishness continues to exist there. A sociological study helps to sustain this judgment. A survey conducted at the Institute for Sociological Research of the University of Cologne found that every second person in West Germany harbors some kind of adverse opinion of Jews. Of these, 15 to 20 percent manifest "distinct antisemitic prejudices of different kinds," while another 30 percent have "latent antisemitic prejudices." The most severe prejudices are found among farmers in the southern part of Germany (a small segment of the population), of whom 52 percent contend that the persecution of the Jewish people is deserved punishment for "their" crucifixion of Jesus.[12] The Cologne study has been criticized for, among other things, employing a type of leading question that tends to weight results on the side of an expression of derogatory attitudes.[13] With due allowance for the probability of exaggeration in the survey findings, it remains the case that those of today's antisemitic people who were living in Germany in 1933 to 1945 would have supported the Nazi anti-Jewish ideology and program, or at least probably would not have opposed Nazism. And, just as evidently, any present or future assault upon Jewish existence would be welcomed or condoned by these people. In the frame of reference of the Holocaust's aftermath, what term other than "collective guilt" can accurately describe the objective moral condition of antisemites in Germany today?

3. *Although precise lines can never be drawn between authentic nonresponsibility and culpable responsibility, the truth is that historical memory is readily seduced by irresponsibility.*

Within humanness—that is, within "radical freedom" (as Reinhold Niebuhr defines humanness)—irresponsibility is an ever-present temptation. Indeed, there could be no such thing as moral obligation without the immanent potentiality of its denial, a denial capable of marshaling great force.

More than once, in different sections of Germany, we were told that Nazism was of course much worse, and was accepted and practiced much more, in regions of the country other than those represented by our informants. The script seemed to read: "Oh, yes, I remember all right. But it did not

35

really happen here. It happened over there." In effect, this means: "We were only the victims; it was they who were the victimizers." These informants were playing the knave at the point of both space and time. It is contended above that historical memory is subject to judgment by the facts. The principle applies equally here.

Jürgen Neven-du Mont's apologetic report upon Heidelberg in *After Hitler* helps sustain the fantasy and deception according to which Nazi behavior was always something that involved the other people. I and my parents and relatives would never take part in such harmful acts, and neither would anyone I know (including, for that matter, party members). Even supporters of the regime did not, so one woman put it, "do bad things."[14] In a word, we are all good people. The truly fanatical Nazis and their supporters are invariably off somewhere else. But if that is so, then just where are they? It is as though Nazism has vanished into the clouds. Were one fully to accept this testimony, he would have to begin wondering how all the people could ever have been killed. The next step would be to ask himself, were they really killed? The final step, perhaps, would be the publication of a work denying that the Holocaust ever occurred.[15]

Among the possible motivations for such testimony is the evident one of seeking to get out from under any form of moral responsibility, of attempting to dissociate oneself from any kind of blame. (Some Germans today claim to have had a place in the resistance movement that they did not in truth have.)

4. *One powerful force in the evasion of the moral demands of memory is the elevating to sovereignty of the self-contained individual.*

It is a historical-moral truism that before the dawn of individual conscience and individuality as we have come to think of these realities, the human being felt himself bound by and responsible for the behavior of his group. One dilemma within any modern moral philosophy concerns the measure in which the total emancipation of the person from collective fate may foster an inadvertent break with humanness. For is it not so that to be human is to belong to, and to be responsible for, the other? From this latter standpoint, atomistic individualism comprises an assault upon the integrity and dignity of the person.

Very few will argue that Germans born during or after the

Nazi period bear "the sins of the fathers" in the sense that these younger ones are subject to guilt and punishment. But are we to conclude, morally speaking, that all the links between the generations can be or ought to be severed? A few German young people have told us that they do feel a special responsibility, on the very ground of their personal identity. They confront themselves with a special obligation to do what they can to see to it that a crime such as the Holocaust does not recur. Their moral outlook recognizes the truth that even though personal guilt is lacking, they have nevertheless "inherited a dark legacy . . . from whose implications and consequences they are unable, if they are sensitive, to dissociate themselves."[16] The decisive words here are "if they are sensitive." And, in point of fact, the "dark legacy" will often adversely affect the younger generation even when sensitivity is lacking and the power of the past is not acknowledged.

In the above context, a distinction may be introduced between the absence of personal culpability and the presence of personal shame.

5. *Some human beings bring themselves to accept a responsibility that, morally considered, is not directly theirs.*

Some individuals will to remember. The guilt they assume is borne vicariously. The memory they forge is an act of grace. This memory then helps to determine their lives, for they incarnate their remembrance within deeds that cannot justly be demanded of them.

We think immediately here of the original purposes behind the founding of the German Reconciliation and Peace Movement (*Aktion Sühnezeichen/Friedensdienste*). Begun in 1958 under the inspiration of two church leaders, Lothar Kreyssig and Franz von Hammerstein, the group started by bringing together teams of German young people who would surrender paid employment or formal education for a year or more in order to engage in volunteer work projects within different lands, including Israel. The initial intent of the organization included the quest for forgiveness and reconciliation, in light of the crimes against Jews and other reputed enemies of the Third Reich. Particularly in the earlier years, participants in this work specifically willed to take upon themselves the sins of their fathers.[17]

6. *One objective way to approach the subjective, psycho-moral condition of a people is through an inquiry into the presence or absence among them of rectifying deeds.*

"You shall know them by their fruits" (Matt. 7:16). How can men legitimately forget their past until they come to terms with it by means of acts? In the measure that rectifying deeds are done, it becomes right to adjudge that the evil chapter of the past ought to be closed and its memory laid to rest. We are then supplied with evidence that the past has been internalized, taken into the collective corpus. But insofar as the deeds are lacking, remembrance is a festering wound, and the nagging question remains: who is entitled to forget?

In today's world, one decisive means of assessing the practical outlook and the moral condition of a people is through the actions of its government. We are permitted to speak here only of the democratic world; accordingly, East Germany is excluded from present consideration. Individual Germans and nonofficial groups in Germany—including church bodies—do of course engage in many charitable and otherwise praiseworthy enterprises. Such acts can only impress and gratify the visitor. Again, the official program of *Wiedergutmachung* ("reparation") to Israel and individual Jews has done much to ease the collective conscience. Yet the truth persists that a primary test of the moral condition of a sovereign people is the continuing, contemporary policies of the government it elects. Within modern civilization, excepting such special times as emergencies brought by natural catastrophes, particular polities have dealings only with other polities.

The implication of the above truth is fairly obvious. A crucial and relatively precise means of applying our sixth proposition to the German condition today is through reference to official government policy toward Israel, for the latter polity comprises the one discriminate Jewish entity to which the German polity is now and can be related. In consequence, we are brought to ask if today's official German policy toward Israel is of such a nature as to justify the conclusion that the remembrance of the Endlösung is morally decisive. As we consider the international scene, is it the case that German policy toward Israel differs qualitatively from the policies of other states which recognize the Jewish polity? Is Chancellor

Schmidt substantially justified in his judgment that his people have learned their lesson from the past?

There are serious differences of opinion on this subject. Our own persuasion is that contemporary German policy offers no special evidence to support affirmative answers to the questions just raised. The archbishop of Munich-Preising, Julius Cardinal Döpfner, declared shortly before his death that it is the duty of all Germans to support the Jewish people in the face of the latter's virtual isolation in world politics, a duty that is rooted in "the full responsibility that [the Germans] must bear with regard to the Jews."[18] Where are the data to show, over subsequent years, that the Federal Republic of Germany has met or even approximated the test implied in Cardinal Döpfner's words? In what ways is Germany specially dedicated to the well-being and survival of the state of Israel? Amidst continuing threats to the life of Israel, Germany's behavior has hardly manifested the distinctiveness that appears to be incumbent upon it because of its Holocaust past.

Should the rejoinder be forthcoming, perhaps in the name of Reinhold Niebuhr and the theology of political realism, that nations do not repent, do not incarnate the altruistic spirituality that is sometimes attained by smaller groupings and particularly by individuals, we may respond that this is not the point at issue. Niebuhr's finding with respect to the morality or immorality of nations is essentially sound. However, we are not here involved in the question of how nations behave, but rather in the question of the ethical criteria that are to be adduced in order to judge whether claims concerning national moral health are convincing or truthful. It is overwhelmingly probable that West Germany will continue to make decisions respecting Israel and the Middle East conflict on the basis of perceived self-interest. We simply inquire: what is the moral status and where is the moral convincingness in Schmidt's testimony, "We have learned our lesson from the past"? Nation-states and their representatives are probably not capable of choosing between perfection and imperfection. But they are never deprived of the choice between hypocrisy and ordinary decency. They always retain the choice of keeping silent. Had the German chancellor kept silent, he could hardly be accused of representative hypocrisy. But he did not do this. He spoke.

The question of the remembrance or amnestia of the Holocaust penetrates our entire study. For the present, two citations are offered. The first is from *Das Brandopfer* of Albrecht Goes: "there comes a time for forgetting, for who could live and not forget? Now and then, however, there must also be one who remembers."[19] The second is from the Baal Shem Tov: "To forget is to prolong the exile; to remember is the beginning of redemption." These words are inscribed upon a wall at Yad Vashem.

3

SINGULARITY

One compelling reaction to the Holocaust is the claim that the event is unique. Our next task is to consider the force of this claim, together with some of its possible applications. The problem of uniqueness is shared by interpreters of the Holocaust who speak from all kinds of viewpoints. Our analysis in chapter 1 of the meaning of the Final Solution has already pointed to the singularity of the event.

A friend has said, "I suppose it was the worst thing that ever happened."[1] A survivor of Auschwitz, testifying at the trial of Adolf Eichmann in Jerusalem, told of what he called "the history of the Auschwitz planet."

> The time there is not a concept as it is here in our planet. Every fraction of a second passed there was at a different rate of time. And the inhabitants of that planet had no names. They had no parents, and they had no children. They were not clothed as we are clothed here. They were not born there and they did not conceive there. They breathed and lived according to different laws of Nature. They did not live according to the laws of this world of ours, and they did not die.[2]

Among the reasons for the obscuring of the Holocaust and its distinctiveness is the omnipresence of human suffering and violence in our time. It is not that these realities are now so monstrous and all-pervasive that we have become obsessed with them. We suggest a much more radical interpretation. Hannah Arendt spoke of "the banality of evil." Emil Fackenheim is quite right that the risk in subscribing to this idea, as an overall historical interpretation, is that we fall into the trap set

41

by the Nazis, who sought to make absolute evil into something routine and boring.[3] There is, nevertheless, an uncanny truth in Arendt's phrase. Evil becomes so terrible that it is no longer terrible. The incredible paradox is that final horror becomes trivial. Accordingly, it is no longer capable of gaining attention. It is boring. Or it is not even that. It is nothing at all.[4]

There is a universalism that is blind and even callous in the presence of particularity. There is a particularism that does not see beyond one's own plight. We are called upon to take a dialectical approach here, to make evident a two-sided truth: each instance of human agony is at one and the same time bound up with all other such cases, and yet it remains sui generis. Unless we maintain both these elements—the factor of continuity and the factor of discontinuity—we end up dishonoring the memory and the name of one or another human sufferer. The insistence that the misery of a single human being in any time or place is "equivalent to" the agony of six million Jews conveys the necessary recognition of the element of continuity. (Taken in and of itself, there is nothing singular in the figure of six million. Out of five and a half million Russian prisoners of war in Germany, some four million were killed.) And the insistence that the Holocaust of the German Nazis "contains no historical or moral parallel" conveys the necessary recognition of the element of discontinuity. The two kinds of declaration have to be made together, for the foundational reason that human suffering is not a quantitative matter subject to some form of objective measurement, but is instead a qualitative condition to be apprehended in existential terms, through the faculty of sympathy. Whenever the stress on continuity is abandoned, the solidarity of all human beings in suffering is lost. (Paradoxically, the special agony of the Jewish people is lost as well, for it is then deprived of its human reality.) But whenever the stress on discontinuity is abandoned, the integrity of the Jewish sufferers is flouted and is dissolved into something abstract. It is often pointed out that the greatest insult to the Jewish victims of the Nazis is to subsume their plight under the generalizing category of mass agony, or, worse, of "war crimes."[5] To address the Holocaust survivor by reminding him of the horrors of, say, Vietnam is obscene. It dishonors his dignity. Yet the other side of the dialectic is possessed of undeniable and equal force. To separate the agony of the Endlösung 'from other sufferings would be to dishonor other victims within the unending tale of human misery.[6] Thus there would be equal obscenity in reminding the Vietnamese sufferers about Auschwitz.

If we are to relate responsibly to human agony, we must adjudge that it is simply wrong to subject different forms and cases of suffering to competitive criteria. Individual and collective pain and agony are just that. They are to be received with unique tenderness and compassion—in sui generis ways, and not in categorical or comparative ways. It is imperative that we do our best to individualize and humanize the figure of six million. Saul Friedman does precisely that when he says, "Sooner or later the Jewish child awakes screaming in the middle of the night with the spectre of the bones of his people before his eyes."[7] But to speak this way need not mean forgetting the other human beings in other times and other places who, each in his own way, have awakened screaming in the night. The one remembrance can feed the other remembrances.

It is hoped that the above dialectic will be kept in mind, in order that our own stress upon the singularity of Holocaust suffering will not be construed as implicit insensitivity to non-Holocaust sufferers.

FROM THE UNIQUE TO
THE UNIQUELY UNIQUE

The question of the moral uniqueness of the Holocaust is at once complicated and refined by the question of extramoral uniqueness. Insofar as the Holocaust is a singular event, that fact can be made manifest through historical, philosophical, and theological reflection. Before we enter substantively into these areas, it may be helpful to distinguish alternative treatments of the concept "uniqueness." At least three interpretations vie for attention.

1. One interpretation emphasizes the kinship of all historical events, stressing the elements of continuity within the happenings of human life. From this standpoint, the Endlösung, for all its peculiar features, is held to manifest essential continuity

with other deeds of human genocide, such as the earlier Turkish slaughter of over a million Armenians during 1915 and 1916, or, for that matter, the Nazi persecutions of the Gypsies contemporaneously with the Jews.[8] The late eminent historian Hermann G. Adler opposed the view that Nazism introduced an entirely new dimension into human destructiveness. In Adler's epigram, from the day of Original Sin the Holocaust became possible.[9]

2. There are also undoubted elements of discontinuity (*Einmaligkeit*, "historical singularity") and discordance within the multitudinous events of time or history. In accord with this obvious fact, many interpreters of the Holocaust emphasize the unparalleled character of the obliteration of European Jewry. They single out such matters as the bureaucratization of murder, the combined technological and ideological "perfection" of the destructiveness, and the obsessiveness and even self-defeating character (from a military point of view) of the Nazi concentration upon the Jewish enemy. Within this same general category of interpretation falls the historical contention by a scholar in Darmstadt, West Germany, that the Endlösung represents the singular culminating point of a centuries-prepared denial of Jewish integrity at the hands of the Christian world.[10] Again, historian Klaus Scholder of Tübingen identifies Nazism, not as a form of nihilism, but as a primitive dualistic system of absolute good and absolute evil, within which all of human history embodies a war of the two forces. Capitalizing upon the powerful presence of traditional antisemitism, National Socialism uniquely applied these two foundational categories to Germans ("good") and Jews ("evil"). The Nazis saw in the Jews a deadly bacillus threatening the very being of the healthy Aryan people. They had to be mercilessly objective and wipe out the death-bearing agents.[11] Here is a primary difference in the Nazi ideologies of Jews and of Gypsies, although of course the Germans considered the Gypsies highly inferior people and slaughtered a half-million of them. (In this book "ideology," following Karl Marx, is used in a more or less pejorative sense, to denote the use of ideas and arguments to serve collective self-interest.)

3. We may occasionally glimpse a transhistorical level for which, in English, the somewhat cumbersome expression "unique uniqueness" seems required (in German, perhaps,

ganze Einzigartigkeit, uniqueness in the connotation of "only-ness"). Now we are met, not just with an unparalleled happening, or one that is discontinuous with other genocidal acts, but instead with a truly transcending or metahistorical event, an event that twists our journey through space-time by 180 degrees. It is an event that raises the question of *Heilsgeschichte* ("salvation history") or perhaps of the total eclipse of salvation history, an event that, if it is "comparable" at all, can only be compared with a very small number of other "incomparable" events, such as the Exodus or the giving of Torah, or the Crucifixion and the Resurrection. Thus, in Elie Wiesel's *Beggar in Jerusalem,* it is testified that at Sinai the Torah was bestowed upon Israel, but then in the kingdom of night, in the flames of the Final Solution, the Torah was taken back.[12] Such radicalizing of uniqueness has the effect of placing the Holocaust within the same general frame of reference as certain traditionally sacred happenings or affirmations.

Presumably, one may reject this third understanding of uniqueness by, for example, rejecting all transcending, *heilsgeschichtliche* events. But once the rejection comes from a source that demands *heilsgeschichtliche* responses to alternative events (e.g., Exodus, Sinai, Calvary, Resurrection), we are obliged to answer, as a German saying has it, "ein Esel schimpft den andren Langohr" ("the one jackass is calling the other one 'Long-ears' ").

Fresh dating procedures serve the function of recognizing and symbolizing watersheds of human history. Thus it is that in Christendom reference is made to "B.C." (Before Christ) and "A.D." (Anno Domini, "in the year of the Lord"). Some Jews and Christians have mutually agreed to the usage "B.C.E." (Before the Common Era) and "C.E." (Common Era). In Islam, "A.H." stands for the all-decisive year of Muhammad's *Hijra* (Migration). The year 1941 is perhaps best identified as year 1 of the Holocaust. On this reckoning, 1984 is to be renumbered the year 44. We propose "B.F.S.," Before the Final Solution, and "F.S.," in the year of the Final Solution. Accordingly, 1984 (A.D. or C.E.) becomes 44 F.S.[13]

Clearly, the altered symbology remains quite unconvincing unless one is persuaded that the advent of the Endlösung has meant an ontological redirecting of the course and the fate of human history. We now follow out certain implications of this controversial persuasion, first from a philosophical and historical standpoint, and then from a theological and moral one.

The philosophical issue of human nature and destiny and the theological issue of the divine nature and destiny converge under the power of the twofold question of responsibility (*Verantwortlichkeit*) and fate. What do we mean by human accountability-blameworthiness and its consequences? And what do we mean by divine accountability-blameworthiness and its consequences? Yet we scarcely need remind ourselves that these questions have been raised and must be raised in any time and in any place. The philosophical question and the theological question are here broached strictly within the frame of reference of a single event, the Holocaust. Wherein, then, lies the historical-existential peculiarity of these questions?

All historical events are unique. History does not and cannot repeat itself. That various historical happenings appear to replicate other events is accountable in part through our temptation to be content with surface resemblances and in part through the powerful impulse within the human mind to subject successive happenings to generalizing categories. All too chillingly, the Holocaust contains its own peculiarities—such as the truth that never before in human history was systematic genocide conducted by a government in the name of a pseudo-scientific doctrine of race, and to the end of final blessedness.[14] Morality was transvaluated. Those who murdered were doing "the right thing."[15] Again, the *intent* of the Holocaust was unparalleled in human history, most especially the intent to eradicate human compassion.[16]

However, we must always keep in mind that uniqueness does not necessarily entail unique uniqueness. A kind of continuum impresses itself upon us. We move from the surface level of repetitive events (e.g., the births of thousands of kittens), to the deeper level of relative uniqueness (continuity flavored and altered by discontinuity), and finally to an ultimate level, which transcends the other levels: the level of incomparability or unique uniqueness (e.g., God, the Jewish people, the devil, or, for that matter, this particular dear and incredible little kitten in contrast to all other kittens.) There is a real sense in which every historical being participates in absolute uniqueness or "onlyness," because no other being can ever duplicate its exact history. We see, accordingly, how any such wording as "Is the Holocaust unique?" is exceedingly trivial. To answer yes to such a query is to make the same trite reply that is to be made respecting any happening in history.[17] Instead we have to ask, *in what senses* is the Holocaust unique? Is it indeed *uniquely* unique?

Before further pursuing questions such as these last, we may point out that the level of relative uniqueness is often able to assist in the understanding of uniquely unique events. Thus, in his introduction to *The Echo of the Nazi Holocaust in Rabbinic Literature*, H. J. Zimmels enumerates and then explains several factors that "made the persecution of the Jews by the Nazis unique in the history of mankind in general and in that of the Jews in particular":

1. the nature of the persecution;
2. the plan of the extermination of the whole Jewish race;
3. the number of countries affected and the number of their victims;
4. the use of modern methods of science and technology in the extermination of Jews;
5. the misuse of the victims and their bodies for forced labour, for medical, commercial and private purposes; and
6. the difficulties of finding places of refuge.[18]

Special attention is called to the second item in Zimmels's list. The question of the Endlösung is not that of the destruction of some or many Jews, but that of the total obliteration of Jewry as such. This latter, historically determined eventuality is to be balanced against the moral thesis set forth near the beginning of this chapter, where the qualitative, noncomparable character of humankind's miseries is emphasized. For the truth is that in the Endlösung the qualitative question of Jewish survival and life was so completely overpowered by the quantitative factor that the quantitative element became the all-decisive determinant of qualitative reality. The decision that there were to be no more Jews on Planet Earth constituted an absolute convergence of quantitative and qualitative reality. That decision points us, accordingly, in the direction of the uniquely unique character of the Holocaust. Here is the sense in which the singularity of the event is tied to the identity of the victims: it was the Jews, only

47

the Jews, who were to be removed from human existence. Differently expressed, the *Einzigartigkeit* of the Holocaust rests in the fact that all Jewish babies and children were to die along with older people. It is at this point that the varied forms of understanding (historical, philosophical, moral, and theological) begin to converge: there is a historical-phenomenological link between the Jewish people and the Creator and Judge of the world.

We are summoned to embark upon a journey that leads us beyond purely historical uniqueness into a land of paradox and mystery, of the heights and the depths of human experience and sin, of demonic forces and divine imponderabilities. If we are to gain understanding, we have no choice but to travel along that way.

A singular apprehension of the *Endlösung* appears attainable only if that event is itself sui generis—or, to put it more cautiously, only if, along with the evident continuities between the Holocaust and other acts of genocide and human destructiveness, there are qualitatively unique discontinuities. To the end of testing the assumption that the philosophical question of the nature and meaning of the Holocaust demands uniquely unique conceptualization, we proceed in what appears to be a self-contradictory fashion: we call to witness the phenomenon of antisemitism as such. A contradiction seems to enter here, for the simple and forcible reason that to place a particular event (e.g., the Holocaust), or even a series of consanguine events, within a wider category (e.g., antisemitism) appears to threaten the integrity of the event or events. However, in the present case this difficulty may not in fact intrude, provided that the larger category of antisemitism is itself sui generis, and provided also that the specific event (the Holocaust) is to be grasped as the uniquely unique climax-incarnation of antisemitism.

Once more, dialectical understanding is essential, where each integral side of a paradox points to the force and validity of the other side. If, on the one hand, we treat the Holocaust as absolutely or transcendently unique, we may appear to suppress the long history of antisemitism of which the *Endlösung* is the culmination. Furthermore, were the Holocaust identifiable as absolutely different from all other events, we could not then find any specific lessons in it.[19] On the other hand, in the very act of attending to the history of antisemitism, we are

brought to the singularity of the Holocaust. No longer were
sporadic persecution, various kinds of social denigration, and
partial destruction the orders of the time. Instead, every Jew
had to be slaughtered as quickly as possible. Thus it is that,
within the very frame of reference of the ongoing course of
history, the Holocaust manifests discontinuity as well as continuity with the past.

The decision to assign the Holocaust to the developing
story of Christendom points to both the continuity and the discontinuity of the event. On the one hand, the Endlösung is
enmeshed within a large, enduring structure of conviction and
action. On the other hand, although the event constitutes the
climax of a certain historical development and fate, the Holocaust nevertheless erupts beyond the structure, since its specific acts had no precedential incarnation.

Sometimes the claimed uniqueness of the Holocaust is derived from the claimed uniqueness of the Jewish people. There
is much plausibility here, as is suggested at different places in
these pages. Historically speaking, the peculiarity of an event,
or composite of events, means nothing apart from the special
subjects, the human individuals and groups involved. However,
we are again faced by a dialectical state of affairs. To point out
that human events are made unique by their actors is to imply
that the Holocaust has no greater distinctiveness than any comparable event involving a group of non-Jews. Yet here too we
must move to the other side: those facts about the treatment of
Jews that mark off the fortunes of these people from the fortunes of others become the ground for attesting to the distinctiveness of the Holocaust.

Reinhold Niebuhr used to stress that the peculiarity and
the persistence of antisemitism arise from the fact that the targets diverge from the hostile majority in two crucial ways, religiously and also culturally. Niebuhr was addressing himself to
the uniqueness of antisemitism, but he was not coming to terms
with its uniquely unique character. Like others, he would refer
as well to the condemning of Jews for their virtues as much as
for their reputed vices. Yet in that too we are met by uniqueness, as perhaps by a hint of unique uniqueness.

The world-shattering consideration behind such glimpses
of truth is that the phenomenon of antisemitism is simply in-

comparable. There are no parallels to it. There simply is no historical analogue to antisemitism. It is not a question of "human prejudice" in a general sense. The practice of some social scientists of remanding antisemitism to the category of "human prejudice" is a temptation and a snare, whatever the superficial resemblance of antisemitism to ordinary prejudice. The incomparability of antisemitism is tied to that phenomenon's peculiar spatio-temporal character. Whether we speak of space or of time (the two primordial dimensions of human existence), no prejudice comes anywhere near antisemitism. No prejudice can approach antisemitism for either geopolitical pervasiveness or temporal enduringness. Other prejudices remain, by contrast, localized and fleeting; they are instances of spatial contingency and historical transience. In the last reckoning, and after their having been contrasted with antisemitism, they become slightly reminiscent of child's play.

In the history of Christendom only the Jewish people is charged with a world conspiracy against humankind. And the traditional Christian ideology has managed to nurture a variegated progeny. The centuries are awakened from the past to testify with a single voice to their having been permeated by *Judenfeindschaft,* enmity to Jews as Jews, as in the United Nations of recent years the international wrath reserved for the state of Israel finds no parallel in place or in time. The United Nations, the highest council of the world community, has become a center of antisemitism under the cloak of anti-Zionism and anti-Israelism.[20] At no time in the history of humanity has there been a counterpart to such a phenomenon. Thus, Saint John Chrysostom's allegation in fourth-century Antioch that the Jews are "a nation of assassins and hangmen" is duplicated word-for-word by Russian and Arab propagandists sixteen centuries afterwards.

THE "NECESSITY" OF
THE DEVIL

The philosophical-historical understanding of the unique uniqueness of the Holocaust may be aided by the concept of "the devil." This concept appears to be of seminal use in coming to grips with antisemitism and thence with the Endlösung. However, it is with a certain diffidence that we introduce the concept. Our reference to the devil is hardly designed to disaffect readers, though the usage will doubtless have exactly that impact upon many, perhaps through their wariness of obscurantism and superstition.[21] One of our personal bafflements is that, despite the destructive force of so much in human experience, many religious people still find it easier to go on believing in God than to consider the reality of the devil. We, the authors, are disturbed by those remnants of modern idealism, utopianism, and sentimentality that wish to decree, almost mechanically, the nonreality or even the inconceivability of the devil. If the abiding and omnipresent persecution of Jews raises fateful questions concerning the reality of God, certainly it ought to pose the question of the devil. (To seek to work out specifics of the relations of devilish action and human action presents no problems that are not equally present in the effort to reckon with the specifics of the divine and human relation.) Our simple persuasion is that it is extremely difficult to speak meaningfully of the hatred of Jews without speaking of a demonic force or a concatenation of such forces.

We should be among the last to sanction a "devil theory of history," for that view despoils the sovereignty of God, or at least the much more compelling affirmation of God's love. Nor should we ever agree that membership in the devil's work force frees human beings from responsibility or culpability. The protestation "I only obey orders" is no valid defense. Human guilt persists, and it must be judged and punished. Furthermore, we do not suggest that there is no substitute for the word "devil"; we are willing to settle for such a term as "demonic power," provided only that the specificity and the other elements of the phenomenon in question (as discussed below) are not obviated. Above all, we should certainly not desire our theory of the distinctive character of antisemitism to stand or fall upon the usage of the concept "devil."

It is not our intention to offer an exhaustive clarification of, or "apology" for, the devil. Doubters would probably remain unconvinced, just as many persons remain wholly unimpressed by proofs for the existence of God. We may, however, be permitted one literary and substantive gloss: the devil does not

51

deserve a capital *D*. In point of truth, he deserves nothing. That the devil deserves nothing is related to his own nature. While we appear to be referring at present to the reality of the devil, this is a manner of speaking. Strictly, and on the basis of the absolute ontological gulf between God and the devil, it is more accurate to speak of the devil's unreality. However, this consideration does not lessen in any way the usefulness and appropriateness of the concept of the devil within our current context.

We are the witnesses of a haunting combination of particularity and universality. The Jew is the particular victim, but for no particular reason. That is to say, the Jew is not to be destroyed because he has done something specific, committed some special crime. He is to be annihilated, not on the ground of doing, but on the ground of universal being—or, better, of nonbeing. He is universal evil.[22] Accordingly, there is no reason for his destruction; instead, the destruction is simply the inevitably and logically opposite category from the being of universal goodness.

The integrity of human beings has always been attacked by one or another foe. But antisemitism singles out the Jew for denigration and death. What is the relation between the general and the specific attacks? Is antisemitism simply another technique within the devil's stratagems, just one more campaign within the eternal war upon man? Or is antisemitism of the very character of the devil? Is it a special malady that may eventually entice the divine-human creation back to a state of realized nonbeing? The daring assertion is sometimes made that the very edifice of our social libido, at least in the West, is somehow linked to antisemitism. For example, David Polish writes that "the truth of every cause is validated or found fraudulent in the way in which it confronts the Jewish people."[23]

The word "God" is our imperative symbol for the transcendent, persisting power of righteousness and creativity in the world. The word "devil" is the symbol of the transcendently unique and persisting power of evil and destructiveness, a concept marked, therefore, by a necessity comparable with that of God. The devil is not the reality of evil in any abstract or generalized sense; he (*sic*) is other than the power of evil as such (just as God is anything but abstract or generalized goodness or divineness). The devil is the totally unique power that concentrates upon totally unique evil. The meaning and force of this affirmation are contingent, obviously, upon the convincingness of the idea of "totally unique evil." Is there an evil in this world that is uniquely unique? Yes. We have already spoken of it. That evil is antisemitism.

The "devil" and "antisemitism" are correlative symbols: antisemitism is born of the devil, and the devil receives his sustenance from antisemitism. The elucidation or disclosure of the devil is required etiologically and existentially because the hatred of Jews is not, in essence, a matter of evil as such. It is *this* evil, an evil at once incomparable and incredible, as incomparable and incredible as the original election of Israel by God. Although incredibility is normally or linguistically the opposite of credibility, it is not necessarily the opponent of truth. To speak of the unbelievable destiny of the Jews is somehow to testify to God, for he is the unbelievably unique One. Were the divine election of the Jewish people comparable to other elections, we should have to settle for "the factor of the gods" or some other mundane accounting. In the same way, were the ongoing persecution of Jews comparable to other persecutions, we should have to settle for "the element of evil forces" or some equally profane explanation. But there is nothing like antisemitism. Accordingly, it is appropriate to speak of the devil.

It follows from the above that, within one frame of reference, the devil may be denominated "god." He is the god of antisemitism. The devil seeks to emulate the real God. The kingdom of the true God extends to humankind, yet God sustains his chosen people. So too the devil covets a universal empire, yet he also retains his elected ones, his "faithful remnant," his special witnesses. These are the antisemites. Through the millennia and across all boundaries, the devil's faithful persist. The banality and the vapidity of the recent vogue of the devil in Hollywood and elsewhere lie in the ignorance of the truth that the devil does not work with just anybody. Satan's universality transcends his particularity, but it is implemented through the particularity. As we have observed, it is only the Jews who are opposed without any limitations of date or boundaries of place. The devil is universal, but he is very particular. The unique connection between the devil and antisemitism is authenticated through the incarnating of antisemitic depravity in so diverse and abiding a congeries of sources. The singularity of the devil is manifest in his tie with the world's one uniquely unique evil; the incomparability of the devil stands in horrible correlation with the incomparability of antisemitism. Men and nations who are normally foes always have the opportunity to join hands, in the devil's peace, against the one enemy, the Jew. Membership in the religion of antisemitism is ever open to all. It is the only universal faith. The language of antisemitism is the devil's native tongue; it quickly becomes the second language of the devil's disciples, and after a while it takes command of their original language.

We are beset by the unbelievable proposition that the devil acts to deceive the world into seeing in the Jew his own incarnation. The devil's final deed is to seek to coalesce with the Jew. This is the only possible masquerade for him. Who then could accuse him of being the real father of antisemitism? Here is the devil's uniquely unique work, for only the devil himself could "uncover" the devil in the Jew. Only the devil can fabricate and deliver devilish accusations. Thus, while the Fourth Gospel was written down by a man who may have carried the name of John, the hidden source of John 8:42–47 may be understood as the devil himself. In that passage "the Jews"—note the indiscriminateness—are informed that they are not children of God but are, by deliberate choice, children of the devil. The accusation of Jewish devilishness is an ultimate proof that the non-Jewish, antisemitic soul is invaded by Satan, for only the devil could stoop to the demonic depth of claiming the Jew as his singular confrere. In sum, both psychoanalytically and spiritually speaking, the "Jewish world conspiracy" in fact comprises a world conspiracy planned by demon-ridden Christians and other conspirators against Jews.[24]

When thousands of Japanese were killed and maimed in Hiroshima and Nagasaki there was a goal beyond the acts, a goal variously identifiable (convincingly or unconvincingly) as resistance to aggression, the restoration of peace, and so on. Early in 1974, Cambodian leaders lamented the silence of the world community over terror shellings of Phnom Penh. *Le Republican*, a semiofficial Cambodian newspaper, asked: "Is it that the Communists alone are worthy of compassion while their victims merit only silence and oblivion?"[25] A prevailing rejoinder to such laments is tiresomely familiar to us all: the cause of the people's revolution must be served. However, these and other historical examples embody, at most, only superficial affinities to antisemitism. In contrast to them, the destruction of Jewry is subject to no purpose beyond itself. On the contrary, it is the end of all ends; it is at once the fulfillment (*telos*) and the conclusion (*finis*) of every end. To obliterate the Jewish people is the one goal of existence—or, more accurately, the one goal of nonexistence, the realization of nonbeing, for the destroyer as well as for the destroyed. It is, at one and the same time, sadism sui generis and masochism sui generis. To offer an aphorism for all this: in the categories of satanology, the Jew is the devil not because he is evil; he is the devil because he is the devil. Insofar as it may be felt that attention to the devil will have the effect of mystifying the identity of antisemitism, we suggest that so mysterious a phenomenon as antisemitism may well require consideration of a demonic force or forces if it is ever going to be reasonably comprehended.

Any who doubt the singularity of the Endlösung may well reflect upon the current conspiracy to deny that it ever took place.[26] Such denials kill the sufferers a second time, by taking away the victims' first death. Thus do these devil's representatives offer a kind of grisly witness, if a self-contradictory one, to the distinctiveness of the Holocaust.[27] The unique uniqueness of the event is validated through the satanic pretense that it did not happen. Of what other comparably monstrous event in human history has there ever been a plot by reputedly civilized people to say that the thing never transpired? We are reminded forcibly of Arthur Hertzberg's observation that the antisemite invariably attacks Jews at "precisely that aspect of their current selves which is most uniquely theirs, which most exactly expresses the specificness of their own life"[28]—be it their religion, their national homeland, or whatever. The antisemite always denies the reality or validity of whatever, in different periods, is the bearer of peculiarly existential meaning for the Jewish people. Today, accordingly, the slaughter of the six million and its remembrances must be taken away, must be obliterated.

Emil L. Fackenheim writes:

While even the worst society is geared to life, the Holocaust Kingdom was geared to death. It would be quite wrong to say that it was a mere means, however depraved, to ends somehow bound up with life. As an enterprise subserving the Nazi war effort the murder camps were total failures, for the human and material "investment" far exceeded the "produce" of fertilizer, gold teeth and soap. The Holocaust Kingdom was an end in itself, having only one ultimate "produce," and that was death.

It is false to comprehend Nazism and the murder camps as but an extreme case of general technological dehumanization.

In essence, Nazism *was* the murder camp. That a nihilistic, demonic celebration of death and destruction was its animating principle . . . [became] revealed in the end, when in the Berlin bunker Hitler and Goebbels . . . expressed ghoulish satisfaction at the prospect that their downfall might carry in train the doom, not only (or even at all) of their enemies, but rather of the "master race."

Fackenheim concludes:

Even this does not exhaust the scandalous particularity of Nazism. The term "Aryan" had no clear connotation other than "non-Jew," and the Nazis were not anti-Semites because they were racists, but rather racists because they were anti-Semites. The exaltation of the "Aryan" had no positive significance. It had only the negative significance of degrading and murdering the "non-Aryan." Thus Adolf Eichmann passed beyond the limits of a merely "banal" evil when, with nothing left of the Third Reich, he declared with obvious sincerity that he would jump laughing into his grave in the knowledge of having dispatched six million Jews to their death. We must conclude, then, that the dead Jews of the murder camps (and all the other innocent victims, as it were, as quasi-Jews, or by dint of innocent-guilt-by-association) were not the "waste product" of the Nazi system. They were *the* product.[29]

Philosophically and historically speaking, we are now in a somewhat better position to reckon with the question, wherein lies the singularity of the Holocaust? Our answer is a simple one. (What are we saying? There could be no paradox more reason-defying than this: to propose a simple interpretation of the essence of the modern world's most impossible event, that event before which reasoned analysis seems so terribly help-less. Yet we contend that the truth is a simple one.) The Holo-caust is the final act of a uniquely unique drama. It is the hour that follows logically, inexorably, and faithfully upon a particular history of conviction and behavior. It is a climax that succeeds the drawing up, over many centuries, of the requisite doctrinal formulations. It is the arrival of the "right time" (kairos) following upon all those dress rehearsals, those practice sessions of the Crusades, the Inquisition, and the like. The Holocaust is the consummation of all of them. Yet within this very simplicity, within this very paucity of originality, there implodes all the insane and demonic complexity. Only in our latter years could we finally ready ourselves for the eschatological deed, the Endlösung. Only the final destruction remained to be carried out. True, the labor would have to be back-breaking, but the consummation was nothing, really. All that remained to be done was to "manage" and to follow out the correct technical steps. Antisemitism "became professionalized and mass murder became an administrative process."[30] The German Nazis were nothings: they lived out and applied a deep historical inevitability.[31] Here was the implementation of the dominant theological and moral conclusions of the Christian church, as also of the philosophical ideas of certain so-called great men of western culture (Voltaire, Nietzsche, Fichte, and others), now aided by technological instrumentalities not previously marshaled or available. All in all, *we were following orders*—the remorseless, gathering commands of nineteen centuries.[32]

THE QUESTION ASKED
OF GOD

We move now into a more theological province.

The unique uniqueness of happenings summed up in words such as "Exodus" and "Sinai" is expressed theologically through a concept such as "positive revelatory significance," a revelation of life. By contrast, the Holocaust may be identified through the concept of "negative revelatory significance"—that is, as a uniquely devilish event, a revelation of death itself.

However, such an observation is not distinctively theological. It reflects a sharing by philosophy and theology: death is as much a philosophical theme as a theological one.

Under the promptings of unique uniqueness, the theological province is entered through this inquiry: is it or is it not the case that, in the shadow of the Holocaust, God and the relationship between God and his people ought to be apprehended in radically new and transcending ways? Is it or is it not the case, theologically speaking, that F.S. is the polar opposite of B.F.S.? The question of the uniqueness of the Holocaust thus becomes the other side of the question of the intentions and behavior of the God of history.

The integral link between philosophical analysis ("the philosopher's task is the critical examination of our collective self-image")[33] and theological analysis is conveyed in the title of act 5 of Rolf Hochhuth's play *Der Stellvertreter:* "Auschwitz or the Question Asked of God." Thus does the subject before us become more than a question of the devil and more than a question of human infamy; it becomes as well a question of the divine fate. What is the life story of God? May it be that, in the end, God becomes the devil? In Hochhuth's drama the character known as the Doctor puts God, not man, on the stand of the accused (although Hochhuth never annuls human diabolism). True, we are brought to see that it is the Doctor, rather than God, who is dead, dead inside. (The Doctor has already confessed that he is the devil.)[34] But it is impossible to allow God to leave the courtroom because the question of Auschwitz is addressed, primordially, to him. And he must give an answer.

The Holocaust is a "trial" in the two major meanings of that word. It is a trial of singular agony and a trial of accusation, the first for Jews and certain quasi Jews, and the second for the Christian and pagan world. But the Endlösung is also the trial of God. We do not refer to his suffering or his possible death there, although we are not here questioning those eventualities. We think rather of the second meaning, of God's being "on trial." In the Holocaust God is brought to trial as codefendant with men (as also with the devil). It is to no avail to seek to exonerate God by loading all the blame upon human beings. Men are culpable, of course. But the ultimate responsbility for the evil of this world is God's, for the plain reason that it is he who made the world and it is he who permits monstrous suffering to take place. "God is responsible for having created a world in which man is free to make history."[35]

Once upon a time, some Polish Hasidim conducted a court trial of God. The basis of their charge was dismay over the way Jews were suffering. The Hasidim decreed that God was guilty.[36] But in the presence of the Holocaust, that earlier sentencing of God must remain relatively light. A special moral indictment is now entered against the Ruler of the Universe, because in the kingdom of night, his chosen ones were turned into vermin and worse than vermin, by his permission. We are now met by the accusation of a most infamous crime: the complicity of God in the obliteration of the Six Million. (The capital letters are designed to stand for the coalescence of qualitative and quantitative reality.) The new charge against God is no less than one of implicit satanism. No plea of innocence is open to him. No appeal is available to him. The only conceivable plea would have to be either weakness or absence from the scene, but these are hardly divine characteristics. The question stands: has the Lord of life and love become the Lord of death and hate? Has he been transmuted into the devil?

For the sake of the memory of the Polish Hasidim alluded to above, as well as for the sake of all human sufferers in each time and place, we must reaffirm the sense in which the anguish and death of one human being, and particularly of a little child (yet without forgetting every bird and spider and deer and goat), are as terrible evils as the anguish and death of great numbers of people. But our real heartache arises from a different consideration: what is God to say or to do now in his defense? Or, rather, since he in fact has no defense, what penance must he perform if he is to escape a sentence of execution or if he is at least to rectify the unspeakable injustices for which he is plainly blameworthy?

The only penitential act we know for God is for him to express genuine sorrow for his place in the unparalleled agony of his people, and to promise that he will do his best never to sin again, never to have anything to do with such suffering in the future. Do any signs come now of the transmutation, the repentance of God? This brazen but inexpugnable question is grappled with at some length elsewhere in our study, and particularly in the next chapter. In these strange days, testimony (*torah*) sometimes comes to us from strange and fresh sources. For the present we adduce a single tale.

In Elie Wiesel's *"Ani Maamin": A Song Lost and Found Again*, God remains silent before the pleadings and denunciations by Abraham, Isaac, and Jacob, who protest and agonize over the unending sufferings of Jews. But when Abraham snatches a little girl from before the machine guns and runs like the wind to save her, and she tells him weakly that she believes in him, in Abraham, then at last a tear clouds God's eyes (though Abraham cannot see that). When Isaac beholds the mad Dayan singing "of his ancient and lost faith," of belief in God and the coming of the Messiah, God weeps a second time (though Isaac cannot see that). And when Jacob finds a camp inmate asserting that the Haggadah lies, that God will not come, that the wish to be in Jerusalem will never be granted, but that he will continue to recite the Haggadah as though he believes in it, and still await the prophet Elijah as he did long ago, even though Elijah disappoint him, then yet a third time (though Jacob cannot see that) God weeps, "this time without restraint, and with—yes—love. He weeps over his creation—and perhaps over much more than his creation."[37]

It may be that God is being saved now, that he is being made whole. If so, there is a sense in which B.F.S., the age until the Holocaust, is beginning to pass. In that case, the words *Ani ma'amin* ("I believe") may yet be repeated again in some small moment, down some out-of-the-way street.

FILLING THE CIRCLE OF CULPABILITY

To this point we have had much to say about the Jewish people, the German Nazis, the devil, and God. We have said little of the church and of Christians. The bearing of the latter identity upon the uniqueness of the Holocaust derives from the peculiar Christian contribution to that event. The singularity of the Endlösung is manifest, among other ways, through the role of Christendom and Christian teachings and behavior in helping to make possible the kingdom of night. Christianity created a social atmosphere of contempt for the Jewish people, which could be readily capitalized upon by secular antisemitic forces. Within the churches there was even some encouragement of Christians to believe that in the Holocaust, as in earlier persecutions, the Jews really had it coming to them.[38] It is scarcely necessary to point out that a great deal in Christian teaching and life has served to oppose antisemitism and the influences that issued in the Holocaust. Yet the essence of the Christian problem remains: its ambivalence toward the Jews and Judaism. Recent historiography has brought home the negativistic and hostile Christian influences. It is a significant and hopeful sign that many of these works are by Christian scholars.[39]

In relation to each other, the Jewish community and the Christian community tend to emphasize or to face different questions arising from the Holocaust. Among Jews, stress naturally falls upon problems of God, suffering, the covenant, and the land. (It may be interjected that, in the measure Christians feel an affinity with Jewishness, they ought to be concentrating on the same questions.) By contrast, in the Christian community the primary question is that of the culpability of Christians for the denigration and agony of Jews. Of course, such culpability often is denied. This question is not ignored by Jewish representatives,[40] but the difference remains. Thus the Jew tends to ask, "How can we continue to trust in God?"; the perplexed Christian tends to ask, "What has become of the credibility of Christianity? In the light of the Christian place in the Endlösung, how can the church ever regain its moral integrity?"

These latter two questions receive primary stress in the work of the United Methodist historian and churchman Franklin H. Littell. Littell writes:

> The cornerstone of Christian Antisemitism is the superseding or displacement myth, which already rings with the genocidal note. This is the myth that the mission of the Jewish people was finished with the coming of Jesus Christ, that "the old Israel" was written off with the appearance of "the new Israel." To teach that a people's mission in God's providence is finished, that they have been relegated to the limbo of history, has murderous implications which murderers will in time spell out. The murder of six million Jews by baptized Christians, from whom membership in good standing was

61

not (and has not been) withdrawn, raises the most insistent question about the credibility of Christianity. . . . Was Jesus a false messiah? No one can be a true messiah whose followers feel compelled to torture and destroy other human persons who think differently.[41]

The Canadian Catholic theologian Gregory G. Baum asserts: "What Auschwitz has revealed to the Christian community is the deadly power of its own symbolism." The "anti-Jewish thrust of the church's preaching" is not a historical, psychological, or sociological matter; "it touches the very formulation of the Christian gospel." Along with Littell, Baum concentrates upon the realities of Christian triumphalism and supersessionism in the presence of the Jews and Judaism—what John Pawlikowski calls "the theology of substitution"—which (still citing Baum) "assigns the Jews to the darkness of history,"[42] rejected by God and man, in ways that could only end in the murder camps. In the Holocaust "the theological negation of Judaism and the vilification of the Jewish people" within the Christian tradition were at last translated into the genocide of the Jews.[43] And as the Protestant thinker Paul van Buren points out, "the roots of Hitler's final solution are to be found . . . in the proclamation of the very *kerygma* ["message"] of the early Christians"[44]—a message that was to be perpetuated and compounded in influence across the centuries.

On the basis of the above considerations, the Holocaust has to be identified as a Christian event, of fateful significance, as much as a Jewish or German event.

We do not mean to suggest that in the Holocaust the church is confronted only with moral challenges and with no specifically theological questions. On the contrary, the entire Christological issue is reopened,[45] as are the related questions of the Resurrection and of what it means to speak of the church as "the Israel of God." The confluence of theological and moral issues is typified in an observation of Robert McAfee Brown. The Jew laments: since the world is so evil, why does the Messiah not come?; the Christian wonders why, since the Messiah has come, the world remains so evil.[46]

In the course of our analysis of the Holocaust's singularity, we have been required a number of times to reason in dialectical and paradoxical fashion. A final instance of this necessity is tied to the identity of the human culprits in the suffering of Jews. The paradox is that the Jewish people are supposed to have rejected God and yet also to represent him. These two elements become unendurable to the world. On the one hand, the Jews must be punished for their alleged repudiation of the Christ. Yet, on the other hand, the pagan soul cannot bear the presence of a transcendent Absence. As George Steiner affirms in his powerful essay "A Season in Hell," "by killing the Jews, Western culture would eradicate those who had 'invented' God, who had, however imperfectly, however restively, been the declarers of His unbearable Absence. The Holocaust is a reflex, the more complete for being long-inhibited, . . . of instinctual polytheistic and animist needs."

> Monotheism at Sinai, primitive Christianity, messianic socialism [which is directly rooted in messianic eschatology]: these are the three supreme moments in which Western culture is presented with what Ibsen termed "the claims of the ideal." These are the three stages, profoundly interrelated, through which Western consciousness is forced to experience the blackmail of transcendence. "Surmount yourself. Surpass the opaque barriers of the mind to attain pure abstraction. Lose your life in order to gain it. Give up property, rank, worldly comfort. Love your neighbour as you do yourself—no, much more, for self-love is sin. Make any sacrifice, endure any insult, even self-denunciation, so that justice may prevail." . . .
>
> . . . Three times, Judaism produced a summons to perfection and sought to impose it on the current and currency of Western life. Deep loathing built up in the social subconscious, murderous resentments. The mechanism is simple but primordial. *We hate most those who hold out to us a goal, an ideal, a visionary promise which, even though we have stretched our muscles to the utmost, we cannot reach, which slips, again and again, just out of range of our racked fingers—yet, and this is crucial, which remains profoundly desirable, which we cannot reject because we fully acknowledge its supreme value.* In his exasperating "strangeness," in his acceptance of suffering as part of a covenant with the absolute, the Jew became, as it were, the "bad conscience" of Western history.[47]

Christianity is disclosed (along with Judaism) as at once the effectuator and the crisis of Nazism. The phrase in parentheses here must be very carefully received. It does not at all mean

63

that Jews, through their religion or anything else, are somehow to be blamed for antisemitism. What it does mean is that non-Jews, in their evil, resent and destroy Jews on the ground or pretext of Jewishness and/or the Jewish religion. Saul Friedländer makes clear that "whatever the Jews did or did not do, they could not alter the fact of antisemitism as such, and in particular the emergence of the murderous antisemitism of the Nazis which was fed by an element of true insanity on the one hand, and growing social disintegration on the other, both totally independent of the Jews themselves." Nazi antisemitism could attain its full power because "there were no strong countervailing forces in European society." Western society considered the Jews "undesirable elements which had to be excluded, whatever this would entail for the victims of exclusion."[48] But of course the undesirability was thoroughly Christian in its origins and largely Christian in its perpetuating motivations. Western society was a Christian society.

Historically speaking, the Holocaust, like all great events, was the outcome of multiple influences: German nationalism, conditions in Germany following World War I, Hitler and other leaders, international machinations, and the Christian and extra-Christian antisemitic traditions. Ismar Schorsch argues against assigning Christian prejudice a paramount place in the working out of Nazi antisemitism; it is, for him, just one component in a complex matrix.[49] There is no necessary conflict of interpretation here. In historical analysis, differences between general causation—the creating of an atmosphere—and more specific causative factors must always be recognized and honored. A responsible interpreter will hardly restrict the Christian contribution to the Endlösung to the second of these categories. The Christian contribution fell primarily, though by no means exclusively, within the first category, the propagation and maintenance over many years of an atmosphere hostile to Jews.

To return to George Steiner: the effectuative element killed the Jews, but the summons to perfection had the same consequence, for both elements were joined in the need to dispose of the Jews once and for all. Jesus was, after all, a Jew. In disposing of the Jew, we take vengeance upon our humanity, yet, being pagans beneath the baptized surface, we will fend off the gas and the flames.

Is there any real hope that Christian teachings and behavior respecting the Jewish people and Judaism may be altered in any morally telling way? This question is given much attention in subsequent pages. Our circle of culpability is, at any rate, now filled out: moral responsibility for the Endlösung clearly extends to the Christian community. For the Christian today, here is to be found the most singular quality and lesson of the Nazi Holocaust.

A consequence of the Christian condition as portrayed in this chapter is that every affirmation of faith and every moral judgment and hope become existentially problematic. So shattering an event as the Holocaust has opened a crisis within every facet of Christian, Jewish, and other thinking. The singularity of the Endlösung connotes, at once, uniqueness, momentousness, revolution. Insofar as the Holocaust is a uniquely unique happening, this is because it is *metanoia,* a climactic turning around of the world (*eine Weltwende*). In the Endlösung, *die Stellvertreter* ("the surrogates," the agents of the devil) bring his nefarious work to consummation. And through the culpable actions of many men, the history of humankind reaches a fateful watershed. But so too does the history of God. In the Chinese language the word for "crisis" contains two components: *wei* ("danger") and *chi* ("opportunity"). The Holocaust is a crisis for man and God alike. For both, it is much more than a danger, but it need not be less than an opportunity.

4

DANGERS AND
OPPORTUNITIES

In chapter 3 we connected the singularity of the Holocaust
to "the question asked of God," the indictment and trial of the
Ruler of the Universe. The divine-human relation is fundamental to the entire question of the Endlösung, and it requires,
accordingly, painstaking and painful reflection. Is it right to
hold God accountable for human suffering? Is the history of this
world moving toward a meaningful climax, or is human history
a meaningless flux? Is the voice of God somehow to be heard
from out of the hell of Auschwitz, or is there only silence, desolation, a "hiding of the Face"? Elie Wiesel writes that, on the
level of God, the Holocaust "will forever remain the most dis-
turbing of mysteries."[1] There seems to be no way to explain it
with God, and no way to explain it without him.

We are confronted with two interrelated challenges: the
issue of theodicy, of the divine justice amidst the power of
unique evil; and the issue of the character and purposes of the
covenant of God and his people. The Endlösung is inseparable
from the covenant with Israel, because the covenant was made,
not with an individual and not with another people, but with
the one people whose total extinction was decreed by the Nazis. This is what makes possible the assertion that the uniqueness of the Holocaust is ultimately theological in nature.

On the one hand, we have to grapple with the question of
meaning. Does life make sense, come what may, because it is
finally ordered and blessed by a righteous and loving God, or
is life "a tale / Told by an idiot, full of sound and fury, / Signi-
fying nothing"? On the other hand, we must try to cope with
the question of the will of God. Does God, essentially, make

demands of his people, commanding them, especially, to suffer for his sake, or does he not do this? However, these two challenges are fused into one by their shared content: the murder of the Jews. As William Jay Peck has written, after Auschwitz, "the very being of God" is "tied up with the problem of murder."[2]

THE RULER WHO IS
REALLY RULER

Before the fact of the Holocaust, is it morally defensible to retain the traditional faith in God taught by Judaism and Christianity? Those who cannot answer this question affirmatively must nonetheless acknowledge that many Jews and others who went through the agony of the Endlösung continued to live as believers, and they died the same way. The Holocaust did not succeed, and has not succeeded, in destroying the faith of certain people.

For some, the rationale of faith is tied to the persuasion that puny and sinful men have neither the moral nor the spiritual right to question God. Who is man to think that he can indict the Ruler of the Universe and bring the Lord to trial? "My thoughts are not your thoughts, neither are your ways my ways, says the Lord" (Isa. 55:8). In the face of the divine query, "Where were you when I laid the foundation of the earth?" (Job 38:4), some believers will simply bow their heads in fearful humility and devout silence. It is told that a Rabbi Israel Shapiro of Grodzisk said to his people, as they were about to die at Treblinka, that their ashes would purify Israel and help to redeem the world.[3] "Though he slay me, yet will I trust in him" (Job 13:15).[4] For such believers, the Holocaust is, in effect, a nonevent—or at least it is no different in kind from other evils that have beset the people of God throughout history. Terrible as the happening was, it ought not be allowed to turn men to apostasy. Indeed, the argument has been put forth that were the Jews of today to surrender their faith, they would be offering a posthumous victory to Hitler.[5] This, great numbers of them will not do.

67

LIFE AGAINST FAITH

For other persons, faith in God is no longer possible after Auschwitz. The human situation is devoid of transcendent meaning, and the very idea of the covenanting purposes of God is grisly, nonsensical, or both. Jakov Lind writes that when the Germans marched into Austria one Friday morning, "God lost his last chance to be recognized by me."[6] In Lind's story "Resurrection," a character named Sholom Weintraub responds to a religious outlook by saying:

> Frankly, Mr. Goldschmied, I have no sympathy for you. . . . You talk and talk. Religion, holiness, the Jews' mission. All a lot of phrases, slogans. Choice, dog, guilt. I don't give a shit about all that. In a few days they'll strangle me and burn me like a leper, and that's the end of Sholom Weintraub. They'll give me a number on a mass grave, colored with gold dust, and I'll never, never be alive again. Resurrection is nothing but Talmudic hair-splitting, mystery, smoke and sulphur, hocus-pocus, theological speculation. There is no second time, not before and not after the Messiah, and He doesn't exist anyway. I want to live, Mr. Goldschmied, I want to live and breathe, and I don't care how—like a dog or a frog or a bedbug, it's all the same to me. I want to live and breathe, to live.[7]

Sholom Weintraub was proved to be an optimist. In Bergen-Belsen we witnessed mass graves with single stones (erected long after the liberation) that read only, "Hier ruhen 5000 tote" ("Here lie 5,000 dead"). To be identified in death by one's number would have been *something*, a message of piteous spite for the darkness to read: "Here I am! I am only a number, but here I am!" (Or here I was.)

Another survivor, Alexander Donat, protests that in the ghettos and camps, day in and day out, "we cried for a sign" of God. But "God was not present at our indescribable predicament. We were alone, forsaken by God and men."[8]

Richard L. Rubenstein's point of view is among the most compelling revisions of traditional Jewish faith in light of the Holocaust. In his pioneering study *After Auschwitz*, Rubenstein tells of the radical change that occurred in his religious outlook following a conversation in 1961 with, paradoxically enough, one of the very few German Protestant pastors who had

68

steadfastly risked his own life and the lives of his family by opposing the Nazis on Christian grounds and extending all possible aid and comfort to Hitler's victims. Various Christians in Germany made the same point to Rubenstein, but it was made with special force by Heinrich Grüber, renowned provost of the Evangelical Church of East and West Berlin. He insisted upon the "very special providential relationship between Israel, what happened to it, and God's will," not just in biblical times but continuing to this very day. However, unlike other German clergy and churchmen who, when Rubenstein pressed them, seemed to back away from the conclusion that the Nazi slaughter of Jews was somehow God's will, Grüber responded quite assuredly. With openness and a complete lack of guile, he quoted Ps. 44:22, "for thy sake are we slaughtered every day," and continued: "For some reason, it was part of God's plan that the Jews died. God demands our death daily. He is the Lord, He is the Master, all is in His keeping and ordering."

Rubenstein writes that Grüber

> dramatized the consequences of accepting the normative Judaeo-Christian theology of history in the light of the death camps. After my interview, I reached a theological point of no return—If I believed in God as the omnipotent author of the historical drama and Israel as His Chosen People, I had to accept Dean Grüber's conclusion that it was God's will that Hitler committed six million Jews to slaughter. I could not possibly believe in such a God nor could I believe in Israel as the chosen people of God after Auschwitz.[9]

Commenting further in a later source upon the same unforgettable episode with Heinrich Grüber, Rubenstein writes that if one is a traditional Jew,

> it is impossible to regard the sorrows of Jewish history as mere historical accidents. They must in some sense express the will of God as a just and righteous Creator. Either such a God is a sadist who inflicts pain because he enjoys it or he has a reason for the misfortune he inflicts. The only morally defensible motive for a superior to inflict pain on an inferior would be punitive chastisement which has as its purpose altering the victim's mode of behavior. If one takes Covenant Theology seriously, as did Dean Grüber, Auschwitz must be God's way of punishing the Jewish people in

order that they might better see the light, the light of Christ if one is a Christian, the light of Torah if one is a traditional Jew.

Rubenstein is fully aware of the price to be paid for rejecting the God of the covenant.

> If the God of history does not exist, then the Cosmos is ultimately absurd in origin and meaningless in purpose. . . . I have elected to accept what Camus has rightly called the courage of the absurd, the courage to live in a meaningless, purposeless Cosmos rather than believe in a God who inflicts Auschwitz on his people.

Rubenstein believes that such a belief is simply obscene.[10]

Rubenstein came to the realization that "as long as Jews are thought of as special and apart from mankind in general, they are going to be the object of both the abnormal demands and the decisive hatreds" of which Heinrich Grüber spoke, as well as of the kind of theology which holds that "because the Jews are God's Chosen People, God wanted Hitler to punish them." Accordingly, Rubenstein rejects all notions of special vocation or peculiar responsibility for the Jewish people. After Auschwitz, it is immoral to believe such things.[11]

Rubenstein is convinced that

> the problem of God and the death camps is the central problem for Jewish theology in the twentieth century. . . . The catastrophe of 1939–45 represents a psychological and religious time bomb which has yet to explode fully in the midst of Jewish religious life. . . . God really died at Auschwitz. This does not mean that God is not the beginning and will not be the end. It does mean that nothing in human choice, decision, value, or meaning can any longer have vertical reference to transcendent standards. We are alone in a silent, unfeeling cosmos. . . . Morality and religion can no longer rest upon the conviction that divinely validated norms offer a measure against which what we do can be judged.

Yet, despite his avowal of cosmic emptiness, he has not given in to despair. "Death and rebirth are the greatest moments of religious experience," and Jews have known both in this century. In Europe, he writes, we Jews have tasted the bitterest and most degrading of deaths. Yet death was not the last word. . . . Death in Europe was followed by resurrection in our ancestral home. We are free as no men before us have ever been. Having lost everything, we have nothing further to lose and no further fear of loss. . . . We have passed beyond all illusion and hope. We have learned . . . that we were totally and nakedly alone, that we could expect neither support nor succor from god or from our fellow creatures. . . . We have lost all hope and faith. We have also lost all possibility of disappointment.[12]

BEYOND THE OPPOSITES

Between unquestioning fealty to God and the abjuration or melancholy abandonment of God—in the name of life—other variations of existential argument and witness vie to be heard.

Prompted by an awareness of Christian antisemitism and its genocidal consequences, Gregory Baum has written a study entitled *Man Becoming,* in which he comments upon that aspect of traditional Christian thought which has insisted that God is not responsible for evil and suffering.[13] As he points out, the church's persuasion of God as Lord of history necessarily implied that human sins and crimes are somehow not out of accord with God's permissive will. God permits evil for the present, in order that a greater good will be achieved in the future. Thus, even Auschwitz fills a place in the divine providence. Yet it seems to Baum that this line of thinking makes a monster out of God. Accordingly, certain traditional understandings of the divine providence, omniscience, and omnipotence must be rejected.

God is not provident . . . in the sense that as ruler of the world he has a master plan for human history by which he provides help for the people in need, especially those who ask him for it, and by which he guides the lives of men, even while acknowledging their freedom. . . . [or] in which God has permitted evil and . . . calculated its damaging effects and compensated for them in the final outcome. . . . [Rather] God is provident in the sense that in whatever trap a man falls, a summons continues to address him and offer him new life that makes him more truly human.

71

Baum concludes that God is omniscient only "in the sense that there exists no human situation, however difficult, however obscure, however frightening, in which God remains silent or . . . in which a summons to greater insight is not available." Similarly, God is omnipotent only in the sense that there is "no situation, however destructive, in which an inner strength is not offered to man, allowing him to assume greater possession of his humanity." Through this understanding, we are enabled to affirm "the radical opposition between God and evil." Evil is not permitted by him.

> God overcomes evil. God is constantly at work among men, summoning them and gracing them to discern the evil in human life, to wrestle against it, to be converted away from it, to correct their environment, to redirect history, to transform the human community. The death that destroys is never the will of God. On the contrary, God is the never-ending summons to life.

The expression "this is God's will" must never be taken to mean that God wishes or even permits terrible calamities or injustices to happen. But it can mean, for a person of great faith, a continuing trust that God will summon forth new insights and create life out of death in new ways. Baum writes: "Jewish men and women on the way to the extermination chambers may have said to themselves that this incomprehensible and groundless evil was in some mysterious way God's will—in the sense that they continued to trust in God. But on the lips of an observer such a statement would be a dreadful blasphemy. . . . God's power over the world is not the miraculous action by which he makes things happen as he pleases, but the redemptive action by which he enables men to deal with their own problems." He calls people to "resist evil and find ways of conquering it."[14]

A Lutheran scholar, Franklin Sherman, carries forward Christian reasoning on the subject of how we may continue to speak of God after the Endlösung. Sherman concentrates upon the divine suffering as a religious solution to the problem of theodicy in light of the Holocaust. Neither the conception of a God of judgment nor that of a God of moral education will do, as we are confronted by Auschwitz. The same must be said, religiously and morally speaking, of a reputedly self-limiting God. We may, however, speak of a suffering God, for "God participates in the suffering of men, and man is called to participate in the sufferings of God." And while it is true that the Christian will, accordingly, turn to the cross "as the symbol of the agonizing God," this cannot be allowed to mean any kind of triumphalism. "A God who suffers is the opposite of a God of triumphalism. We can speak of God after Auschwitz only as the one who calls us to a new unity as beloved brothers—not only between Jews and Christians, but especially between Jews and Christians."[15]

Rabbi Arthur J. Lelyveld is prepared, with Gregory Baum, to raise questions about the divine omnipotence. According to him, we have no choice but to grant that gargantuan evil exists and is uncontrolled by God. "We cannot pretend to know why—we can only cling stubbornly to the conviction that there *is* meaning—*lam'rot hakol*, in spite of everything." However, Lelyveld refuses to forsake the demanding side of God. On the contrary, he divides the Christian and Jewish faiths precisely in that way. "The God of Christianity is the God who *gives;* the God of Judaism is the God who *demands*." In the cosmic scope "there is that which is demanded of *us*." "The central stress of Judaism has been: 'Thou *shalt* be unto me a Kingdom of priests,' '*Choose* life!,' and 'Thus saith the Lord. . . . ' The covenant obligation that is central in Judaism calls upon the Jew to be co-worker in perfecting the world—not to *be* saved but to *participate* in the redemption of mankind." Accordingly, as a Jew "I must interpret my responsibility as it is defined by the covenant task." As Lelyveld puts it, "the greater the evil, the more insistent and the more intense, even to the point of anguish, is the demand."[16]

However terrible the evil of the Final Solution, it was not uniquely evil. Lelyveld sees Auschwitz as "a new phenomenon only in a quantitative and technological sense." The more efficient instruments for carrying out human destruction "give the nature of evil new dimensions," but they do "not change its essential nature." What, then, is to be said of God in making a demand that Jews, and humankind in general, confront this ever-increasing efficiency of evil? Lelyveld responds by attesting to the sympathy that dwells "at the heart of the universe"—

sympathy for the very creatures upon whom the divine demands are made. "In this sense, while I cannot say that God 'willed' Auschwitz, I can say that God 'wept' over Auschwitz." God also suffers from anguish. It is this divine sympathy that "enables man to enter into 'partnership' with God." Thus, while Lelyveld, like Baum, finds it a "repelling, blasphemous idea" to adjudge that God willed the destruction of the six million, he insists that we cannot withdraw from the sufferers "the dignity that lies in recognition that there existed among them a willingness to die in fulfillment of a distinctive role." Some had the "incredible courage" to fight "despite the certainty of the futility of resistance"; others were sublimely ready to march, in defiance, "to the freight cars that were to carry them into Hell with the *Ani Ma-amin* on their lips." (The *Ani Ma-amin* is part of the Jewish liturgy: "I affirm, with unbroken firmness, that the Messiah will come. And even though He tarries, even so, I affirm it.") "We have said that Hitler's victims were offered no alternative. This is not wholly so. They had the alternative of dying as cravens, of cursing God and their identity. All the evidence says that in overwhelming numbers they died with dignity."[17]

All in all, Lelyveld believes that we can affirm general providence—that is, meaning and purpose in the whole, and the thrust of cosmic evolution "toward greater love, greater harmony, and greater justice." But we must reject special providence, the juvenile notion of God as a personal protector and coddler. This is to ask "the impossible of the universe." In the relationship of genuine covenantal responsibility, "when God is the guarantor of value and the source of demand, then the confrontation of evil elicits not the plaintive 'Why did God do this?' but rather 'What does God ask of me?' "[18]

Viktor Frankl, a survivor, complements Gregory Baum's and Arthur Lelyveld's theological views through his experiential, psychiatrically oriented conclusions. Camp inmates had to stop asking about the meaning of life and instead think of themselves "as those who were being questioned by life—daily and hourly." The inmates' usual question had been, "If we don't survive, what meaning will all this suffering have?" Frankl turned the question around. If all this suffering and dying have no meaning, then what meaning has life itself? After all, a life whose meaning stands or falls upon the happenstance of one's own survival would not be, ultimately speaking, worth living at all. Frankl was led to conclude that the very meaning of life extends to suffering and death. Potentially, therefore, we can supply meaning to our own lives by suffering as well as by creating and loving, "by the way and manner in which we face our fate, in which we take our suffering upon ourselves." In the last analysis, man ought to realize "that it is not up to him to question—it is he who *is* questioned, questioned by life; it is he who has to answer, by answering for life. His role is to respond—to be responsible."[19]

A variation upon the refusal to have one's faith destroyed while yet conceding that the object of our faith is also our enemy is found in Zvi Kolitz's reconstruction of the last thoughts of a pious Jew named Yossel Rakover, who was apparently murdered in the *Judenvernichtung*. Rakover addresses God:

> You may insult me, you may castigate me, you may take from me all that I cherish and hold dear in the world, you may torture me to death—I shall believe in *you*, I shall love you no matter what you do to test me!
>
> And these are my last words to you, my wrathful God: nothing will avail you in the least. You have done everything to make me renounce you, to make me lose my faith in you, but I die exactly as I have lived, a *believer!*
>
> Eternally praised be the God of the dead, the God of vengeance, of truth and of law, who will soon show his face to the world again and shake its foundations with his almighty voice.
>
> Hear, O Israel, the Lord our God the Lord is One.
>
> Into your hands, O Lord, I consign my soul.[20]

Rakover's invective-prayer is highly paradoxical and dialectical. God seems to be the unquestioned superior of men, and yet his evidently sadistic wrath, in conjunction with the resoluteness of the believer's faith, almost seems to make the human being morally superior to God. The reader is left wondering who is the better God: the One of Jewish tradition, or the man whose vituperation is washed by a holy assent. It is hard, psychologically speaking, to separate scorn, piety, and self-flagellation in Rakover's words.[21]

TOWARD CONCILIATION

Our ultimate challenge is fully to recognize the reality of evil for what it is, including human and divine responsibility for suffering, without at the same time betraying the foundational conviction that God is active in history, a conviction requisite to the belief that human life has meaning. In the words of Ulrich E. Simon, "nothing can be made of this mass dying if man is the measure of all things, except the message of an anthropology of despair: the only thing that matters is to be outside, and not inside, the cage."[22] Eliezer Berkovits helps, we submit, to reconcile the yes of faith in God with the no to God that is required for the sake of human dignity, the very image of God. Unlike many interpreters, Berkovits confronts head-on the ineluctable fact of the divine culpability for evil and suffering. Yet he does not end up in the denial of God.

Berkovits makes clear that he has no intention of explaining and certainly not of justifying the silence of God during the European Holocaust. This very caution enables him to speak existentially and forthrightly, yet not with impiety. ("The one who is silent may be so-called only because he is present.") Berkovits emphasizes that nothing can exonerate God for the suffering of the innocent in history. (We may interject that while man is sinful and blameworthy for his actions, this simply does not exculpate God. Berkovits has already been cited on this in chapter 3: "God is responsible for having created a world in which man is free to make history." No human being ever had anything to do with his own birth into this world. It is in this sense that we are required to declare the continuing innocence of men.) Now there simply is no justification for the tragedy and suffering of men in the world. "God's dominion over the world is not a dominion of justice. In terms of justice, he is guilty. He is guilty of creation." There is no justification for the ways of God, the ways of providence. Within the dimension of time and history, such ways are simply unforgivable. Yet it is possible for us to accept these ways, and hence to forgive. What is the moral basis of this acceptance, this forgiveness? There is the possibility of a trust in God, in a dimension beyond but fulfilling history, in which the tragedy of man will find a transformation.

One of the teachers of the Talmud notes that when God asks Abraham to offer him his son Isaac as a sacrifice, the exact rendering of the biblical words reads: "Take, I pray thee, thy son." In the view of this teacher the "binding of Isaac" was not a command of God, but a request that Abraham take upon himself this most exacting of all God's impositions. In a sense we see in this a recognition that the sacrificial way of the innocent through history is not to be vindicated or justified! It remains unforgivable. God Himself has to ask an Abraham to favor Him by accepting the imposition of such a sacrifice. The divine request accompanies all those through history who suffer for the only reason that God created man, whom God himself has to endure. Within time and history God remains indebted to His people; He may be long-suffering only at their expense. It was hardly ever as true as in our own days, after the Holocaust. Is it perhaps what God desires—a people, to whom he owes so much, who yet acknowledges Him: children, who have every reason to condemn His creation, yet accept the creator in the faith that in the fullness of time the divine indebtedness will be redeemed and the divine adventure with man will be approved even by its martyred victims?[23]

Perhaps we are a little better situated now to address the problem of the covenant. For the question remains searingly with us: can the assertion continue to be made that central to the covenant is the obligation of the Jewish people to be "suffering servants" of the Lord? Can this assertion be defended morally today, after the Final Solution, or has it become an affront to the image of God in man?

An enigmatic passage in *A Beggar in Jerusalem* grasps us. We cited the end of the passage in chapter 3; its context is the ecstatic Jewish return to the Old City of Jerusalem.

The crowd keeps getting larger. Military personnel and officials, celebrities and journalists, all are streaming by in one continuous procession, along with rabbis and students, gathered from all over the city, from every corner of the land. Men, women, and adolescents of every age, every origin and speaking every language, and I see them ascending toward the Wall, toward all that remains of their collective longing. Just like long ago, at Sinai, when they were given the Torah. Just like a generation ago, in the kingdom of night, when it was taken back.[24]

77

What was it that we witnessed in the Endlösung? Was it the recantation of the covenant? If so, to where was the covenant taken? To oblivion? If not to oblivion, then to what place? Could it be that the covenant was received back in order to be incarnated in a fresh form?

To some, the taking back of the covenant is as legendary as its bestowal. In consonance with this view, there was in fact no singular kingdom of night, for there never was a singular kingdom of day.

For others, God recanted because of the sins of his people. Israel betrayed the divine statutes and had to be judged. In response to this point of view, we cannot refrain from observing that there is much laughter in *A Beggar in Jerusalem*. For the most part, it is fearful, maniacal laughter. According to Rabbi Nachman of Bratzlav, somewhere in the world there is a certain city that encompasses all other cities. In the city is a street that contains all the other streets of the city; on that street is a house dominating all the other houses; it contains a room that comprises all the other rooms of the house. "And in that room there lives a man in whom all other men recognize themselves. And that man is laughing. That's all he ever does, ever did. He roars with laughter when seen by others, but also when alone."[25] Is there something special for him to laugh about now, F.S., in the shadow of the Final Solution? Yes, there is a special cause: the man is laughing because it was *in the kingdom of night* that the Torah was taken back. (This fact determines eschatologically all other transformations of the covenant.) We believe—we hope without falling into unkindness—that someone who identifies the Endlösung as an act of judgment by God upon his people makes himself subject to confinement in that room of laughter, where he will have to listen, without surcease, to the laughing man.

The teaching that the divine election of Israel requires the Jewish people to suffer distinctively and unendingly for the sake of God and his purposes was sent to perdition in the gas chambers and crematoria. The symbolic declaration may be made that God recanted with reference to the Torah because he could no longer live with himself. The kingdom of night proved too much, even for him. Elsewhere in *A Beggar in Jerusalem* a young madman, one of only three survivors who had escaped the deportation, asks: "How does God justify Himself in His own eyes, let alone in ours? If the real and the imaginary both culminate in the same scream, in the same laugh, what is creation's purpose, what is its stake?"[26]

It is because of the torment carried by the "blasphemous" implication of the necessary penitence of God and the burden of the singular horror of the Holocaust that some of us have no choice now but to range ourselves against the covenant of demand, the demand to Jews to suffer, to be uniquely obligated. Rather, there must be some other form of covenant: of promise, of freedom, of defiance, of survival, of normality, of something, of anything, but *not of Auschwitz,* not a religious sanction to the murder of Jews.

It is just here that morality and theology are welded together and made wholly one. The flame that fuses them thereby burns down our prison, and we are set free. How is the past to be redeemed? How is the Final Solution finally to be annihilated? There is no way, save through the radical transformation of the covenant. The covenant of demand means divine consent to Jewish oppression. The elect were informed that they were going to have to be "a kingdom of priests and a holy nation" (Exod. 19:6). There is no theological or moral way to give answer to the Endlösung unless we arrange a decent and fitting burial for this entire idea. There is no way to give answer until we beat into the dust the myth of the Jew as "suffering servant." The gestalt beyond all covenantal demands, the forming of full Jewish humanity, is the birth of the epoch F.S., after the Final Solution.

Yes, the Torah was taken back in the kingdom of night. Does this mean that it will not be renewed? No. It is renewed. But it is transformed. The covenant between God and his people no longer bears the stigma of demand—and not even (to return to Eliezer Berkovits's exposition) the character of a request. As Irving Greenberg has helped us to see, the covenant is resurrected as a wholly voluntary readiness on the part of Jews to continue to bear the yoke of Torah. They are in no way required to do so, nor even asked to do so. But they may will to do so, in service and therefore in joy. Here is the ever-potential incredibility of Jewish existence today: to honor the life of Torah after the death of Auschwitz, and without having to do it.

79

This, we dare to say, is today's revelation of God.[27] But it is left to each generation, to every Jew, to make the decision.

The final and sublime logic in the avowal of total liberation is that the honoring of the life of Torah cannot be used as a weapon against those Jews who choose not to be "religious." Where freedom is truly reigning, it has to be indivisible. After the Holocaust, the sanctifying of the divine Name (*Kiddush ha-Shem*) is carried forward and accomplished in new ways through the sanctifying of human life as such (*Kiddush ha-Haim*). This unfolding of the covenant destroys any invidious judgments against the secular human being in contrast to the religious person. The flesh and the spirit are equals.

We fail to meet here the question of how the authentic witness for God and the truth is to identify itself and to be identified, through symbolization or other means, as against the witness for the devil and evil. What are the peculiar marks of those who will to be witnesses? The search for the answer to this question is among the most baffling and fateful challenges to face post-Holocaust theology.

FORGIVENESS

After the Endlösung, the question of the meaning of our human existence and the question of the will of God are brought together and given an existential (nontheoretical) answer with the aid of a rethinking of the covenantal relation. When we speak of an "answer," we do not pretend to have attained ultimacy, for there are no ultimate human answers to the problems of life; at best, we may express fragmentary truths that simply help us to keep going, to get up in the morning and to face another day. As Yehuda Aschkenasy of Holland has said, it is impossible to write a theology of suffering, because when you meet real suffering yourself, you won't get an answer through theology—though you may eventually learn to live with suffering.[28] The covenant is both transcended and fulfilled once the compassion of God stands in judgment upon the divine demand, once God, forgiving us, is also forgivable and forgiven. This kind of affirmation is fully post-Holocaust in character; that is to say, it takes the Endlösung with utter seriousness as a morally and theologically

80

determinative event. Yet this view does not fall into cynicism or unbelief, for that would indeed grant a posthumous triumph to the Nazis as surrogates of the devil.

There is a passage from Reinhold Niebuhr that, when given wider application than Niebuhr had in mind, conjoins him and Elie Wiesel. The passage brings as well a little focus to these poor midrashim upon the tale of that strange beggar who reaches out to us from the deep shadows of Jerusalem—no, from amid the sunshine of that city. The words are almost thirty years old now.

> Nothing that is worth doing can be achieved in a lifetime; therefore we must be saved by hope. Nothing which is true or beautiful or good makes complete sense in any immediate context of history; therefore we must be saved by faith. Nothing we do, however virtuous, can be accomplished alone. Therefore we are saved by love.[29]

One vital thrust of post-Holocaust theology, Jewish and Christian, is the asseveration that the "we" here must refer as much to God as to human beings.

5

BETWEEN SERVITUDE
AND FREEDOM

If it is so that the history of God and men is afflicted radically by the Endlösung, the very least that ought to be done is the altering of Christian dogma (as, in some measure, Jewish dogma). However, at the end of chapter 3 we raised the question of whether there is any hope that Christian teachings and behavior will change. In order to carry this question forward, we suggest a working typology or continuum, with the usual proviso that different parties do not always exactly fit one type and often cross the lines between types.

RESPONSES TO THE
HOLOCAUST

1. For some Christians, the Holocaust remains, morally speaking, a nonevent. (We speak of "nonevent" now in a quite different way from the spiritual refusal to permit the Holocaust to destroy one's faith, the way the term is applied in chapter 4.) Evaluatively stated, the Christians involved remain servants of the church's unholy past. Large numbers of persons, within Germany but also beyond, live and act in ways quite unaffected by the Final Solution. They think and behave as if there had been no kingdom of night. Nothing essential is learned or changed.

2. For others, the Holocaust manages to gain the status of a partial event; it is partial in that it is able, objectively speaking, to exert a greater or lesser impact upon Chris-

tian thinking and action. Evaluatively expressed, the door to freedom from the past is at least being set ajar for Christians within this category.

3. In a third model, *metanoia*—total revolution—is achieved within and through the Holocaust. Evaluatively put, Christians are granted the power and joy of liberation. Liberation means not only complete self-acceptance, but also freedom from the idolatry of triumphing over the other, the Jew. Once we are enabled to accept ourselves, we can begin to accept the other. Such deliverance may be approximated collectively, as well as being realized individually.

In the present chapter the first two of these models are explored, with greater attention being given to the second. The third possibility is given voice in our two final chapters; it is represented as well through our critical comments upon the other two types.

MODEL 1: THE PRE-HOLOCAUST PAST AS SLAVEHOLDER

From among many candidates, we choose one instance of recent Christian advocacy which proceeds, to all intents and purposes, as though there never was any such event as the Holocaust. This small book, *Die Judenfrage* ("The Jewish Question"), by the Christian writer Friedrich Gruenagel, is part of a series devoted to "the strengthening of biblical faith and Christian life."[1] A major reason for our selection of the volume is that *Die Judenfrage* is popularly written and was designed to reach large audiences in the churches.

Gruenagel's monograph initially prompts high expectations in its call for the reconciliation of Jews and Christians. At first the author appears to be directing us to a revolutionary position, a radical rethinking of Christianity, as the required moral reaction to the crimes against Jews. He emphasizes that the unparalleled events of the past remain unmastered (*eine unbewältigte Vergangenheit*). Satanic forces ever put us in their grasp, quite

as readily as do divine powers. This truth lay incarnate in the
dark events before 1945. Gruenagel laments the continuing and
incorrigible antipathy to Jews, abetted as this is by the ideology
of antisemitism, a pathological disease of the spirit that can
break out in any time and in any land.

In addressing himself to the work of Vatican Council II, this
Protestant writer praises Pope John XXIII's attempt to strike at
the theological roots of antisemitism, and he regrets that the
pope's effort was to be partly despoiled by Arab Christian inter-
ference. He identifies the human machinations that sought to
undercut the council's striving to provide a statement on Judaism
and the Jews. Regrettably, the theological question was in-
terfered with by political interests. Gruenagel lauds Augustin
Cardinal Bea's struggle against the "absurd Christian ideology"
which teaches that the Jewish role or presence in the event of
Golgotha meant God's damnation of the Jews. Vatican Council II
clearly proclaimed the common origins of Jews and Christians
and attained an out-and-out condemnation of antisemitism.[2]

In light of these statements, how is it possible to link Gruenagel to the ideology of the Holocaust as nonevent? It seems
astonishing, but immediately after his commendatory reference
to the council's utilization of Holy Scripture, Gruenagel feels
called upon to insert the traditionalistic contention that "the
law" (*das Gesetz*) is the true and fateful cause of the woes of the
Jewish people. He attributes to the apostle Paul an apprehension of a certain depravity (*Verworfenheit*) within his own
people despite their acknowledged election by God, which
prompts Gruenagel to refer to the "spiritual torment" in Heinrich Heine's conclusion that "the Jewish religion is not really a
religion; it is a disaster." To be sure, this judgment did not
make Heine an enemy of his people. Yet he "saw through" to
the cause of their misfortune. In Gruenagel's words, "the pre-
tension to the absoluteness of the law stood in the way."[3]

It is not long before Gruenagel explodes into anti-Jewish
sentiments, cataloguing many supposedly fundamental and lasting Jewish sins. At the center of these transgressions, he asserts,
lie Jewish hardheartedness and nationalism. In fact, readers are
advised that the German Nazi self-application of the idea of
election, of being the chosen race, simply represented a reincar-
nating of the mentality of Jews. Today, Jews and Israelis main-

tain the threatening outlook of claiming a monopoly upon the blessedness of God, whom they utilize in order to make themselves victorious at the expense of other peoples. As Gruenagel's argument develops, it becomes clear that, as he sees it, the only basic fault of the Christian church in its entire relationship with the Jewish people is its failure to bring the Jews to Christ, as their solitary savior from "the law," nationalism, and other evils. Antisemitism becomes primarily a matter of Jewish culpability, the consequence of the hardness of heart of Jews. All in all, only when the Jews conquer their sins and "return" to Christ will antisemitism be overcome and Christians and Jews reconciled.[4]

Gruenagel's exposition brings forcibly to mind a concept or, better, an eventuality that is being argued over in some German church circles today: *eine geistliche Endlösung,* "a spiritual Final Solution." Among concerned Christian scholars in today's Germany stands Rudolf Pfisterer of Schwäbisch-Hall, who emphasizes that the Christian attempt to "save" Jews is, in his words, "nothing more than the continuing work of the Holocaust."[5] For, in the last resort, what is the moral and practical difference between stuffing Jews into gas chambers and mass graves and striking at the very heart of their religious and human integrity through seeking to convert them? There are, of course, other telling means of subverting Jewish rights and dignity—through, for example, Gruenagel's varied accusations against the Jewish people. As an alternative to the term "non-event," we may speak of the Endlösung as a "perpetuating event"—an event that serves to give continuing life to certain stereotypes and prejudices, which in turn nurture a spirit conducive to future Holocausts.

Friedrich Gruenagel and others of similar persuasion are living corporally in the years after the Holocaust, but their efforts and outlook are essentially pre-Holocaust in character. Franklin H. Littell attests that the Endlösung is and will remain "the major event in recent church history," because it "called into question the whole fabric of Christendom," exposed in the most awful measure the church's rebellion and betrayal, revealed "the final blasphemy of the baptized gentiles," their "open revolt against the God of Abraham, Isaac, and Jacob," and showed the thinness of the veneer with which a sham

Christianity covered "the actual devotion of the European tribes to other gods."[6] It is not to be wondered at, therefore, that Gruenagel and those who share his views are forced into a situation where, to all intents and purposes, the Holocaust did not really happen. That is to say, it is as if there never were any murder camps.

MODEL 2: CRACKS IN THE PRISON BARS

Major exemplification of the second model, the Holocaust as a partial event, is found in an official pronouncement of the Council of the Protestant Church in Germany (EKD; Evangelische Kirche in Deutschland) entitled *Christen und Juden* ("Christians and Jews"). This document is the product of five years of discussion and study.

The EKD's declaration goes farther theologically and morally than that church has ever gone before. The German churchmen and theologians who prepared the statement remain acutely aware of the Endlösung; plainly it is much on their conscience. They speak of the deep trauma that the event created for Christians, of the church's latter-day rediscovery of its Jewish roots, and of the abiding integrity of the faith of Judaism. They confess the appalling role of the Christian world in the historic persecution of the Jewish people, including the causative power of Christian antisemitism in the annihilation of the European Jews. The council emphasizes that a special obligation falls upon the Christians of Germany to oppose the new antisemitism that appears in the form of politically and socially motivated anti-Zionism. Christians have a particular duty to support the independence and security of Israel—not alone as a political reality or human achievement, but also within the very frame of reference of the history of the people of God.[7]

On the other side, these spokesmen are beset by a traditional and familiar Christian dilemma. The EKD pronouncement goes on to reflect the conflict over the *Judenmission*, the mission to the Jews, that continues to divide German Christians. The authors pose the question of how the Christian is to bear witness to the Jew. Asserting that Christ is the "Savior of all men," they insist that while certain ongoing missionary practices have given Jews reason for mistrust, Christians cannot remain silent concerning the ground of their hope and faith. Indeed, they contend that, according to the newer Christian understanding, mission remains equal to dialogue as a dimension of the one Christian witness to Jews. Thus, in the end, the council is not totally prepared, so the evidence goes, to accept Jews simply as equal brothers and sisters.[8]

The dominating challenge faced by the EKD council is how to reconcile its call for unqualified justice and love for the Jewish people with its Christological and other theological assurances (including the Resurrection), as plainly and forcibly stated throughout *Christen und Juden*, according to which the Christian faith comprises the fulfilled truth of God, the real consummation of Jewish (as of human) hopes and expectations.[9] *Christen und Juden* thus typifies the unending and tragic plight of the Christian church in the presence of the Jewish people: human equality is compromised and threatened by a presupposed inequality of decision, behavior, and faith.

Finally, *Christen und Juden* fails to surmount or exclude the ancient canard of Jewish responsibility, or coresponsibility, with the Romans for the execution of Jesus.[10] Even were such responsibility a reality, the moral and psychological question remains: what is the purpose of repeating this charge within a church statement devoted to Christian-Jewish reconciliation, and this in the land of the Final Solution? (Moreover, there is implicit in it encouragement to the Christian community to repeat the canard each church year throughout the world, as is still the dreadful custom.) In a word, the Council of the EKD is living, simultaneously, a post-Holocaust life and a pre-Holocaust life.[11]

JÜRGEN MOLTMANN AND MODEL 2

Our second model is additionally represented in the developing point of view of Jürgen Moltmann of the University of Tübingen. In keeping with Moltmann's considerable influence, we offer a lengthy analysis of, and response to, his position. The intensive discussion will also serve to focus a number of moral and theological issues posed by the Holocaust. The Endlösung has had little impact upon theology in Germany. Will German religious thought continue to live, as it were, before 1933? With special reference to New Testament theology, Charlotte Klein has shown that a pessimistic reply to that question still must prevail. On the other hand, there are some signs of change. Moltmann has explicitly stated that the Holocaust is a most important influence on his rethinking of Christian theology.[12]

We concentrate upon two of Moltmann's important works, *Der Gekreuzigte Gott* (published in translation as *The Crucified God*) and *Kirche in der Kraft des Geistes* (published in translation as *The Church in the Power of the Spirit*). Our study of these materials has been supplemented by personal conversations with their author, which in no way implies that he accepts our judgments of them. It is appropriate to stress, however, that the key issue at this juncture is not whether Moltmann provides a "valid" interpretation of the Christian faith, and certainly not whether we do, but instead whether Moltmann's representation of the Christian gospel in fact confronts the destruction of the Jews of Europe without equivocation, in accordance with his own declaration.

Several areas of discussion are suggested by *The Crucified God*. (We do not see any way totally to dissociate this title from the infamous charge of deicide, but we are assured that Moltmann's usage is not intentionally prejudicial.)

First, there is the morally decisive and even fateful question of Jesus, "the law" (*das Gesetz*), and his reputed rejection by "the Jews." Moltmann makes Jesus "a scandal to the devout," which becomes a fundamental reason for the Crucifixion. Jesus was sentenced to die by "the law." He was cursed and condemned by the "guardians of the law" and of faith, and killed as a "blasphemer," having been "handed over to the Romans to be crucified." His "sufferings and humiliation" are linked to "his freedom towards the law." Jesus placed himself "above the limits of the contemporary understanding of the law," demonstrating through his forgiveness of sins "God's eschatological law of grace towards those without the law and the transgressors of the law." Moltmann discerns a clash between Jesus' gospel and "the law" which led to a legal trial. He underwent "a trial before the Sanhedrin" as well as before Pilate. At stake were "the righteousness of faith and the righteousness of works, . . . the justification of the godless and the justification of the righteous." The Jews "condemned Jesus and delivered him to crucifixion" out of ignorance and lawlessness, "against the will of god and therefore against the law," and as evil men. "The purpose of the sending of the son of God is liberation from slavery under the law for the freedom of the children of God." Through faith in Christ men become "free sons of God." The unconditional love of Jesus for the rejected "made the Pharisees his enemies and brought him to the cross."[13]

The heart of Moltmann's exegesis is found in this passage:

> [Jesus'] execution must be seen as a necessary consequence of his conflict with the law. His trial by the guardians of the law was in the broader sense of the term a trial about the will of God, which the law claimed to have codified once for all. Here the conflict between Jesus and the law was not a dispute about a different will, or the will of a different God, but about the true will of God, which for Jesus was hidden and not revealed by the human concept of the law. Jesus' claim to fulfill the law of the righteousness of God, the claim made in the Sermon on the Mount, and his freedom from the law should not be understood as contradictory. For Jesus the "radicalization of the *Torah*" and the "transgression of the *Torah*" basically both amount to the same thing, the freedom of God to show grace. Thus the right which he claimed to forgive sins goes beyond the *Torah* and reveals a new righteousness of God in judgment, which could not be expected according to the traditions of the law.[14]

Moltmann does not take sufficiently into account the insistence within much contemporary scholarship that, very largely, the conflicts and happenings he describes do not reflect historical truth. Minimally speaking, his interpretations are off balance. They fail even to acknowledge, much less to respond to, the massive historical work that maintains the precise opposite of his claims. Given this other increasingly accepted conclusion, it is just incorrect to say that Jesus stood in opposition to contemporary Judaism, its representatives and its teachers. He did not come into conflict with "the law" or with his people. He lived and died a faithful Jew, standing indeed for the best in the tradition of the Pharisees. Pharisaism sought fundamentally to keep "the law" alert to human needs; Jesus and the Pharisees were in this respect reformers (against the Sadducees).[15]

Moltmann is quite aware of the general historical question, "Is the preaching of the church in continuity and harmony with Jesus and his history?" He acknowledges the place and the use of historical criticism. Yet he then writes that critical scholarship must "ask what the testimonies have to say about those to whom they bear witness, and what faith has to say about the one who is the object of faith, and whether it is in accordance with him."[16] We respond that surely critical scholarship must also ask whether elements or data that are allegedly "in accordance with him" are also in accordance with the truth.

To refer to a most grave subject, is it possible or the case that Jesus could have been condemned in the manner Moltmann reports? There is simply no way around or through the formidable conflict between New Testament claims of what Jesus said and did and what he may actually have said and done. Fundamental and responsible historical scholarship requires that we continually look behind the New Testament documents, and indeed that we study these documents with full attention to independent knowledge of first-century Judaism and Palestine. In this latter context, particular attention is called to the charge of blasphemy reputedly leveled against Jesus.[17] On grounds at once juridical and historical, Justice Haim Cohn of the Supreme Court of Israel argues convincingly against the possibility of this charge. He also corrects certain other errors. Thus, the whole notion that Jesus was given a Jewish trial on a charge of blasphemy, that he was found guilty of blasphemy on his own confession, and that he then received a capital sentence through the Sanhedrin runs hard against no less than seven well-established provisions of Jewish law.[18]

Again, how could it be possible that Jesus, a God-fearing Jew, would claim to forgive sins against God himself? Moltmann says that "the right of showing mercy belongs to the judge alone. When a man who cannot but be under the law arrogates to himself this exclusive right of a judge, and puts himself in the judge's place, he reaches out his arm towards God and blasphemes the Holy One. This is not the blasphemy of cursing God, according to the law, but the blasphemy of self-deification." Moltmann also maintains that in Jesus' time blasphemy was understood broadly, extending even to impudent talk against Torah or "stretching out" one's hand against God—this as against the narrower post-Christian Halakah, according to which the blasphemer must have expressed the name of God clearly in the form of a curse. "In the case of Jesus it cannot have been a renunciation of God by a curse, but can only have been the blasphemy of a false Messiah made by a 'hand stretched out against God,' someone intervening in a matter where rights are reserved for God alone."[19] However, as Cohn points out, the incompatibility of the alleged trial with the actual facts rests upon everything we know from reliable sources respecting the law and procedure obtaining at that particular time.[20]

Jürgen Moltmann equates "blasphemer" with "demagogic false Messiah," and claims that Jesus' identification as a blasphemer in these terms "is difficult to dispute in view of the whole of his scandalous message."[21] In addition to the most debatable character of the assertion that, religiously speaking, Jesus' teaching was in fact "scandalous," the trouble here is that "blasphemy" is interpreted much too loosely. Messianic claims, even extreme ones, simply were not received as blasphemous; that is to say, there is no biblical or rabbinic law on the subject. (We do not discuss the controversial issue of whether Jesus in truth claimed to be "messiah"; it appears that he did not.) Finally, were Jesus in fact found guilty of blasphemy, why was he not stoned to death, as required by the religious law? Moltmann fails to meet these all-decisive difficulties.

What is there to exercise us within the question of "the law"? Its bearing upon a concern with the Holocaust is weighty. We know that Nazi ideologists and the Deutsche Christen (the German Christian Movement) outdid each other in insisting that the Jewish "law" meant evil and slavery. Of course, it cannot be overstressed that the "higher law" of ostensible liberation through Jesus is the archenemy of Nazi "liberation." Yet the unhappy truth remains that persisting Christian negativism toward the Jewish "law" offers, however unintentionally, a negative form of alliance with National Socialist ideology, and in this respect helps to perpetuate pre-Holocaust influences. Moltmann asks, "Does inhuman legalism triumph over the crucified Christ, or does God's law of grace triumph

91

over the works of the law and of power?"[22] This question is
posed on the same page where he refers to "the cries for righteousness of those who are murdered and gassed." Moltmann's
query and his subsequent reference, when put together, form
an added, fateful question: did not the charge of "inhuman legalism" against Judaism and the Jewish people contribute to
the murdering and the gassing?[23] Irving Greenberg declares:
"Since even God should be resisted [were he to order a
Holocaust], we are called to challenge such central *sancta* as
the Gospels, the Church Fathers, and other sources for their
contributions to the sustenance of hate."[24] How can Moltmann
escape Greenberg's indictment once he has made the "guardians of the law" into the enemies of Jesus? In this crucial respect, his interpretation of the New Testament appears to be, at
one and the same time, pre-Holocaust and precritical.

There is some ground for suggesting that when Moltmann
makes Jesus the victim of his religion, of the "guardians of the
law" as well as of society and the state, he does so to the end of
establishing the absoluteness of Jesus' rejection[25]—in other
words, to the end of filling out his own theological system or
argumentation. Insofar as this is the case, Moltmann has subjected himself to the perils of ideology. As the British historian
James Parkes often asks, how can true theology ever be
grounded in false history?

JUDAISM AND THE JEWS

We consider next the related question of Jürgen Moltmann's description of, and attitude to, Judaism and the Jews, as
given voice in *The Crucified God*. The affirmation, expressed
by Moltmann, that God's grace is revealed in sinners and his
righteousness in the unrighteous, hardly originated with Christianity. For untold numbers of Jews, not "this faith" (Christianity), but Judaism is fully capable of setting them "free from
their cultural illusions, releasing them from the involvements
which blind them, and confronting them with the truth of their
existence and their society." In addition, to identify the Judaism of Jesus' day as a matter of works-righteousness is a basic
misinterpretation, one that echoes prevailing German biblical
scholarship before and since 1933.[26] Judaism is being misread

through the eyes of Pauline and Lutheran thought. (Moltmann is Reformed, but, as Wilhelm Pauck once remarked, it is very hard for German theologians to sever the umbilical cord that ties them to Martin Luther.) The New Testament scholar Krister Stendahl identifies the theological model of "Law" versus "Gospel" as a subtle and powerful form of anti-Jewishness in Christian theology, particularly in Protestantism and most prominently in Lutheranism.[27] The issue falsely becomes one of free divine grace versus the self-justifying acts of men. Significantly, when it comes to the Gospel of John, for example, Moltmann successfully avoids fundamentalism,[28] but not when it comes to the Jews, "the law," and such other tenuous claims as the one that Jesus forgave sins.

In truth, according to the historic and prevailing Jewish view, "the law" (better, Torah) means liberation. It is, indeed, "sweeter than honey" (Ps. 19:10). We think of the daily prayer of the Jew: "Our Father, our King, be gracious unto us for we have no works. Save us according to thy grace." This prayer is only made possible by Torah. Among many Christian faults is the failure to recognize that the whole Jewish attitude to Torah and to God's grace found its source and origin well before Christianity was born. Unhappily, Christians have been conditioned to misrepresent first-century Judaism, and thence later Judaism. In the traditional Jewish viewpoint, Torah constitutes God's gift of undeserved grace and freedom, of hope for the future, and of guidance for everyday life. Moltmann makes much of the ecstasy of freedom in Christ. But what does it mean to say, practically and in real life, that Christians are free and Jews are not? In what concrete way is the Christian "set free" more than the Jew? And what does it ever mean to include Jews among the "godless"?[29]

Moltmann also speaks of the positive effect that the Resurrection of Jesus may have on men "who are open to the world and to the future." Yet surely Jews and Judaism are widely and abidingly marked by such openness. Therefore, in going on to say that men who are closed to the future and without hope are not reached by the Resurrection, Moltmann does not honor the dignity and self-identity of Jews. Further, we must grapple with this consideration: the Christian form of the claim that the un-righteous are declared righteous is open to a charge of moral insensitivity. We do not quarrel with the note of universalism in Moltmann's denial that the unrighteous are punished with eternal condemnation, nor do we deny that "in the end the victims will not triumph over their executioners." But unless we allow a place for some form of essential condemnation, we deprive ourselves of theological and moral criteria for distinguishing between the exploiters and the exploited, between the Nazis and their victims. The problem here is the perennial temptation within the Christian community, especially within modern Christendom, to be deficient, in principle, at the point of justice. This is a fault against which Judaism has always retained safeguards. More seriously expressed, does not the Christian proclivity to stress the divine forgiveness constitute an ideological transgression against the victims of unrighteousness, a transgression that comes, ironically, from within the very circle of those who have been, historically, the victors, the powerful? Moltmann himself may be called to witness here: "indifference towards justice and injustice would be a retreat on the part of God from the covenant."[30]

Moltmann declares that he has "related the conflict between law and gospel to the promise of Abraham, the promise of life, and [has] argued that through the gospel this promise was liberated from the shadow of a legalist understanding of the law and given universal force for everyone who believes, whether Jew or Gentile." But what of the Jew who does not so believe? He must remain in some way unregenerate, upon Moltmann's own reasoning. Moltmann once remarked to Ernst Bloch that "only a Christian can be a good atheist."[31] The fact is that Jews beat Christians to this by dedivinizing the world long before Christianity came. And they thereby rewrote in advance Bloch's original judgment (turned around, approvingly, by Moltmann) that only an atheist can be a good Christian. The rewriting reads: only an atheist can be a good Jew; that is, can be one who denies the power of man's foolish gods, his idols.

It is important that there be a greater and more concrete stress upon the truth that the crucified man to whom Moltmann bears witness was a Jew. Moltmann attests that God became "the kind of man that we do not want to be: an outcast, accursed, crucified." But we must avoid the abstraction of "a" man who is then also taken to be the Christ of God. It is essential to emphasize just here that it was *this Jewish man* who was put to death, a declaration that in addition to its other necessities also helps to point to the singularity of antisemitism in time and place. Lastly, Moltmann contends that the Jewish answer to the question of redemption "could be described by saying that God forces Israel to repent through suffering." What is the ground of this allegation? Moltmann seeks support for the judgment in Emil L. Fackenheim, but this is not licit. To Fackenheim, God is anything but a coercive presence.[32]

THE CHRISTIAN IMPERIUM

A third issue for discussion raised by Jürgen Moltmann's work is the crucial matter of Christian absolutism and triumphalism. Moltmann attests that "*only* the crucified Christ can bring the freedom which changes the world because it is no longer afraid of death." The church of the crucified Messiah can liberate all men, including Jews. The preaching of the cross "is the *only* adequate access which the godless have" to the God who was crucified. "In the face of Jesus' death-cry to God, theology either becomes impossible or becomes possible *only* as specifically Christian theology." "*Only* from him [Jesus] and through him does the resurrection hope then extend to the living and dead." The way through judgment and Godforsakenness "is *only* passable for men in his company." Moltmann does concede that Israel demonstrates to the church "that the redemption of the world is still to come," yet earlier he denies any such function to Israel, holding that the church and the gospel meet the problem. Now, however, he goes on to explain the lack of redemption by adjudging that "the church of Christ is not yet perfect and the kingdom of God has not achieved full revelation as these two communities of hope, Israel and the church, continue to exist side by side."[33] This appears to imply that the absence of redemption centers essentially in the incompleteness of the church. Yet how is this anything but eventual Christian triumphalism, despite the consideration that elsewhere the "success" of the church and the redemption of the world are distinguished?

Again, while Moltmann asks for "an openness on the part of Christians to the existential basis of Judaism," his pages in

many respects also mirror an opaqueness to the Jewish apprehension of Judaism and of faith. Thus, he declares that

> when we have spoken of the conflict into which Jesus came with
> the "law," this does not refer to the Old Testament *Torah* as instruc-
> tion in the covenant of promise. The more the understanding of the
> *Torah* became remote from the promise, the more violent became
> the conflict with the gospel. The closer the understanding of the
> *Torah* draws to the original promise and election of Israel, the
> greater the possibility of an understanding for the law of grace, of
> the gospel and for the hope which it gives to the hopeless and to the
> gentiles.

Here it seems that Moltmann is either cutting the ground from
under the uniqueness he has earlier insisted upon respecting
the Christ-event, or he is telling the Jew, in effect, what he
ought to believe respecting the essential nature of faith—
namely, that faith is a matter of "promise" in contradistinction
to "law." The latter process certainly seems to be in force on
pages 134–35. The question is, within the bounds of *The Crucified God*, what is the ground for asserting that Israel "rightfully
exists alongside the church" and in consequence "cannot be
abolished"?[34]
      We are further told: "For a Christian there can be no
question of any guilt on the part of the Jews for the crucifixion
of Jesus—for his history is a theological history; there can only
be a question of an offer of God's law of grace, and therefore
only a question of hope for Israel."[35] But unfortunately it is not
only a "theological history" that Moltmann has been representing. Ostensibly he has been speaking in behalf of truth, which
for him entails the union of history and theology. Accordingly,
on the one hand, the Christian of whom he speaks is here
being instructed in a view different from the one Moltmann
claims to have led up to respecting Judaism; on the other
hand, the view he presents here can hardly avoid conversionism respecting Jews.
      Triumphalism is a serious enough problem for Christians
when it is being explicitly avowed. However, certain passages
in *The Crucified God*—inadvertently, we believe—fall into a
more serious condition: triumphalism in the guise of antitriumphalism. For example:

The gospel assumes this promise [to Abraham, the promise of life] and leads the believer out of the uncertainties of a legalist understanding to the point of trust in the faithfulness of God, "who gives life to the dead and calls into existence the things that do not exist" (Rom. 4:17). The conflict of Jesus with this contemporary understanding of the law and the conflict of the kerygma [proclamation] of Christ with the nomist understanding of the law in Paul in the following period consequently invalidate neither the promises of Israel nor the election of Israel; rather, they give force to the latter and make it universal. . . . The proclamation of the cross is "Christianity for all the world" (Blumhardt), and may not erect any new distinctions between men, say between Christians and non-Christians, the pious and the godless. Its first recognition leads to self-knowledge: to the knowledge that one is a sinner in solidarity with all men under the power of corruption. Therefore the theology of the cross is the true Christian universalism. There is no distinction here, and all will be made righteous without any merit on their part by his grace which has come to pass in Christ Jesus (Rom. 3:24)[36]

Alas, what Moltmann does here is precisely to erect distinctions between Christians, who "know" and "agree" with what he says, and Jews, the essence of whose faith is, for him, only grasped through the advantage of the true Christian gospel. And this result is brought to pass in the very course of denying that any distinctions or divisions between human beings are being erected. Here is moral and theological irony in its most dire form.

Is there something more grievous than saying that Christians understand the meaning and goal of Judaism and the promises and intentions of God better than Jews do? Yes, at least one thing: to do this while claiming that we are not doing it. Christian triumphalism is unfortunate enough, but it is not as unfortunate as the triumphalism that denies, or does not see, the truth that it is being triumphalist. It is very painful for us who are Christians, but we cannot escape from the judgment made by a participant at the Hamburg Holocaust Conference that there is a crying need for an unqualified relativization of absolute claims and loyalties of the kind that made the Endlösung possible. Jürgen Moltmann's own strictures against triumphalism and absolutism only appear to be that; in the end they are, we fear, representative of this very outlook. The declaration of "the freedom of God in faithfulness to his promises"[37] is, regrettably, not the end of division. It is a cause of division. More than that, it has issued in the persecution of the Jewish people, as well as of many other peoples.

Part of the famous episode in Elie Wiesel's *Night,* where a youth is murdered at a death camp and a voice in the watching crowd whispers that God is hanging there on the gallows, is reproduced in *The Crucified God.* Moltmann declares that any other response "would be blasphemy. There cannot be any other Christian answer to the question of this torment." But why has "Christian" been inserted here? The sufferer was a Jew. Further, the voice whispering a religious affirmation is that of a Jew. However, a more shattering consideration is involved. It may be asked why Moltmann's section, "The fullness of life in the trinitarian history of God," is placed immediately after the story from *Night.*[38] In these ways he implies a spiritual impotence and even emptiness for the faith of Judaism that does not, we fear, honor the command of love for the sufferers.

Moltmann moves quickly from the tale of the youth's hanging into a disputation between Christian theology and Jewish theology. Thus, for example, we are counseled that "only in and through Christ" is the "dialogical relationship with God opened up." And again, "no relationship of immediacy between God and man is conceivable" that is separated from the person of Christ. He refers to the church as the "universal community" of God, in explicit opposition to Jewish "particularism." It is sad that Moltmann should say these things at this place in his study. We plead for nothing more than respect for the dead children, women, and men who could never accept propositions such as those just cited. Let us enable the sufferers of Auschwitz and of the other hells to have their moment alone with God, or without him; let us not intrude with our theological caveats, however much these may stem from conscience and from conviction. Those who were murdered in the camps willingly or unwillingly represented the viewpoint Moltmann directly criticizes (although with some inaccuracy)[39] and not the Christian view he proclaims. Would it not be infinitely more fitting just to honor these persons as human beings, and let things stand that way?

Moltmann goes on to confess that "a 'theology after Auschwitz' may seem an impossibility or blasphemy." His own presentation is surely not blasphemous in any sense implied in that passage, but it is so in another way. It moves, in all inadvertence to be sure, against the God who dwelt in the destroyed Jews. The author testifies: "Even Auschwitz is taken up into the grief of the Father, the surrender of the Son, and the power of the Spirit."[40] Again Christian triumphalism intrudes itself in the guise of its very opposite. For what could be more uncompassionate than the trinitarianization, the Christianization, of Auschwitz, of those poor souls who, had they been allowed the choice, would have in many instances willingly inhaled the gas and entered the flames rather than accede to any trinity of the Christian God? Had Moltmann taken Christians who died in the camps and argued in a parallel way, our reaction would be entirely inappropriate. But these are Jews of whom he speaks.

THE FATE OF GOLGOTHA

An appraisal of *The Crucified God* cannot very well avoid a fourth issue, that of the cross. We are confronted by a two-sided question: the historical-moral fate of the cross as a Christian symbol, taken in the context of the fortunes of the Jewish people; and the moral and theological difficulty posed by Moltmann's linkage of the cross with ultimate horribleness. We must not pass over Moltmann's testimony that the crucified Christ is a powerful counterforce to Christianity as "an accomplice of oppression."[41] Full acknowledgment also must be made of the beauty and the strength of Moltmann's call for identifying the Christian gospel with the alienated, the poor, the rejected, and the godless. Nevertheless, we must comment critically upon certain additional passages in *The Crucified God*.

We read that Christ's "death is the death of the one who redeems men from death, which is evil." Yet in the Nazi time the cross assisted in bringing death, the polar contrary of the "pains of love." The "crucified Christ" simply cannot be separated from what has happened to the cross. Moltmann insists that "the cross does not divide Christians from Jews."[42] In truth, countless Jews of our world will never be able to distinguish the cross from the swastika, nor ought they be expected to do so. It was after the Holocaust that a Jewish woman, catching sight of a huge cross displayed in New York City each year at Christmastime, said to her walking companion, Father Edward

H. Flannery, "That cross makes me shudder. It is like an evil presence."[43] It was in and through the Endlösung that the symbol of the cross became ultimately corrupted by devilishness. When asked by two bishops in 1933 what he was going to do about the Jews, Adolf Hitler replied that he would do to them exactly what the Christian church had been advocating and practicing for almost two thousand years.[44]

Moltmann further writes: "The poverty and sufferings of Christ are experienced and understood only by participation in his mission and in imitating the task he carried out. Thus the more the poor understand the cross . . . as the cross of *Christ,* the more they are liberated from their submission to fate and apathy in suffering." No, in stark truth the six million Jews were not liberated, from death or from other suffering. They were not liberated at all, through "understanding" or anything else. " 'Resurrection, life, and righteousness' come through the death of this one man in favor of those who have been delivered over to death through their unrighteousness." In actuality, the Jews did not really qualify as unrighteous—nor, for that matter, as righteous. They were just murdered. And they were murdered just because they were Jews—not good or bad or any other kind of Jews, but just Jews. What does it mean to say to the Jews of Buchenwald or Bergen-Belsen that "through his suffering and death, the risen Christ brings righteousness and life to the unrighteous and the dying"?[45]

Much further along in *The Crucified God* we are advised that

> in becoming weak, impotent, vulnerable and mortal, he [the crucified God] frees man from the quest for powerful idols and protective compulsions and makes him ready to accept his humanity, his freedom and his mortality. In the situation of the human God the pattern formations of repressions become unnecessary. The limitations of apathy fall away. Man can open himself to suffering and to love. In *sympatheia* with the *pathos* of God he becomes open to what is other and new. The symbols which show him the situation of the human and crucified God give him protection as a result of which he can allow his own self-protection to fall.[46]

Moltmann may be right in asserting that some gentiles can still speak in these terms; many, of course, have done so. But the

utterly disarming fact is that before, within, and beyond Auschwitz, many Jews have been able to do the very same thing, and
this without faith in Christ. (To insinuate that the power of a
"hidden Christ" is present here would be to fall into a *deus ex
machina.*) The God of these Jews has long since freed them from
all kinds of idolatries. However, the truly decisive consideration
is that in the presence of Auschwitz, the claims Moltmann makes
for Christian symbols and virtues have come to have the very
opposite meanings and consequences from those he indicates.
For now, within his own history and within ours, the categories
of "weakness," "impotence," "vulnerability," "mortality," "re-
pressions," "openness to suffering and love," and "protection"
have all been transubstantiated into demonic structures. As Irving Greenberg observes, in our world suffering only helps to
"strengthen rampant evil and to collaborate in the enthronement
of the devil."[47] The endlessly woeful consequence is that the
Crucifixion is robbed of its redemptiveness. All that survives
upon the hill of Golgotha is unmitigated evil. After Auschwitz,
the Crucifixion cannot be accepted as a determinative symbol of
redemptive suffering. From the point of view of the Holocaust,
God is not met on the cross, even in his "Godforsakenness."
Once upon a time he may have been met there, but he is not met
there any longer. As we seek to behold Golgotha now, our sight
is blocked by huge mounds of torn bodies and ashes.

On Moltmann's own reasoning, the only two allowable pos-
sibilities appear to be that the Jews of the death camps were
either redeemed or remained in some way unregenerate or perverse. If we opt for the first possibility, what does the redemption of these Jews mean? They were piled into heaps of corpses
and either buried or burned. With respect to the second possibility, they did not identify with the suffering Christ, and this at
the very boundary-situation of their lives. Therefore, did they
deserve their suffering? It is obscene to say that the Jews of the
death camps were somehow redeemed, and it is outrageous to
suggest that they were perverse for not identifying with the
suffering Christ.

The measure of our disquietude here is tied to the ironic
truth that Jürgen Moltmann's ideals are the very highest: he
struggles against blasphemy, against hopelessness, against ex-
ploitation. Reinhold Niebuhr taught that the most formidable

temptations of man assail him not at his lowest moments, but at his highest. There is at this place in Moltmann's work a temptation to the greatest blasphemy of all, as he himself uses that concept. For it was the very faith he identifies as offering the ultimate assurance to man which itself played a major role in bringing the Jews of the Endlösung to their state of horror and forsakenness. Accordingly, Moltmann's theory turns out to be, at this precise point, not one of assurance and hope, but one of hopelessness. It purports to deliver men, but it does the opposite: it helps to subject certain human beings to the most terrible suffering and degradation, and for the sole reason that they do not or cannot accept "the faith." We are met here, not by the humaneness and the freedom for which Moltmann so passionately and honestly pleads, but by their very antitheses. Any faith that is capable of this evil outcome will have to be radically regenerated, along with the blasphemous and hopeless faiths Moltmann so admirably and rightly condemns.

A second aspect of the question of the cross is more decisive, because it is not eligible for the possible claim or rejoinder that the cross, after all, transcends and is immune to a certain historical-moral fate and thereby is able to retain its redemptive power, come what may. (We have to make clear, however, that any such claim or rejoinder remains steeped in ideology, for, no matter how valiantly we twist or turn, *the* truth always proves in the end to be *our* truth.)

Moltmann points out that his earlier *Theology of Hope* "began with the *resurrection* of the crucified Christ" and that in *The Crucified God* he is "turning back to look at the *cross* of the risen Christ."[48] We may have the temerity to envisage a next step: the nonresurrection (as yet) of the crucified Jesus and the crucifixion of the nonresurrecting Christ. This potential development may be formulated in at least two alternative ways: 1) absolute Godforsakenness (until the still-future resurrection, which means the future resurrection of Jesus, as of others); or 2) the pure faith of Christian Judaism (not to be confused with Jewish Christianity, which is the faith of Jews and not of gentiles). If we are to "turn back" with radical and total validity, and radical and total resoluteness, then let us really turn back— to the facts of the crucifixion of the Jew Jesus, and thence to the suffering Jews (of whom Jesus remains, to be sure, in a real sense the representative, the *Stellvertreter*). However, we here comment only upon the first of these two formulations.

We have just implied that there is an "absolute Godforsakenness" which transcends and overcomes Moltmann's advocacy in *The Crucified God*. His testimony to the event of Jesus' death upon the cross as comprising the center and existential focus of the Christian faith—this in unique association with Jesus' allegedly utter Godforsakenness—will not do. Moltmann adjudges that due to Jesus' "full consciousness that God is close at hand in his grace," his abandonment and deliverance up to death, as one rejected, are the very torment of hell, and put at stake the very deity of Jesus' God and Father.[49] We suggest that this particular "abomination of desolation" simply does not stand up as the absolute horror upon which Christian faith can and should, dialectically, build its hope. We contend that in comparison with certain other sufferings, Jesus' death becomes relatively nondecisive.

Here is a description of the disposal of Jewish children in Auschwitz in the late summer of 1944:

> ... when the Hungarian Jews arrived we used a music camouflage. At the time the children were burned on big piles of wood. The crematoria could not work at the time, and therefore the people were just burned in open fields with those grills, and also children were burned among them. Children were crying helplessly and that is why the camp administration ordered that an orchestra be assembled by a hundred inmates and should play. They played very loud all the time. They played the Blue Danube or Rosamunde; so that even the people in the city of Auschwitz could not hear the screams. Without the orchestra they would have heard the screams of horror; they would have been horrible screams. The people two kilometers from there could even hear those screams, namely, the ones that came from the transports of children. The children were separated from their parents, and then they were put in Section III camp. Maybe the number of children was several thousand.
>
> And then on one special day they started burning them to death. The gas chambers at the time were out of order, at least one of them was out of order, namely, the one near the crematorium; it was destroyed by mutiny in a special commando operation in August, 1944. The other three gas chambers were full of the adults and therefore the children were not gassed, but just burned alive.
>
> When one of the SS people sort of had pity with the children,

103

he would take a child and beat the head against a stone before putting it on the pile of fire and wood, so that the child lost consciousness. However, the regular way they did it was just throwing the children on to the pile.

They used to put a sheet of wood, then the whole thing was sprinkled with petrol, then wood again, and petrol and wood, and petrol—and then people were placed there. Then the whole thing was lighted.[50]

It is no longer possible, if it ever was, to make the passion of Jesus of Nazareth the foundation of Christian faith. Jesus of Nazareth was at least a grown man, a mature man, a man with a mission, and by all the evidence a courageous man, who set his face steadfastly to go up to Jerusalem (Luke 9:51). In contrast, there has occurred within this world and within the present epoch an evil that is more terrible than other evils. This is the evil of little children witnessing the murders of other little children, while knowing that they also are to be murdered in the same way, being aware absolutely that they face the identical fate. Before this kind of event, the death of Jesus upon the cross is lost in relative moral nonsignificance. At most, its representation reflects pre-Holocaust theology; it is not theology "after Auschwitz." The Godforsakenness of Jesus has proven to be nonabsolute, if it ever was absolute, for there is now a Godforsakenness that is worse by an infinity of infinities, and that bears within itself an ultimate *Einzigartigkeit:* that Godforsakenness of Jewish children which is a final horror. In adducing the present point we do not renege upon the judgment put forth in chapter 3 that any and every instance of human agony must be received in equal and qualitative terms, rather than comparatively or competitively. We submit that there is a moral and existential difference between human suffering as such and the suffering of children, due to such factors as innocence and, above all, the uncomprehending quality of the anguish of these little creatures of God. The adult sufferer has at least had a chance to realize some kind of personal fulfillment.

KIRCHE IN DER KRAFT DES GEISTES

A number of welcome changes and advances appear in Moltmann's later study, *Kirche in der Kraft des Geistes*. We

104

refer primarily to the chapter "Die Kirche des Reiches Gottes" ("The Church of the Kingdom of God"), and notably to the sections concerned with the church, the Jewish people, and Israel. Especially commendable are Moltmann's new emphases upon unique Christian solidarity with Israel, upon the Christian relation to Israel as being preeminent over, and determinative of, the other salient relations he considers (to the religions, to human society, and to the world of nature), and upon the need for the church's return to its foundations in Israel. Moltmann pays serious attention to the views of Franz Rosenzweig. Israel is fully acknowledged as the Christian's abiding source, his brother in hope. For centuries, anti-Judaism has meant the paganization of the Christian church. Moltmann now most effectively laments and criticizes the centuries-long triumphalism of the church, in which the church has sought to represent itself as the uniquely sovereign authority of God upon the earth, with the consequence that it has separated itself from the history of Israel. Such absolutism "cuts the church off from its origin," but also from its future.[51]

Fundamental and requisite presuppositions for the end of Christian triumphalism include the rediscovery of the relevance and truth of the Old Testament (Torah), a new discovery of the unfulfilled elements within the messianic hope, and the placing of Israel in a relation of partnership with the Christian church. Israel retains her sacred calling, alongside the church, until the End. Particularly noteworthy is Moltmann's assertion that hatred of the "obdurate" Jews is ultimately grounded within Christians' self-hatred. Noteworthy as well is his observation that the refounding of the state of Israel, whose integrity he honors, has put the relation of Christians to Jews upon a completely new plane: Jews now meet Christians not just as "the synagogue," but as citizens of a sovereign state. Moltmann manifests an entirely fresh attitude to Torah and to Jewish obedience to it, in marked contrast to many assertions and implications in *The Crucified God*. His condemnation of Christian supersessionism is a high point of *Kirche in der Kraft des Geistes*.[52]

Are we to conclude that the point of view of Moltmann's earlier study has been surmounted? Unfortunately, no. We comment upon two decisive points: the issue (discussed in our

105

chapter 4) of the perpetuating of special demands upon Israel, and the nagging question of the Christian imperium.

First, for Moltmann, the special calling of Israel consists in or remains the sanctification of the divine Name.[53] We must acknowledge, to Moltmann as to the Jewish community, that many Jews will continue to insist upon this role. Insofar as the Jewish people, or some among them, desire to perpetuate a special calling or task, that is their business, or at least it is their right. For Christians to deny that right out of hand is to fail to honor Jewish integrity. But we must also suggest to Moltmann that Christians are forbidden to make any special demands upon the Jews. Here abides a serious shortcoming in Moltmann's continuing work. Christians have no right to inflict spiritual and moral requirements upon the Jewish people that may perpetuate or compound Jewish suffering. Even were the protestation to be forthcoming that Christians earlier possessed the duty to be prophets unto Israel (itself a most dubious claim), the nineteen hundred years of Christian antisemitism that culminated in the Holocaust have surely betrayed and canceled any such role. As long as the Christian community tries to make Israel something special, to trumpet forth that Israel has obligations greater than or different from those of other human beings, the burden of the Christian past will not be lifted. Christians will continue to share in God's original sin (so to speak), the insinuating of the divine powerlessness, the divine perfection, into the life of ordinary mortals. As a matter of fact, Jürgen Moltmann may be called to witness against himself at this very point: he states again and again that the life and character of God entail suffering, not the making of demands.

The problem of making demands upon Jews is revealed especially sharply in Moltmann's section on the land of Israel.[54] Granted that his allotting of a special and positive role for Israel overturns erstwhile Christian condemnations of Judaism, the special requirements he amasses for Israel nevertheless flout his assertions in The Crucified God that human beings should be accepted in all their individual and collective dignity, without any conditions.

Second, while Moltmann deplores Christian triumphalism in his later volume, he does not in fact surmount it. He maintains, or at least reports, the view that the second advent of

106

Christ will bring to fulfillment not only the Christian but also the Jewish hope. And he himself asserts that at the Parousia, Christ will manifest himself as the Messiah of Israel. Moltmann contends that however one judges the Christian *heilsgeschicht-liche* apocalyptic as he describes it, it undoubtedly succeeded in overcoming anti-Judaism. The truth of the matter is that it did not have this consequence, and neither does Moltmann's point of view. He testifies that through their "rejection" of Christ, the Jews become the "last" to "come in" (after the gentiles). Yet such testimony is made possible only through denying that the Jews are, in Franz Rosenzweig's phrase, "already with God," thus denying that God remains faithful to his promise. Hence, the anti-Judaism of *The Crucified God* is only tempered in the second volume, not really vanquished.[55] (We have to remember in this frame of reference that the actual replacing of the Jews by the gentiles within the church is what made possible the entire anti-Jewish development of Christianity.) From the standpoint of the relevant pages in *Kirche in der Kraft des Geistes*, the Christian church does constitute the practical replacement of Israel in the work of salvation. The church remains, in Moltmann's view, the roundabout instrument of the salvation of Israel.

For all the changes as between the two studies under review, Moltmann remains impaled upon the dilemmas of the apostle Paul and subject to all of the latter's ambivalence respecting Israel and his fellow Jews. We simply do not understand what it means for Moltmann (following Paul, as the evidence has it) to aver that Israel remains the hope of the church.[56] The fact is that, according to the Pauline outlook, original Israel betrayed its soteriological calling, its place in salvation history (see Rom 9–11). For all Paul's eschatological insistence that "the whole of Israel will be saved" and that "God's choice stands" (Rom. 11:26, 28), there is no way to avoid, as the apostle's own, the persuasion that the church has effectively replaced original Israel and inherited the divine election.[57] There is no denying that for Paul, Jews as well as gentiles are justified in God's sight only by coming to Jesus Christ (Rom. 10:9–17). Within this context, the only substantive difference between *The Crucified God* and *Kirche in der Kraft des Geistes* is that the latter propounds what might be called

107

"postponed triumphalism," or proleptic triumphalism, in partial distinction from "pure" triumphalism. Moltmann may now be fighting anti-Judaism at the essential point of opposing churchly triumphalism as a present historical evil. But his own absolutism and triumphalism have not been overcome at the all-decisive point of living human relations with Jews today.[58] The knowledgeable Jew will simply ask, how does your new position differ in substance from the old view you now appear to be criticizing? For there is really no difference between saying Jesus Christ is the one whom Jews must accept now and in the final reckoning it is Jesus Christ who will redeem them. In truth, from a moral standpoint the second position may be identified as more lamentable, because it acts to subject the Jewish future to a fate over which the Jewish people are deprived of any say or control. Their dignity as human beings is impugned as much as or more than ever.

ASSESSMENT FROM WITHIN

To conclude our exposition and evaluation of Jürgen Moltmann's work, we suggest that the version of Christian faith this theologian advances is not to be criticized upon arbitrary or external grounds, but instead deserves to be approached as though from within—that is, upon the moral foundation that he himself provides. Certain of his own presuppositions and reasoning combine to offer the foremost argumentation against his conclusions. Moltmann is struggling courageously to create a post-Holocaust theology. Yet he cannot escape the fact that *The Crucified God* comprises, in essence, pre-Holocaust thinking, and that the same is the case, in somewhat qualified measure, with *Kirche in der Kraft des Geistes*. (In fact, Moltmann explicitly denied to us that his later volume involves any shift within his theological point of view.)[59]

Specifically, the problem centers in the nature and genuineness of human liberation. It is our conviction that the historical fate of Christianity, considered especially from the standpoint of that world-transforming event called the Endlösung, has seriously called into question many dogmatic Christian affirmations and claims. In social, psychological, and political terms, that faith has been taken prisoner by ideology, an ideology which is pervaded by a terrible irony because it seems to be deprived of any means to transcend itself and to learn thereby the truth of its own entrapment. The Christian faith, which is supposed to bring freedom, is transmuted into an apologetic weapon, all the while identifying itself as transapologetic. Christians are reputedly enabled, with the aid of the gospel, to expose the falsehoods, evils, and wiles of those who do not assent to, or benefit from, the gospel of liberation. But a grim specter stands over the world Christian community. What of the dreadful eventuality that many of those whom Christians seek to identify as slaves may in truth be free men and women, while those they endeavor to portray as free (namely, themselves) are in truth slaves—for example, slaves to a pre-Holocaust (and Holocaust-preparing) past that extends all the way back through Martin Luther to Chrysostom and to Paul, to the fate-bearing and enslaving dichotomization of "gospel" and "law"?

Is there any exit from this moral plight, a means whereby the Endlösung itself is transfigured? At the close of chapter 3 we spoke of the Holocaust as *metanoia*, a turning around of the world. Can a comparable revolutionary ferment somehow invade the church? Can Christians come under the power of *metanoia*, total revolution, genuine liberation, under "the power of the Spirit," to resort to Moltmann's Pauline terminology? We shall have more to say concerning this possibility, this hope, but for the present there may be some positive relevance in a judgment of the Catholic theologian Rosemary Ruether, who finds the resolution of the Christian moral-theological problem only in the church's unqualified repudiation of its antithetical theology (*gegensätzliche Theologie*) and its "realized eschatology." Ruether asks, "Is it possible to say 'Jesus is Messiah' without, implicitly or explicitly, saying at the same time 'and the Jews be damned'?" She answers, only if the Christian affirmation is relativized into a "theology of hope," which will free it of anti-Jewish imperialism, and indeed of all religious imperialism. The "theology of hope" is, of course, linked to the name of Jürgen Moltmann. But, as we have seen, there is much that appears hopeless in his theorization. Is Christian thought of necessity marked with moral hopelessness? Or can there be a theology that sustains genuine hope, the joy of liberation? Ruether further states: "The self-infinitizing of the messianic sect

109

that empowers itself to conquer all mankind in the name of the universal" is essentially "a false messianism. What Christianity has in Jesus is not the Messiah but a Jew who hoped for the coming of the Kingdom of God and who died in that hope."[60] Short of this kind of judgment, is there any way to face up to the double crisis of Christian relevance and Christian identity as emphasized by Moltmann himself?[61] And, of incalculably greater importance, is there any other way to receive ultimate Christian liberation from complicity in the Final Solution? In alternative terminology, is there any resolution of our problem apart from the total humanization of theology? Perhaps Jürgen Moltmann's developing thought may yet come to complete a journey along such possibly saving roads, and one day become, accordingly, a true theology of hope.[62]

6

LIBERATION

We have considered two responses to the Holocaust: the Endlösung as, in effect, a nonevent, and the Endlösung as a partially influential event. In the first case, the Christian church's unholy past is perpetuated. In the second case, deliverance from that past is initiated. Our two final chapters are entered in behalf of a third possibility, the Holocaust as determinative of theological and moral revolution.

From the Roman Catholic side, Gregory Baum declares:

The message of the Holocaust to Christian theology . . . is that at whatever cost to its own self-understanding, the church must be willing to confront the ideologies implicit in its doctrinal tradition. We must be willing to sever ourselves from the ideological deformations, whatever they may be, even if we do not know as yet how to formulate the positive content of God's revelation in Jesus Christ. . . . We cannot afford, at this time, to be afraid. And in my mind, this ongoing conversion of the church to truth includes the correction of *all* its implicit ideologies, not just the anti-Jewish trend.[1]

And, from the Protestant side, Paul van Buren adjudges:

Having begun by taking Jews into account in a way not known before in the history of Christianity, at least a few Christians have begun to realize that a reconsideration of what Christians have been saying about Judaism and of Christian-Jewish relations must lead to a reconsideration of Christianity itself. . . . Theology can shut its eyes and pretend that the Holocaust never happened and that Israel doesn't exist. Theology has shown itself capable of such blindness before! But if there are prospects for serious theology, for a theology

111

not hopelessly blind to matters that pertain to the heart of its task, then the time has come for a reconsideration of the whole theological and Christian enterprise of the most radical sort. . . . [The command out of Auschwitz] is that we accept a judgment on something false lying close to the very heart of our tradition, and that like Abraham, we have to set out on a journey of radical reconstruction not knowing the final destination. If theology does not hear that voice of command to go, if it shuts its ears to the voice of Auschwitz, then I see no reason to bother ourselves or anyone else with a discussion of the prospects for theology.[2]

The Christian churches and Christian thinking are challenged by two inseparable questions. How seriously are they going to treat the singular event of the rediscovered Holocaust? How seriously are they going to take the moral consequences of the traditional Christian teachings concerning the Jewish people and Judaism? Emil L. Fackenheim suggests that the link between Christian affirmation and Christian antisemitism has become *the* question for contemporary Christianity.[3]

As a means to the end of Christian *metanoia,* we shall be dealing with selected areas of the church's teaching and experience in the light of several compelling norms: the dictates of historical truth; the consensual standards of Jewish and Christian morality; the loving faithfulness of God; the subjecting of certain affirmations of faith to judgment at the hands of historical event; the challenges of existential rationality; and the indispensableness of political power and political values.

THE OBJECTIVITY OF GUILT

It is imperative that we first dissociate ourselves from a particular form of subjective fixation upon Christian "guilt feelings" respecting antisemitism. This judgment is harmonious, we suggest, with James Parkes's persistent stress upon the critical, all-decisive character of objective historical truth and its lessons. In making the point, we in no way turn our backs upon the new historiography, with its finding of the massive Christian contribution to the Holocaust. Himself a singular pioneer in this very historiography, Parkes has nonetheless always avoided a fixation on guilt.

The indefatigable editor of *Encounter Today*, Sister Marie-Thérèse de Sion of Paris, has lamented what she calls "certain masochistic trends" among today's Christians who, finding their lives darkened by the shadows of Auschwitz, "burden themselves" with guilt feelings for a presumed collective guilt. Such Christians, she contends, only "surprise their Jewish friends who detect here a pathological 'lack of dignity.' "[4] Sister Marie-Thérèse, who has labored tirelessly and even heroically for Jewish-Christian reconciliation, nevertheless utters here only a partial truth. Were she speaking of certain parties, she would be presenting the whole truth, but she is alluding to Rosemary Ruether and her *Faith and Fratricide*. That work is surely not above criticism, but it is not properly subject to the particular criticism Sister Marie-Thérèse makes. As a matter of fact, in *Liberation Theology*, Ruether herself rightly insists that no reconciliation with a person who exploits and defames others is possible, until and unless the humanity of the evildoer is somehow acknowledged together with the humanity of those he has oppressed.[5] The difficulty with Sister Marie-Thérèse's appraisal is that she does not distinguish between subjective guilt feelings and the objective pathology of the Christian world, as the latter is chronicled by Ruether.

Will D. Campbell, in reckoning with American racism, observes that this phenomenon is not a mere subjective attitude or prejudice; it is the condition, the objective structure in which the American people live and move and have their being. In consequence, so Campbell attests, if we are white, we are racist.[6] This applies not only to all American gentiles, but also to all American Jews, excepting, of course, Jews who are also blacks. So too with those of us who are Christians, and this by no means excludes black Christians: to be a part of the Christian domain is to participate in that objective demonic structure called antisemitism.

Accordingly, while we must not put on display subjective guilt feelings or in any way abide masochism, the truth is that Christians are enmeshed within a special objective condition. They are assailed by an ontology of guilt, by the being of guilt, a condition that is inexorably bound to a particular story, to

113

certain given historical facts. Nevertheless, a partial qualification is necessary. Not all of the Christian world has been entangled with the objective condition of antisemitism. Some Christians have been spared the moral culpability and fate of Roman Catholic, Eastern Orthodox, and Protestant Christians within the western world. We cannot rightfully impute to other Christians our own historic hostilities to the Jewish people. Thus, many Christians in the so-called Third World have not even known of the Christian contribution to Nazism, and have been kept rather free of the antisemitic influences associated with, and made politically inevitable by, the entrenched social and cultural power of western Christendom. (At a recent international meeting in Jerusalem of the Consultation on the Church and the Jewish People, World Council of Churches, we met a number of such Christians from different African countries.) However, at least two facts point to the solidarity in sin of all Christians: contemporary antipathies toward the Jewish people of Israel within Christian segments of the Third World; and the universal Christian possession of, and allegiance to, the New Testament (with its antisemitic proclivities) as a decisive spiritual authority. It is impossible to overcome Christian enmity toward Jews without vanquishing the absolutism of the Christian gospel.[7] All Christians face the challenge to reconcile the reputed Word of God in the New Testament with justice and understanding for Jews.

From the foregoing analysis it follows that the duty of Christians, as against beating their breasts in self-hatred and self-agonizing, is to turn away from their subjectivities and fight for the objective transformation of the relevant teachings and moral condition of modern Christianity. If it is the case that the German Nazi Endlösung comprises an ultimate incarnation of the church's teaching of contempt for the Jews and Judaism, the only way to wage effective war upon this consequence is through a pervasive revolution in Christian doctrine and Christian behavior, involving the most radical surgery and the most radical theological reconstruction. Without such a revolution, the church and its adherents will quite possibly contribute to future obliterations of the Jewish people. The one thing Christians of today can do about the Holocaust is to work against a repetition of it.

What revolutionary Christian responses are to be advised? What steps must the Christian community take, out along the frontier, out along the pathway to human liberation? We shall be speaking ideally, in large measure, although in truth certain signs of hope have already manifested themselves within the Christian world.

The exposition to follow in part offers proposals not yet made in this book and in part summarizes and reviews affirmations already given voice. Under the heading "The Jews and Jesus Christ," we respond to the traditional Christian charge of Jewish unfaithfulness. Under "The Faithfulness of God," we represent God's fidelity to his people, in opposition to Christian supersessionism. Under "Reaffirmations," we refer briefly to two proposals made in earlier pages—a post-Holocaust understanding of the cross of Jesus, and the abolishing of special demands upon Jews—and we further assess the morality of the "trial of God." Under "The Issue of the Resurrection," we address the most serious of all theological problems in the Christian-Jewish relationship. And under "Political Power and the People of God," we endeavor to apply the lessons of the Holocaust to the morality of political sovereignty. Throughout, we try to honor Irving Greenberg's principle that no statement, theological or other, can be made "that would not be credible in the presence of the burning children."[8]

THE JEWS AND JESUS CHRIST

The claim that the Jewish people are deservedly chastised by God for rejecting the one true faith is among the most socially fateful Christian traditions. The Christian revolutionary will identify this allegation for what it is, a calumny.

Every year the defamation gains a renewed lease on life during so-called Holy Week, more correctly identifiable as Unholy Week. (James Parkes, the historian and Anglican clergyman, recently attested that his Christian conscience no longer permits him to enter a church during Holy Week, while the Christian educator Heinz Kremers of the University of Duisburg observes that the Passion story remains "the most dangerous root of anti-Jewish emotions among German school-children."[9] The calumny recently has been aided and abetted all across the United States by a television film *Jesus of Nazareth*, directed by Franco Zeffirelli. The blame is not, however, exclusively that of filmmakers or even of succeeding generations of clergy. Such people are simply carrying forward the falsehoods of the New Testament and of the ecclesiastical tradition.

There are two sides to the matter: the reputed spurning of Jesus as the Messiah, the Christ, on the part of "the Jews"; and alleged Jewish blameworthiness in the Crucifixion of the "Son of God."

On the first side, the Jewish community cannot and will not accept Jesus as the Christ. An all-decisive reason for this is that our world remains unredeemed. Hence, Jesus could not be the promised Messiah. While this is not to imply that Jewish teaching treats the Messiah as a divine savior,[10] yet the coming of the Messiah is peculiarly linked in Jewish thought to an objective transformation of life wrought by God. Jewish insistence upon the fact that Jesus cannot have been the Messiah, sustained as it is by almost two full millennia of experience, received climactic vindication in the Endlösung, the ultimate act of unredemptiveness. (Here lies the source of the lament that with the Holocaust, it is too late for the Messiah to come.) Theologically and positively speaking, the Jewish nonacceptance of Jesus as the expected or promised Christ is a case of Israel's persisting faithfulness to the covenant.

On the question of the Jews and the fate of Jesus—an issue that rates only summary treatment at most—the fact is that they and their leaders would have had nothing to do with any betrayal of one of their countrymen to the hated Roman occupying power. This consideration is discussed in the important but predictably ignored study by Haim Cohn, *The Trial and Death of Jesus.* We earlier alluded to Cohn's analysis of the impossibility of any Jewish legal or religious condemnation of Jesus. When we keep in mind the numerous provisions of Jewish law that would rule out any capital sentencing of Jesus through a "Jewish trial" on the charge of blasphemy (see n. 18, chap. 5, above), as well as such other factors as the falsity of the tradition that the Romans were accustomed to release malefactors at Jewish

116

festival times (see the account of Barabbas; Mark 15:6–15), we are enabled to recognize the massive speciousness of the New Testament on the subject of Jesus' trial and death. Haim Cohn concludes his work with these words:

> Hundreds of generations of Jews, throughout the Christian world, have been indiscriminately mulcted for a crime which neither they nor their ancestors committed. Worse still, they have for centuries, for millennia, been made to suffer all manner of torment, persecution, and degradation for the alleged part of their forefathers in the trial and crucifixion of Jesus, when, in solemn truth, their forefathers took no part in them but did all they possibly and humanly could to save Jesus . . . from his tragic end at the hands of the Roman oppressor. If there can be found a grain of consolation for this perversion of justice, it is in the words of Jesus himself: "Blessed are they which are persecuted for righteousness' sake: for theirs is the kingdom of heaven. Blessed are ye, when men shall revile you, and persecute you, and shall say all manner of evil against you falsely, for my sake. Rejoice, and be exceeding glad: for great is your reward in heaven" (Matt. 5:10–12).[11]

It is necessary to insert a caveat in the name of realism. Regrettably, historical analysis is a highly limited weapon in making wholesome the emotional commitments of human beings and in counteracting their volitional prejudices. The New Testament documents are not objective history; they are polemical, evangelical tracts. But this datum cuts two ways. On the one hand, it reflects the fact that the records cannot be finally received as bearers of objective truth. On the other hand, it also points up the consideration that the Christian world is wedded to these documents. Scholarly analysis is severely restricted in its function of redeeming the human bias that is derived from, and perpetuated by, them. As the Christian scholar Ulrich Simon of King's College, London, points out, the defamation of the Jewish people in the Gospel of John, that New Testament book most dear to Christian piety, constitutes in and of itself an incitement to corporate murder.[12] It is ridiculous to maintain that the New Testament is an inherently antisemitic document. But to shut our eyes to the antisemitic elements in the New Testament is equally foolish and irresponsible.

The Christian reformer has his work cut out. His chances of

117

exerting creative influence are not great if he limits himself to
the idealistic notion that disseminating the truth about history
will bring about changes in human behavior. It is essential,
therefore, that he not hamstring himself by espousing one
method alone.

In a single sentence, Ignaz Maybaum points up the necessity for extrahistorical strategies and also authenticates our judgment that the alleged Jewish responsibility for the death of
Jesus deserves no more than cursory treatment: "The ancient
tradition that 'the Jews killed Christ' . . . has its origin in the
twilight between myth and history and is therefore not acces-
sible to historical research."[13]

THE FAITHFULNESS OF GOD

Christian supersessionism is the notion that the Christian
community of faith has replaced the people Israel as the divine
instrument of salvation. The view has as its corollary that Jews
must be missionized if they are to be brought to the truth,
which means the Christian gospel. What may the Christian
revolutionary say to this?

Is not the persuasion that the Christian church has superseded Israel an affront to the Ruler of the Universe, who has
promised that he will be forever true to the people of Abraham,
Isaac, and Jacob (Gen. 17:13, 19; Lev. 24:8; 2 Sam. 23:5; 1 Chron.
16:17; Ezek. 37:26; etc.)? The General Synod of the Reformed
Church of Holland has declared that the election of Israel is
continued in the Jewish people today, because the faithfulness
of God does not falter or come to an end.[14] Accordingly, any
assault upon the ongoing integrity of original Israel, the chosen
of God, is an assault upon God himself. The Dutch Christians do
not make the point, but the reason Christian conversionism is
forbidden is that the effort to change the Jewish community into
a part of the Christian church is a veiled attack, often unknowing,
upon the foundation of the church and hence upon the Christian
faith itself. The foundation of the church is the Israel of God. If
the Jewish people are not the elder brothers and sisters within

the family of God, it follows that the gentiles as reputedly adopted younger brothers and sisters actually remain lost and without hope (see Eph. 2:12). The covenant into which they are ostensibly led by means of the event of Jesus the Jew becomes a delusion. Conversionism aimed at Jews reverses the true course of the history of salvation and turns upside down the structure of salvation history. Such conversionism implicitly assails Christianity. It is a Christian impossibility—not for pragmatic reasons, which are so dear to some religious thinkers, but for reasons of theological principle.[15]

Reinhold Mayer of the University of Tübingen, although a member of the study commission that produced the EKD statement *Christen und Juden,* writes that the mission to Jews is, in whatever form, "anachronistic and degrading," a kind of behavior that Jews "in faithfulness to their calling cannot take seriously." Two other members of the EKD commission speak in the same way. Rolf Rendtorff insists that Jews are not to be treated as potential Christians; they possess their own inner integrity. And Heinz Kremers believes that Christians are called, as Pope John said, simply to accept Jews as equal brothers.[16]

Although it is not the Holocaust that motivates the Christian reformer's struggle against conversionism (as is evident from the foregoing paragraphs), that event has served nonetheless to bring home the consequences of the erstwhile Christian program to convert Jews. We referred in chapter 5 to the interpretation of the missionary stance toward Jews as a form of spiritual Final Solution. Here is a terrible reminder that the Christian supersessionism and triumphalism which helped ensure the Endlösung also serve today, in effect, to sustain the German Nazi program. Supersessionist theology is a carrier. It carries the germs of genocide, the genocide only of Jews.

REAFFIRMATIONS

Three additional and essential elements in the work of Christian revolution have already been introduced in the course of our analysis, and hence are placed under the heading "Reaffirmations."

1. The Christian revolutionary will strive to rethink certain understandings of the cross of Jesus, and particularly the assertion that the cross represents the ultimate in human Godforsakenness. We spoke of this matter in our assessment of Jürgen Moltmann's work.

2. The Christian revolutionary will oppose that aspect of the asserted religious covenant that makes abnormal demands upon the Jewish people, a psychology helpfully identified by Rabbi N. Peter Levinsohn of Heidelberg as the "suffering servant syndrome."[17] While at this stage we are enumerating the major obligations of today's Christian revolutionary, at this particular point the Christian may be joined by the Jew. We say "may be," because a most delicate issue becomes paramount. We have earlier conceded that for the Christian to negate a Jewish resolve to perpetuate a special calling would be to dishonor Jewish integrity. That calling could well involve a readiness to suffer in obedience to the apprehended will of God, Holocaust or no Holocaust. The poignant fact is that Christian opposition to Jewish martyrdom may itself be invaded by Christian imperialism. A great deal depends upon the intent and the content. Is the message from the Christian side the counsel of friends, or is it a fresh, if inverted, form of yet another demand upon Jews? An added complication is that, however the Christian community may behave, special demands upon the Jewish people will continue to be made from various quarters. And a further temptation can enter in: Christians may not wish the Jew to be singled out for abnormal obligations because secretly they themselves—though heirs of the Jew Jesus—desire to escape from special responsibilities. There is no human deliverance from this entire psychology. All in all, it is not here claimed that Jews of a transformed covenant will be spared all unusual suffering. What is being said is that, after Auschwitz, such suffering is opposed and indeed repented of by God himself, and that, if this is so, the next question is, what obligations are given to us, and especially to those who are Christians?

Although today's need for theological reconstruction applies as much to the Jewish community as to the Christian church, the latter retains its particular focus for Christians, for the all-important reason that Christians historically have stood in the forefront in leveling special demands upon Jews. Nevertheless, a serious consequence is to be noted, deriving from our own opposition to those demands. Unavoidably, we are trespassing upon an intra-Jewish conflict. In expressing our own conviction, we inevitably take the side of those Jewish representatives who subscribe to a position paralleling ours, in opposition to those for whom the sanctification of the divine Name through suffering (whenever required) will remain an abiding commandment, until the very "end of days."

The requiring of special behavior from the Jewish people continues to be found even among Christians who evince a new solidarity with Jews. Thus, in *The Burden of Freedom* Paul van Buren avows that the Jewish people "do not possess freedom as their own treasure, to enjoy for themselves," but rather for the serving of mankind's freedom, and in order that God's freedom "might be Israel's consuming passion." Israel "is no more free to be other than God's people."[18] Doubtless without intending to do so, van Buren here reflects an ideology that has beset the Christian church for hundreds of years—or, more accurately, one half of an ambivalent ideology which, on the one hand, fabricates abnormal obligations for Jews and, on the other hand, and with glaring inconsistency, faults them for "always" behaving in sub-Christian fashion. Jews are expected to be both angels and devils—everything but ordinary human beings. The reply to the first of the two aspects of this ideology might well be Emil L. Fackenheim's admonition that the Jew today "is commanded to descend from the cross and, in so doing, not only to reiterate his ancient rejection of an ancient Christian view but also to suspend the time-honored exaltation of [Jewish] martyrdom."[19]

The import of Fackenheim's wholly post-Holocaust counsel can be directed equally to would-be taskmasters in the Christian world, to a type of Jewish traditionalist, to those other persons and collectivities that have become apostles of the perfectionism in question, and, if need be, even to God himself. To all these eligible parties the response is, "You have entered your last demand against us"; to such parties as need an added word, the judgment is forthcoming that "in the name of reputed freedom and divine opportunity for the Israel of the past—the life of 'holy obligation'—you have only made certain that succeeding generations of Jews would be brought to degradation and agony and death." The one immorality that equals the visiting of the "iniquity of the fathers upon the children and the children's children, to the third and the fourth generation" (Exod. 34:7) is that of visiting the presumed covenantal obligations of the fathers upon generation after generation of their children, independently of the children's consent.[20] The Jewish children of the murder camps rise in silent refutation of both these forms of immorality. The myth of the Jew as "suffering servant" will be relieved of its horrible force only as the victims of the myth say no to it—aided in their determination by the efforts of some Christians.

A widely shared objection to our denial of the covenant of demand is that this viewpoint flouts the will of God. But the objector himself has a problem. It centers in the arbitrariness versus the morality of God. If the objector bases his complaint upon the sovereign abritrariness of God, the discussion ceases because no common ground is available for carrying it on. But if the objector seeks to retain a moral deity, the challenge to him is to show that it is not morally wrong to take requirements once imposed upon the fathers and to impose them upon succeeding generations, even at the cost of the latter's safety and security. The objector is asked: in which epoch are you living, B.F.S. or F.S.?

Today a plea often is made for the secularity of theology. Within the context of relations with Jews, Christians may honor that plea by receiving Jews simply as people, ordinary people. Any other stance helps to perpetuate a pre-Holocaust outlook.

To annul the covenant of demand is to witness against Jewish suffering from the human side. But this does not resolve the problem of God and Jewish suffering. We are brought to a further step.

3. The Christian revolutionary will appear as a witness, together with numbers of his Jewish brothers and sisters, before a special tribunal where a special trial is being conducted: the trial of God. We have referred to such a trial in chapter 3, but the "blasphemy" of post-Holocaust thinking is nowhere made more necessary than in our present chapter. We have celebrated God's faithfulness to his people; now we are so brazen as to join in his trial, to covet his penitence. Yet the reader is asked: is there a choice? The fatefulness of history must be consummated. Of moral necessity, B.F.S. is to be succeeded by F.S., for

the sake of truth and goodness. It is said that God himself has the highest stake in these virtues, much higher than ours.

Many persons are doubtless shocked and offended by the very thought that human beings have a right to put God "on trial," but we call attention to Scripture. There are biblical grounds for human protagonism before God (e.g., Abraham's contention with God and our patriarch's question, "Shall not the Judge of all the earth do right?" [Gen. 18:22–33]; the protests before God throughout the Book of Job; and, for the Christian especially, Jesus' cry of abandonment on the cross). Of course, we are not permitted to ignore God's accusations against his human creatures in the name of his justice.

At the very least, there has to be a total revolution in the doctrine of election. That teaching has made the agony of Israel an unceasing sentence and has turned God into the equivalent of the devil. If the doctrine of election is to be retained, this can only occur through its radical humanization. Chosenness will become election to life. For the first time in the story of the people of God, their existence will become an unqualifiedly normal reality.

A "commandment" can mean opposite things. There is the command to sacrifice oneself, and there is the command to live. When using the concept of "demand," we mean the first of these; it stretches things unduly to apply that category to survival. Normally, the human will to live does not require prodding. Emil Fackenheim writes:

> In Judaism there are two archetypes of experience—one is the saving experience (the Red Sea), the other is the commanding experience (Sinai). If one tries to hear a redeeming voice at Auschwitz, there is only silence. But a commanding voice speaks to those willing to listen: A Jew is forbidden to give Hitler a posthumous victory, and to consent to despair is to give that victory. The moral-religious contradiction can be resolved only by affirmation that *there can be no second Holocaust!*[21]

The contradiction is to be resolved all right, but Fackenheim is implying that the dialectic of salvation and command must be retained. After Auschwitz, no command is legitimate that does not save, and there is no salvation without the honoring of the command to live. The command of collective self-sacrifice is terminated, and its place is taken by the command to survive.

The original covenant is transformed but nevertheless honored through what Fackenheim calls the 614th commandment, the command to live.[22] This commandment is nothing more nor less than the free choice and right of Jewish existence as such, which is another way of saying that it is not a commandment. It is the commandment that ends or fulfills all others. It is a declaration of independence, a testimony to the utter sanctity of Jewish life.[23] B.F.S. became total dehumanization; F.S. is life with no strings attached. The dehumanization was to be final; so the humanization must be final. The dispensation of the first Torah is ended, for Torah is now embodied, in a definitive sense, within the Jew himself. The Jew is the incarnation of the word, the teaching. F.S. is the era of the incarnation of the Jewish people.

For all time, any human being, not excluding the Jew, can resolve to become a martyr. But after the Holocaust, martyrdom cannot be a collective ideal for the Jewish people.[24] The End-lösung is the eschatological judgment upon a double-standard God and upon all double-standard theology. The Holocaust remains the rational climax of the unholy split between Jewishness and humanity. The holy nation became excrement.[25] In alternate terminology, the dispensation F.S. is the victory of God as love over the devil as hate.

Yet the nagging question persists of whether the command to survive can be wholly set free from the element of demand. If the Jewish people will to survive, but to do so only as human beings and not as Jews, do they not betray their own integrity and fall prey to an abstract existence? And yet, if they will to survive *as Jews,* do they not continue to subject themselves to the arbitrary and impossible demands of others, not excluding God?

We are not able to supply an answer that will finally resolve or silence this question. But we are required to respond to it. Fackenheim has been cited as pleading, not for one command, but for two: that Jews "descend from the cross" and that they survive as Jews, because otherwise a posthumous victory will be handed to Hitler. But how is it possible to call, at one and the same time, for an end to martyrdom and for Jewish survival? One way in which it may be done is through the gaining and retaining of political freedom and power.[26] Otherwise the command to live as Jews is immoral. Fackenheim asks:

> Is not, after Auschwitz, any Jewish willingness to suffer martyrdom, instead of an inspiration to potential saints, much rather an encouragement to potential criminals? After Auschwitz, is not even the saintliest Jew driven to the inexorable conclusion that he owes the moral obligation to the antisemites of the world not to encourage them by his own powerlessness?[27]

We find that the antisemites of the world are owed nothing at all, any more than is their master the devil, but Emil Fackenheim is surely correct in affirming that Jewish martyrdom can no longer be sustained. That is to say, if in the epoch B.F.S. the martyrdom of Jews was empowered to sanctify the divine Name, in the dispensation F.S. such martyrdom will only blacken God's name. It will, indeed, threaten his salvation. We must conclude that as a Jewish option, the theology of victimization, that terrible but natural child of the covenant of demand, was put to death in the murder camps.[28]

THE ISSUE OF THE RESURRECTION

The Christian revolutionary will insist upon a genuine reaffirmation of Jewishness, which entails radical historicalness. (It is not correct to say that Jewish thinking unexceptionally takes history and historical events seriously; many in the Orthodox community do not. Nevertheless, historicalness as a norm within Jewry is supported by a long and weighty religious and moral tradition.)[29]

We must make clear at the beginning of this most decisive of all our steps that the avowal of Jewish historicalness is not to be confused with the efforts of so-called Judaizers, or with Jewish Christianity.[30] We speak in behalf of Christian Jewishness, with the accent always on the adjective. The rediscovery of Jewishness as the bedrock of the Christian faith does not and cannot be permitted to mean reductionism. Against all

125

reductionist temptations, the Christian reformer will assert the integrity of his faith: "In Christ [the Jew] God was reconciling the world [*kosmos*] to himself" (2 Cor. 5:19). There is a universe of difference between this Pauline affirmation and the idolatrous notion that Christ was God, reconciling the world to himself. We must stress *the world* in contradistinction to Israel, God's firstborn, for Israel already lives in his presence, as Franz Rosenzweig put the matter.[31] The event of Jesus is the joy that ends the desolation of those who have been without hope. Jesus is a second Abraham, the Abraham of the gentiles, patriarch to the pagans. We who are gentiles must somehow be rescued from religion, from all those pitiful gods that tempt us, from all our idolatries. When Jesus is turned into an idol—seven words that form a most fitting single title for the whole story of Christendom—we are only returned to our sins, our idolatries, our hopelessness. The Christian is given the chance to live out a unique and independently valid challenge to be an adopted child of God, within the covenant of promise. In the course of his pilgrimage from time to eternity, the Christian must never leave the bedrock of Jewish historicalness. It gives meaning to his life, ever helping him to separate truth from heresy.

We cannot lose sight of the stubborn truth that a nonconversionist viewpoint respecting Jews, however much it may aid reconciliation between Christians and Jews, does not in itself reduce obstacles to solidarity with peoples of other faiths. On the contrary, the very affirmation that, through Jesus, we who are gentiles are enabled to become part of the Israel of God, serves to point up an unhappy division within humanity, the division between Israel (Jews and Christians) and all those who remain beyond the covenant of promise. The only way to counteract possible hostility to these other peoples is through relativization, the unqualified acknowledgment that our way is not the only possible way to salvation or the good life. It cannot be overstressed that this acknowledgment accords with major emphases within the Jewish tradition. Through his very participation in Jewishness, the Christian is helped to surmount exclusivism and intolerance.

The fact stands that a widely accepted theological schema gnaws at the vitals of the Christian church, a schema according to which, in effect, the Cross-Resurrection-Parousia is made into a solely decisive series of events, salvationally speaking. More precisely, as Heinz Kremers comments critically, in the thinking of many Christians such a series of events transcends the ordinary realm of history, forever taking precedence over all historical happenings.[32] Thus, Alan T. Davies speaks of the Crucifixion and the Resurrection, which for him lie along "the margin of history," as qualifying "the extent to which Christian faith can accept new revelatory moments."[33] A ready consequence of this schema is that Christianity itself becomes a wholly transcendent "reality," which moves in entirely "spiritual" ways above the flux of history. History is no longer open to God's presence, in direct contrast to a dominant emphasis within Judaism. This Christian outlook easily turns into forms of absolutism and triumphalism, or of particularism wearing a camouflage of universal truth. As we have seen, by equating the suffering and death of Jesus with the very torment of hell, Jürgen Moltmann in effect denies any crucial theological significance to the Holocaust. At most, the latter event can possess only ancillary significance, because the very hell of Godforsakenness preceded it and, indeed, furnishes prototypical substance for the Holocaust itself.

If we are to be human beings without reservation, that is, fully historical beings, how is it possible for us to remain bound by certain original soteriological processes, which, through dogmatic presentment, rule out the moral and theological decisiveness of other happenings? However, it is not alone as "fully human beings" that we must assert the significance of historical events. We face a strange but fundamental paradox: the Jewish and Christian traditions themselves call us to this assertion. Irving Greenberg writes: "For traditional Jews to ignore or deny all significance to this event [the Holocaust] would be to repudiate the fundamental belief and affirmations of the Sinai covenant: that history is meaningful, and that ultimate liberation and relationship to God will take place in the realm of human events."[34] Once the Christian casts aside this insistence upon historicalness, he abandons the biblical *Weltanschauung*. Again, whatever else is meant by the "third person" of the Trinity, that "person" points us to the significance of post-New Testament historical life. In the worldly unfolding of events, a crucial acting out of the divine-human drama is to be found, and with it fresh apprehensions of God himself.

It must be asserted, however, that when we turn to the question of the Resurrection of Jesus Christ, our problem is seen to be infinitely sharper than the potential denial of the religious significance of various historical events. True, the effort is sometimes made to establish a relation between the allegedly saving event of the Resurrection and the devilish event of the Holocaust. Ulrich E. Simon, for example, testifies that without the Resurrection the Endlösung is nothing other than pure hell.[35] Yet beyond the fact that alternative human experiences can be described as hellish, there remains no comparison between the Crucifixion and the Resurrection at the point of theological and moral decision making. A simple but crucial reason is that while there is no doubt at all that the Crucifixion occurred (granting that the interpretations of the event are legion), there are grave questions respecting what it means to talk about the reality of the Resurrection.

We have cited Emil L. Fackenheim's query of whether the link between Christian affirmation and Christian antisemitism is today the central moral issue for the church. It is as a means of facing up to this query that some Christian theologians have called for a recovery of Jewishness within the church. But what is that recovery to mean? Many times these days we read or hear Christian representatives saying that the persisting presence of Christian antisemitism demands a wholehearted rethinking of the church's teachings. Yet it soon becomes apparent that many such people have no intention of surrendering or even of reformulating major doctrines of their faith, even though these are the very teachings that cause the trouble.

The ultimate test case is the Resurrection, for two reasons. First, the faith of countless Christians has at its center the consummated Resurrection of Jesus Christ. "If Christ has not been raised, . . . your faith is vain"—so writes the apostle Paul (1 Cor. 15:14). Second, the one place for the reaffirmation of Jewishness to happen, if it is to happen at all, is in connection with the momentous and all-determining tenet of the Resurrection. A genuine rediscovery of Jewishness has to mean the taking of historical fact with utter seriousness, in contrast to the negations of Greek and Manichean spirituality. The Christian revolutionary is called upon to be strong and of good courage, to enter the arena where the real battle rages. Jewishness means a denial of any consummated Resurrection, until this time in history and beyond today. The question of rediscovered Jewishness versus continuing Christian anti-Jewishness, or antisemitism (to call the reality by its proper name), turns upon a life-and-death judgment respecting the Resurrection. Within this arena is held the fate of the entire Jewish-Christian relation, including the question of whether the Christian community may yet act to redeem its past.

The Christian moral plight is brought into focus most clearly in the combination of ideas presented by Wolfhart Pannenberg, who asserts that "through the cross of Jesus, the Jewish legal tradition as a whole has been set aside in its claim to contain the eternal will of God in its final formulation." (Where has such a claim ever been made in the Jewish community? The real Jewish point of view is diametrically opposite to Pannenberg's caricature of it. The constant need to rethink and reformulate the legal tradition, a need that lies at the center of ongoing interpretations by scholars and rabbis, is itself the proof that the tradition does not "contain the eternal will of God in its final formulation.") For Pannenberg, "the law" is consummated, fulfilled in Jesus. Typifying as he does the customary false allegation within German and other biblical scholarship that Jesus himself stood in opposition to a hardened Jewish "law," Pannenberg calls upon the Resurrection to vindicate his charge that Jesus came into fundamental conflict "with the law itself, that is, with the positive Israelite legal tradition which had become calcified as 'the law' after the exile." However, through the Resurrection of Jesus, "the emancipation from this law was confirmed by the God of Israel himself." Pannenberg resorts to exactly the same reasoning in the matter of Jesus' "claim" for his own person, and uses this opportunity to speak of Jewish complicity for Jesus' death. Jesus' "claim to authority, through which he put himself in God's place, was . . . blasphemous for Jewish ears. Because of this, Jesus was then also slandered by the Jews before the Roman governor as a rebel. If Jesus really has been raised, this claim has been visibly and unambiguously confirmed by the God of Israel."[36]

Pannenberg's allegations embody the major elements of the

entire Christian predicament vis-à-vis the Jewish people and Judaism: the Cross; the setting aside of "the law" through its "fulfillment" in Jesus; Jesus' own "opposition" to "the law"; Jesus' "authority" as equal to that of God; and, climactically, the Resurrection as the divine verification of these various points at which Christianity stands in judgment upon the Jewish people and their faith. The truth is here pointed up that it is the teaching of a consummated Resurrection which lies at the foundation of Christian hostility to Jews and Judaism, for only with that teaching does Christian triumphalist ideology reach ultimate fulfillment. Only here are the various human and divine claims making up the church's structure furnished with the capstone of an event that is exclusively God's and that in this way vindicates every other claim. The Resurrection is the relentless force behind every other Christian derogation of Jewry. The apostle of this ideology in effect declares, "It is not the fallible Christian theologian to whom you Jews are to listen. He is, after all, a sinful human being. You are much better advised to pay attention to *God* and what he does. Let God decide the matter. But God's decision turns out to be on the Christian side, not yours; *He* raised Jesus from the dead. So the Christian is proved right and you are proved wrong. In the Resurrection God *confirms* the Christian gospel, the Christian cause."

Living as we are in the midst of the Christian plight, a condition solidified by nineteen hundred years of thinking and behavior, how are we going to proceed? Plainly it would be at once morally irresponsible and intellectually untenable to grant to one event (the Holocaust) the right to obliterate an earlier event (the Resurrection). The only course for us is to seek to represent the truth, in the name of historicalness.

Within the bounds of the kind of thoroughgoing historicalness that is represented by Jewishness (but not monopolized by Jewry), there are two alternatives respecting the first Easter Sunday: the somatic Resurrection of Jesus and the nonresurrection of Jesus. Paul van Buren, representing an influential strain within recent theology, opts for a third alternative, an extrabodily Resurrection.[37] From the standpoint of Jewish historicalness, not to mention ordinary common sense, such a declaration is not an authentic possibility, because the avowal of an extrabodily Resurrection is not convincingly allowable apart from

Greek presuppositions and conditioning. Such a declaration does not really become meaningful except on the ground of the Hellenist divorce of spirit and matter. Accordingly, van Buren and others at this point dissociate themselves from Christian Jewishness, Jewish historicalness. Affirming an extrabodily Resurrection tacitly disavows resurrection as such. As Rosemary Ruether writes, the anthropology of body-soul dualism contradicts the biblical understanding of man and creation. The messianic hope of redemption entails the redeeming of life in the body, not flight from the body.[38]

Any demythologizing of the Resurrection of Jesus comprises a logical and substantive impossibility. To transmute that reported event into a "symbol" or "myth" or "vision" or "experience" is to spin intellectualistic spider webs and to become the victim of a vague esotericism. In this context, Christian fundamentalism remains, formally speaking, correct. That is to say, with its literalist teaching of the somatic Resurrection of Jesus, fundamentalism is at least being faithful to Jewish categories of thinking and life, not to mention the attestations of some of the first Christians. It is relevant to observe that, for all his triumphalist protestation, Wolfhart Pannenberg can hardly endear himself to those fundamentalists who insist upon a literal bodily resurrection, for he explicitly denies that the understanding of the first Christians was that of a revivification of a corpse. Through his acceptance of a different view (under the spell of the apostle Paul),[39] Pannenberg places himself in an impossible situation; he strives hard to believe in the Resurrection, and yet he does not afford it its full somatic identity. In point of truth, the original Christian declaration of the event of the Resurrection—before the time of the "appearance" to Paul of the resurrected Lord (1 Cor. 15:8)—made no allowance at all for Paul's distinction between the body that is sown and the body that is raised (1 Cor. 15:35–50). To many in the original Christian community, as reported in the Gospels, it was Jesus who was raised from the dead, not his "spirit" and not even his "spiritual body," but Jesus himself. Thus, as the Lucan account has it—possibly Luke is the earliest Gospel, in spite of the traditional holding among scholars that Mark precedes it[40]— "Jesus himself stood among them. . . . 'See my hands and my feet, that it is I myself; handle me, and see; for a spirit has not flesh and bones as you see that I have.' And while they still disbelieved for joy, and wondered, he said to them, 'Have you anything here to eat?' They gave him a piece of broiled fish, and he took it and ate before them" (Luke 24:36, 39–43). The last we knew, spirits were not possessed of hands and feet subject to human handling, nor did they go about consuming broiled fish. For the Christians whose convictions Luke reports, the risen one was not some "new bodily" successor to, or even a remodeled version of, Jesus. The risen one was Jesus of Nazareth. Either Luke's account represents the truth or Jesus has not been raised. We are not permitted a third alternative.

The Christian believer today who gives himself to a reconciliation with Jewishness and the Jewish people must ever feel the enticements of fundamentalist literalism, because biblical fundamentalism is the one unflagging foe of all things Greek— that is, all things abstract. Yet fundamentalism pays an enormous and fateful price. The fundamentalists are enabled to keep body and soul together all right, but they escape heresy only by violating historicalness, surrendering existential reasonableness, and falling into superstition. With the first Christians, they obliterate the harsh distinction between hopefulness and consummated event. They turn their backs upon historicalness; that is to say, they fail to comprehend the nature and meaning of historical fate. This permits them to fashion the Resurrection of Jesus into an accomplished fact. In the name of the rational truth of Jewishness and of historicalness, Christian fundamentalism has to be rejected. In somewhat more positive phrasing, the error of the literalist notion of the somatic Resurrection of Jesus is its prematurity.

To sum up: most tragically, the new rethinking of Christian doctrine, the very movement which insists that justice be brought to the Jewish people at long last, is, with few exceptions, engaged in a balancing act. It is Christian triumphalism with guilt feelings. The new theology fancies that it can overcome anti-Jewishness while holding onto, among other doctrines, the consummated Resurrection of Jesus Christ. But that dogma is essentially antihistorical and anti-Jewish. The salient moral question, therefore, is not do we or do we not believe in the Resurrection of Jesus, but instead, do we who are calling for a reaffirmation of Jewishness mean what we say? Are we prepared to follow out to their full conclusion the consequences of our summons, or are we fooling ourselves and others? It is neither theologically correct nor morally right to maintain, as Pannenberg does, that God has acted to vindicate the Christian cause as against the Jewish people and faith. But there is only one possible ground for denying Pannenberg's vindication—by testifying that Jesus has not yet been raised from the dead. Thus does the Christian revolutionary work, at the very heart of traditional Christian affirmation, to sever the link between the church's teaching and the convictions that led to the Holocaust.[41]

POLITICAL POWER AND
THE PEOPLE OF GOD

Thomas A. Idinopulos and Roy Bowen Ward point out, in an otherwise faulty appraisal of a work by Rosemary Ruether, that "doctrinal formulations (or reformulations) will not end anti-Judaism, much less antisemitism because history shows both to be complex phenomena which depend heavily on political, social, and economic factors, as well as on the intellectual and theological developments which gave expression to them."[42] This passage reflects the importance of a theology of politics.

The phrase "theology of politics" stands for the responsible application of theological and moral principles to the political domain, the domain of power. A theology lacking relevance to the political realm is not worth anything. As Alistair Kee writes, the "question is not whether political theology is still theology, but whether anything that is *without* political significance deserves the name 'theology.' "[43] A purely theoretical or academic theology is a form of idolatry and even blasphemy, because it takes the name of God and subjects it to the imaginings of the human mind and the ideological self-deifications of the human spirit.

As so often, Irving Greenberg contributes positively to the rethinking of theology in the era after the Holocaust, in this instance through his commentary upon a Jewish woman and her child. The scene is Auschwitz, following upon a horrifying train journey.

In this state, when she suddenly understood where she was, when she smelled the stench of the burning bodies—perhaps heard the cries of the living in the flames—she abandoned her child and ran.

Out of this wells up the cry: Surely here is where the cross is smashed. There has been a terrible misunderstanding of the symbol of the crucifixion. Surely, we understand now that the point of the account is the cry: "My lord, my lord, why have you abandoned me?"[44] Never again should anyone be exposed to such one-sided power on the side of evil—for in such extremes not only does evil triumph, but the Suffering Servant now breaks and betrays herself. Out of the Holocaust experience comes the demand for redistribution of power. The principle is simple. No one should ever have to depend again on anyone else's goodwill or respect for their basic security and right to exist. The Jews of Europe needed that goodwill and these good offices desperately—and the democracies and the church and the Communists and their fellow-Jews failed them. No one should ever be equipped with less power than is necessary to assure one's dignity. To argue dependence on law, or human goodness, or universal equality is to join the ranks of those who would like to repeat the Holocaust.[45]

The worst fate that can befall any people is to be bereft of political sovereignty. As Richard L. Rubenstein says, "theologians or moralists may argue that all men possess some God-given irreducible measure of dignity, but such talk will neither deter future emulators of the Nazis nor comfort realistically their victims. . . . Human rights and dignity can only be attained by membership in a community that has the *power* to guarantee those rights."[46] It is, indeed, a moral responsibility for a people not to be weak. This duty is owed, not alone to themselves, but also in a sense to their foes and detractors, lest the others be tempted into aggressive acts against them. Significantly, the black leader Eldridge Cleaver, who often speaks in these terms, emphasizes that the Holocaust has taught him that if you go along, or have to go along, with tyranny, you simply cannot live. His conclusion was "Black power," in order to encourage the white brethren to be and to behave like decent human beings.[47] The primary way for the Christian community to relate to Jews today is from the standpoint of a theology of politics rather than from that of religion, for the erstwhile political powerlessness of Jews has only guaranteed their persecution and suffering.

134

The Jewish people have at last gained the power that can help keep their enemies at bay, their human foes and their divine protagonist. True, the theology of politics cannot be permitted to mean the theologizing of politics. That is to say, theology cannot rightly subject the political domain to the dictates of religion—for example, by claiming absolute rights, in the name of God, for a particular people to a given land. There are no absolute human rights to anything. All human rights are limited and partial. Nevertheless, through Israel, Jews are enabled to fight for their lives. This, as Pinchas Peli attests, is the very "essence of Israel's meaning."[48] Men do not live by bread and bullets alone, but without them, they become ravening wolves or helpless victims. Those who are bothered by a stress upon sovereignty as the central meaning of the state of Israel have failed to take to heart the Jewish story. *Eretz Yisrael* forms the answer to almost two thousand years of Jewish defenselessness. Within it is contained the most effective reply to those who talk glibly of the "power of the Cross," of spiritual force as the answer to physical force and armed aggression. These persons are not simply wrong in an empirical or political sense. They are, objectively speaking, obscene; that is to say, they are threats to the human creation of God. There is a parallel in the pacifism advocated by some Christians—pacifism in the sense of a political instrument, in contrast to the vocational pacifism of individuals—and the Christian effort tacitly to abolish Jewry through missions. If the latter represents a "spiritual Final Solution," pacifism as an advocated policy directed to Jews reestablishes the threat of a physical Final Solution. Auschwitz throws into clear relief, and once and for all, the demonic character of much Christian spirituality, a type of spirituality that, when applied to Jews, is best summed up in a certain cynic's definition: Christianity is that religion which teaches that the Jewish people are to turn the other cheek.

A perfect illustration of double-standard Christian morality is a piece by a Quaker professor named Calvin Keene. Having sought to dispose of those Christians who relate the reestablishing of the state of Israel to the will of God, Keene introduces his own version of a covenant of demand by declaring that Israel is to be "evaluated" and "the future of this new state" is to be "determined" by "its practice or lack of practice of justice, mercy, and righteousness."[49] The revealing element is not so much what he tries to demand of Israel as what he fails to ask of the Arabs. Evidently the latter's hostile policies toward Israel are acceptable. That Keene should refuse to apply his Quaker-pacifist demands to the Arabs suggests that his purpose is not in fact the making of peace, but instead the end of an Israel turned into defenselessness through the implementing of his brand of "Christian" perfectionism.

Of course, we must not be oblivious to the universal temptations of power. Due to the ontological status of human statehood as a creation of God and not God himself, political sovereignty may never be exalted into an absolute.[50] Nor can we ignore the incapacity of power to resolve problems of ultimate human meaning and the purposes of life. Power is to be lived with in ways advocated by Reinhold Niebuhr.[51] It is neither to be idealized into some kind of messiah nor disdained as some kind of devil. Power is to be used as an instrument for restraining human sin and channeling human creativity in a world that will never be perfect.

Even though the Christian church has, overall, partly corrupted the Jewish doctrine of God, the church has, overall, contributed much to the doctrine of man, thereby helping to refine Jewish anthropology. Much of the Christian insight into human social and political life lies in teaching us to be suspicious of men and their motives, particularly of ourselves. The French Christian scholar Fadiey Lovsky writes that the Holocaust comprised the most striking historical demonstration of "the hereditary reality of human sin."[52] Although the symbolism of sin as a "hereditary" taint wrongly obscures human responsibility for evil, it does have the virtue of pointing to human solidarity in sin.

Power has the best chance to achieve relative responsibility under a system of political democracy, since in that system the destructive dangers and the constructive opportunities of power are alike taken into account. Democracy is a creative alternative to two extreme political views, absolutism and anarchism. Political absolutists, whether of the older kingly and historically tyrannical sort or of the newer totalitarian type, pretend that the masses of humanity are either too evil or too stupid to govern themselves. At the other extreme stand the idealistic anarchists of history who teach that governmental rule is really not required because human beings are, in essence, too good to have to be subjected to arbitrary and artificial political restraints. Against both views Reinhold Niebuhr affirms that "man's capacity for justice makes democracy possible; but man's inclination to injustice makes democracy necessary."[53] In theological language, man is made in the image of God, yet he is also a sinner. He is capable of honoring and achieving a certain measure of justice; hence, the masses of men can rule themselves. But rule is needed, government is necessitated, because men also seek to lord it over their fellows. Accordingly, a political structure of "checks and balances" is required, to protect us from other men and to protect other men from us. Absolutism is unduly pessimistic about man; anarchism is unduly optimistic. Alone among political systems, democracy takes seriously both the heights of human constructiveness and the depths of human sin. None of this is to suggest that there is any such thing as *the* Christian political system. All human systems stand under the judgment of God. Democracy is more a method than a doctrinaire claim.

In the frame of reference of international affairs, the challenge of justice is to render every nation its due, to ensure it of whatever it can legitimately claim simply by virtue of being a nation (a minimal standard of living, the capacity to defend itself, the right to participate in the counsels of nations, and so on). The prime question of international relations is how can power be utilized to contribute to justice among the nation-states? The general answer must be not through annulling power (which would be to turn away from the exigencies and responsibilites of the real world), not through uncontrolled power (which would mean imperialism and international anarchy), but rather through manifold structures of balanced or mutually trammeled power. With the aid of these structures, human collectivities are able to maintain a tolerable coexistence. In sum, the key to relative justice among the nations must always remain the art of compromise.

Because the prevailing emphasis in this book is upon a theological way of looking at life, it is appropriate to include a word about the relation between the ultimate resources and promises of faith and the sphere of political action. There are two polar types of religious believers: those who stay aloof from

137

the world and remain "pure," but thereby commit the sin of irresponsibility; and those who plunge into the world and inevitably, therefore, take upon themselves the dirtiness and nasty compromises of the political scene. The difficulty with many religious people, as Arnold Nash used to say, is that they are always committing the wrong sins rather than the right ones. Martin Luther offered a curious word of advice to his brother Christians: "Sin bravely, if also you have brave faith." All men sin. The question is whether we are going to be irresponsible sinners, those who sin but not bravely, or responsible sinners, those who sin bravely.

There is a final mercy that God in his grace makes available in the realm of human power relations. The political man of faith lives with an uneasy but easy conscience, uneasy because he inexorably falls short of every ideal, but easy because he is assured that the Ruler of the Universe accepts him nonetheless. To those who take on political obligations, a strange assurance comes. Perhaps it can best be called "the peace that passes all understanding." In a word, the ultimate resource behind sustained political action is the divine forgiveness.[54] But is this not the hidden resource behind all that we say and do, the final power that enables life to go on? If so, there is some hope for all, even for those who unintentionally betray the truths of God.

Irving Greenberg refers to the ghastly idea that we try telling the burning children in the pits of Auschwitz that they are burning for their sins.[55] Likewise we may say: try informing the children that they are chastised by the Lord as Jews who have spurned the one true faith and crucified the "Son of God." That they are superseded by the Christian church in God's economy. That the cross of Jesus comprises the ultimate in human Godforsakenness. That they are the suffering servants of the Lord. That God is not to be called to account for their fate. That the Resurrection has taken place and is able to save them. And that political and military power are not for the people of God.

Try it.

7

TURN TO THE
KINGDOM OF DAY

We have told of the attack upon an old man as found in "To the Mound of Corpses in the Snow." It was very soon that night came. The old man had died. His body was but one of many corpses in "the endless field of the Gentiles." Then at once, from a wholly other realm, there appeared a holy seraph. It was Rabbi Uri of Strelisk, come to mourn the father's murder. From the mound of corpses crept a little grandson to ask why the seraph had not sent thousands of angels and seraphim to defend them. But Rabbi Uri was himself kneeling frozen in the field, and the snow kept on falling.[1]

It was but a few moments from the officer's attack upon the father until the death of the holy man. For this book, the space-time between has been but a few fragile chapters. But perhaps it is better to count up to a lifetime: nineteen hundred years of the Christian church. William Jay Peck testifies that in a "structural sense, the whole of Christianity was responsible for the death camps"; accordingly, any "denial of such involvement will doom the message of the church to remain at the level of shallow and impotent argumentation." For Stefan Zeroniski, "the crime itself never dies, regardless of when it was committed—a thousand years ago or early this morning." Yet it seems to this Polish writer that one must also "keep a second ear open to catch the sound of any bells from a new tower, from a temple of the future."[2]

Is there a new temple under construction somewhere? In this study we have returned to the kingdom of night. We have focused upon the remembrance of the Holocaust, the terrible singularity of that event, and the consummate need for a revolutionary transformation of Christian moral and theological teaching and action respecting Judaism and the Jewish people. In conclusion, we direct our thoughts to the future, applying the category of hope to, successively, the people of God, the Christian church, and the world of eschatology.

For Christians to say anything at all about hope and the Jewish people, they must be engaged in their own form of hoping, the hope that they are somehow part of that same people. Some Christians today have set out upon a strange road, a journey of *metanoia* from the epoch B.F.S. to that of F.S., a long night's journey into day. The Exodus from Egypt has become their Exodus, as Sinai has become their Sinai. And now the same is to be said of the Holocaust. To these Christians belong, in an extraordinary way, the murder center of Belzec and the uprising of Vilna. And to these Christians is given the task of addressing others within and beyond the church. Will you not stand with the children of Theresienstadt, the women of Birkenau, the men of Treblinka? Will you not enter within their struggle, their hell? Will you not honor the state of Israel, fighting its afflictions and rejoicing in its blessings? Together with the Jew Jesus, the authentic Christian is conjoined with the unending story of Israel, the people of God, a tale that is pierced by, but then prevails over, "the Final Solution of the question of Jews."

HOPE AND THE
PEOPLE OF GOD

The kingdom of night is hopelessness. Ours is the time after the kingdom of night. All idealism has been put to the torch: God will see after his own—as he did in Auschwitz. By identical reasoning, to enter the kingdom of day is to persist in hope. Yet even the kingdom of day is not the kingdom of heaven: here is the crux of our human problem. No perfection is to be found within human affairs, and there will be no perfection within the bounds of this world. Just as the kingdom of night could not succeed in vanquishing all goodness, so the kingdom of day cannot vanquish all evil. Yet this does not make the kingdom of day unattainable. It can come and it does come, in a fragmentary sense but a promising one.

If the kingdom of night is absolute dehumanization, absolute death, the kingdom of day is simply humanization resought, life regained. The kingdom of night is the slaughter of Jewish infants and children; the kingdom of day is the birth of Jewish babies and the raising of youngsters—though never without risk and always as an act of courage and faith, for what if these little ones should one day be obliterated?

Are we not confined to the hope that our hopes will prove to be authentic ones, consonant with reality? These hopes have to keep struggling against the force of a betraying hope, for, as Manès Sperber teaches, there is the hope that guides and that which misguides. The second kind leads man "in chains to his death." Sperber cites the lamentation of a young Polish poet named Tadeusz Borowski, not a Jew, who was to kill himself at the age of twenty-nine. Borowski said of himself and the other inmates of Auschwitz, "It is hope that provokes men to march indifferently to the gas chamber, and keeps them from conceiving of an insurrection; hope makes them dumb and causes them to resemble corpses. . . . Never has hope provoked so much ill as in this war, as in this camp. We were never taught how to rid ourselves of hope. And that is why we are dying in the gas chambers." Sperber notes that, in contrast with almost all the other insurrections, the revolt of the Warsaw ghetto was not inspired by any hope at all.[3]

But still the resisters fought. We have to be vigilant against the hope that misguides. However, it is not always so that the resort to armed power is bereft of genuine hope. It may foster such hope, because it can sometimes work to sustain life. Political sovereignty for the people of God, as we have understood it, is an essential of the kingdom of day.

The Jewish poet Paul Celan is not right in concluding that only one thing was still attainable during the horror of the Holocaust; that is, language, which remained undefeated despite "a thousand nights of death-dealing speech."[4] We should be the last to hold that the poetic/linguistic calling cannot be a heroic form of struggle against the enemy. We honor Celan, who created the single most powerful poem to come out of the Endlösung: "Todesfuge" ("Fugue of Death").[5] Yet we must speak in behalf of another war, a war for life, humanity, and justice, a struggle at whose heart was the killing of the killers. We have taken note of the Jewish resistance even in Auschwitz and Treblinka. The integrity of power was never wholly annihilated, even among Jews under sentence of death. Here is the partial truth in T. W. Adorno's famous aphorism that no poetry is possible after Auschwitz. For all its cathartic and testimonial value, poetry was snuffed out in the fires. It is so that the fires themselves were finally extinguished—but only by shells and bombs.

Today's free state of Israel, among its many other achievements, reproduces and perpetuates this *Widerstand*, this *Résistance*. It constitutes, so to say, the dowry brought to a new marriage, a new covenant of promise. Israel is the rainbow set again in the clouds. Yet we are obligated to remember that the rainbow seen after the recession of the floodwaters signified the divine remembrance of the covenant with all living creatures (Gen. 9:16). Accordingly, and keeping before us the stress of Eliezer Berkovits upon innocent and vicarious human torment in the context of the unforgivableness of the divine creation, we must speak as well for the political rights of the Arabs of Palestine, who have suffered so grievously as the forgotten people of the Arab world. It is the minority peoples of this world who need political sovereignty the most, if they are to be enabled to protect themselves, to survive, to prosper.

Under the aegis of the relative moral validity and necessities of power, and hence upon grounds not narrowly religious, we answer affirmatively the question of David Wolf Silverman: "Dare we not say today that the founding and preservation of Israel is God's gesture of faith in the midst of His silence?"[6] Bound together as they are, Holocaust and state of Israel create a shattering dialectic for any faith that posits the decisiveness of historical events, an assumption that itself precludes any separation of the transpolitical and political realms. The Holocaust inquires: how can you still believe in the God who delivers Israel? The state of Israel replies: how can you not believe in the God who delivers Israel? On the cross the Palestinian Jew Jesus cried out, with the Psalmist, "My God, my God, why have you forsaken me?" In our time the Israeli poet Yehuda Amichai asks: "My God, my God, / Why have you not forsaken me?"

The unbearable, relentless logic endures that God, the one who does not deliver Israel, is yet the one who does deliver her. Having faith, we are sent into despair. And in despair, we are lifted back into faith. Can we believe in God? No, it is impossible. *Can* we believe in God? Yes, for a fleeting moment.

In the dialectic of Holocaust and state of Israel, each focus takes its opposite into itself.

> ... The smell of our own land is like the smell of our strong wine.
> Our slaughtered dead children come here to rest and play,
> Near to us, face to face with us,
> Cooling their faces, no longer wandering homeless, astray.[7]

On 4 April 1976, we attended a service in the Yad Vashem Memorial, Jerusalem, in honor of Joseph S. Cammerer of Germany, one of the "Righteous of the Nations" who, during the Nazi time, had aided Jews at peril to his life. A cantor was singing. At that moment fighter aircraft of the Israel Defense Forces were suddenly heard. The singing stood for the powerlessness of the Jewish victims; the aircraft represented the power of the state of Israel. To Ilse Aichinger, whose question is inscribed at the beginning of this book, the answer may now be sent with love: here is where the children are, some of them.

If our dialectic of despair and faith is not nonsense, we are granted an alternative to both utopianism and cynicism. We are emboldened to struggle along, not because any final answers have come, but because our plight has been comprehended, the plight that God and Israel share, a condition that makes them friends forever. Mutual understanding is anointed by mutual compassion. The choice of future courses of action becomes one of responsibleness resting upon reality. Yizhak Orpaz tells of the man who is conscious that no way out of his condition is open. "His hope, and, if you like, his salvation, lies in the question: How do I live with this? He does not tire, because he bears with him a kind of ancient memory of a blessing and a breaking. In his quest he makes a flawed world meaningful."[8]

The threat is always bursting into a promise, yet the promise is ever being held back by a threat. On the one hand, strange deliverances emerged out of the very kingdom of night.

I am György Kemény. Live in Budapest as a graphic designer. I work like everybody does. Thirty years ago I was a Jewish boy of nine. My parents put me to an asylum, to keep my life saved. There I was once shot at, but the bullet missed to kill me. Next I was taken to a mass execution at the River Danube. But an air raid dispersed my were-to-be murderers. When liberation came, I weighed 34 pounds. My mother still starts crying, when remembering all this. Today I live in Budapest. I am a graphic designer, work like everybody else.[9]

On the other hand, a menacing shadow casts itself across the promise, a shadow of the kind that, in consonance with the above reasoning, we must ever expect yet ever work to efface: will the kingdom of night reappear?

The people of today's state of Israel have been described as "a concentrated example of siege and dread." Aharon Megged writes that the Yom Kippur War of 1973

re-linked the Zionist period of the last two or three generations, to the old long chain of Jewish history: a history of a people living as a minority—this time within an ocean of Arab hostility—isolated, with no allies to depend upon, and continuously struggling for its very survival. All our life in Israel, which seemed to be a departure from that history, has now apparently come back to it.[10]

Elie Wiesel speaks from a similar point of view.

For the first time in my adult life I am afraid that the nightmare may start all over again, or that it has never ended, that since 1945 we have lived in parentheses. . . .

Could the Holocaust happen again? Over the years I have put the question to my young students. And they, consistently, have answered yes, while I said no. . . . I was somehow convinced that—paradoxically—man would be shielded, protected by the awesome mystery of the Event.

I was wrong. . . . All of a sudden, I am too much reminded of past experiences. The enemy growing more and more powerful, more and more popular. The aggressiveness of the blackmailers, the permissiveness of some leaders and the total submissiveness of others. The overt threats. The complacency and diffidence of the bystanders. I feel as my father must have felt when he was my age. . . .

And so I look at my young students and tremble for their future; I see myself at their age surrounded by ruins. What am I to tell them? . . .

I remember. And I am afraid.[11]

A Christian scholar in Germany shifts the focus somewhat. He refers to the veil draped over the *Sonderbehandlung* ("special treatment") of the three million Jews of today's Soviet Union.[12] *Sonderbehandlung* was the Nazi code word for the extinction of the Jews. Genocide need not take place overnight or even within a decade. It can be a drawn-out business.

Are there any signs of promise from within the threat, and despite it?

Let us admit the worst into conscious analysis. Let us grant—on the basis of very weighty but not absolutely certain evidence—that the unchanged and unchanging position of the overwhelming majority of the Arab states is that Israel has no right to independent and sovereign nationhood in Palestine, and, accordingly, that she must be destroyed as quickly as time and opportunity will permit, and this with the aid of, or despite the necessary prudence of, interim agreements, settlements, and even peace treaties. Let us concede that the Arab conflict with the Jews of Israel has nothing to do, in its essence, with territorial withdrawals or border adjustments; and therefore that Israel could pull back to the pre-1967 armistice lines, or to the 1947 partition lines, or, for that matter, to a single beachhead on the Mediterranean coast, and yet remain as "guilty" as she has always been, and as liable to obliteration, on "moral" grounds.

In this study we have distinguished two fundamental components of the Endlösung: the dehumanization of Jews and Jewish resistance. The difference between resistance in the Nazi time and Israeli Jewish resistance today is that the latter is not doomed. It is representative of the kingdom of day, because it is made possible by a humanized Jewish society, it reflects the regaining of life, and furthermore there is a possibility that it will succeed.

Today there are formidable obstacles to the success of a potential Arab or other Holocaust of the Jews. A number of nations other than Jews and their destroyers are potentially involved. The question, "Are you prepared to support, through

145

silence or in other ways, a *Judenvernichtung?*," is quite a different one today from what it was in 1933. Now the potentiality of betraying Jewish lives—never before a disconcerting matter in the history of the West—has been invaded by international self-concern. The same Elie Wiesel who fears that the nightmare may start all over again properly pointed out—although four years earlier than he expressed the fear cited above—that "for the first time man's fate and the Jewish fate have converged. That means it is impossible to try again another Holocaust without committing the collective suicide of the whole world."[13] Herein lies a most encouraging consideration. A threatened Israel may well take the position (we ought to say, is morally obligated to take the position) that it will not allow a second Holocaust, although the primary decision, one way or the other, will have been the responsibility of its foes. Two thousand years of antisemitic annihilationism would appear to be enough. The ideology of the disposable Jew met its nemesis in the 1940s, in the almost coincident invention of nuclear weapons and the reestablishment of the Jewish state—a very interesting oddity (cf. Ps. 2:4: "He who sits in the heavens laughs; the Lord has them in derision"). The world will simply have to learn that it can no longer dispense Jewish fate. Following Emil Fackenheim, we have alluded to the requirement that Hitler not be permitted a posthumous victory. It is instructive to substitute "the world" for "Hitler."

An analogue from recent history is very relevant. When in 1973 the Soviet Union threatened to dispatch its own troops to join the Syrian army during the fourth war against Israel, the United States officials said no, you will not do that, because if you do, you will be met by American forces armed with tactical nuclear weapons.[14] It is hardly necessary to record that the Soviet Union drew back. As Louis Halle of the University of Geneva points out, thermonuclear weaponry, with the aid of effective espionage satellites, has become a powerful force for coexistence between the USSR and the United States over a full generation and has contributed to world peace.[15] There is every reason to expect that this technology will continue to perform a like function in the years ahead. It is possible, of course, that the Arab nations will decide to consummate their death wish for the Jews through their own self-destruction. Adolf Hitler was perfectly ready to destroy Germany and the entire German people in the course of the Endlösung. However, the price of a new Holocaust is escalating rapidly.[16] A nuclear deterrent can be made to work—not that it ever guarantees anything. We do not speak here of the kingdom of heaven. Our standpoint is that of the kingdom of day. The reminder of John Maynard Keynes is at once apt and gratuitous: "In the long run we shall all be dead."

Yet a dread implication of our analysis remains. Despite appearances, the real tragedy of, and threat to, the Jewish people today centers not in the Middle East but in the Soviet Union, and secondarily in such places as the Argentine and Eastern Europe, where national sovereignty, often a functional good, is manifest as a moral peril. It is true that as long as Israel exists, the Jews of the Soviet captivity are granted a measure of hope. But is this an instance of authentic hope, or is it the kind of hope that cannot deliver? The problem is met in only a most minimal way through those Jews who manage to escape from the ever-so-gradual Soviet Endlösung.[17]

HOPE AND THE CHRISTIAN CHURCH

Would not the Jewish people, as perhaps the world itself, be better off without the church, without Christianity? Those who speak from within the Christian community cannot avoid this question, just as the detractors of Christian faith will not permit them to avoid it. For example, it is argued that one fundamental reason why antisemitism is at a nadir in certain parts of the world is that Christians in those places have, to all intents and purposes, subdued their faith-claims under the impact of secularization, the norms of religious pluralism, and simple humanitarianism. There is much comfort, for Jews as for other men, in the fact of a post-Christian era in which there are no longer hosts of the church to wreak persecution and destruction upon humankind.

However, a moral desire that the Christian church continue, maintaining its integrity and independence, is forcibly expressed not only by Christians but also by some Jews. A parable in Matthew tells of an unclean spirit "gone out of a man" which

147

then "brings with him seven other spirits more evil than himself, and they enter and dwell there; and the last state of that man becomes worse than the first" (12:43, 45). Even if it is so that Christianity has brought great harm to Jews (as to other peoples), would not the church's abolition or demise open the door to equally sinister or more evil spirits? A gentile world freed from the moral constraints provided by the Christian faith may very well, so the argument goes, visit upon us even greater hells than the original Holocaust. Anthropotheism, the effectual divinization of man,[18] can only let loose an infinity of horrors. Nazism was itself an embodiment of a devilish/religious impulse, not only to control human beings absolutely, but also to make man God. Does not the Christian church, at least ideally and potentially, provide a brake upon such self-idolatry? A colleague in Strasbourg writes: "It is regrettable that the virus of dechristianization is rife in the world."[19] It is worth noting that the man who speaks these words is a Jew whose father was murdered in Auschwitz.

Our question resolves itself into another question. What kinds of Christianity are possible? It is clear that the world and especially the Jewish people, not to mention Christians themselves, will be infinitely better off if triumphalist Christianity can be overcome. For there is no escape from exclusivism and intolerance so long as humankind is divided into "the elect and the reprobate."[20] No truth is of greater importance here than this: the faith of Judaism has always been massively free of the idolatries that have pervaded Christendom. We are required to conclude from this that it is false, in principle, to claim that only through the religion of Christianity can the all-decisive human struggle against idolatry be waged. But we can also help to implement this truth by giving ourselves to the restoration of Jewishness within a Christianity infected by seven unclean spirits. In this direction are to be found wholeness and justice and love. And in this way we are enabled to address both groups of friends referred to above: those who fear for the end of Christianity, and those who are sickened by the sins of the church. We are persuaded that a reformed Christian faith—one that is empowered by revolutionary ferment and chastened by relativization (but not subjected to reductionism)—can be a great ally of the Jewish people, as of human beings everywhere.

When all is said and done, there is no equal to the steadfast, vital spirituality that bears as its fruit compassion and a zeal for justice. We refer as an example to an individual who lives this kind of faith. In Denmark today the name of Finn Henning Lauridsen stands out. He is the founder of an agency called For Israels ret til at bestå (For Israel's Right to Exist). An earnest Christian, Lauridsen devotes himself to arousing public opinion within and beyond his own country in behalf of the Israelis' right to live a free life. Outstanding artists contribute to the publicizing of Lauridsen's effort. He is much distraught over the possibility of a new *Vernichtung* of the Jewish people and is insistent upon the moral obligation of Christians and others to act to prevent a second Holocaust.[21]

A Dutch pastor has said, "Only by understanding Auschwitz can we be Christians again."[22]

HOPE BEYOND HOPE

The Israeli poet Abba Kovner shows visitors how the hut in which he works on his kibbutz lies halfway between the children's playground and the cemetery. Is this not where all of us carry on our work? Robert McAfee Brown writes that unless our future is also God's future, the scenario for our future "is too threatening to entertain."[23] The apostle Paul declares, "If in this life we who are in Christ have only hope, we are of all men most to be pitied" (1 Cor. 15:19).

Inexorably, human memory fades, as does human resolve. This will be true of the Holocaust, as of earlier afflictions of the people of God. We can only trust that our own remembrances and intentions will somehow be gathered into the strange work of the Ruler of the Universe. May it be that he is answering, in imponderable ways, our wretched petitions for freedom, our case against him, against the demonic powers, against, most of all, ourselves? Should he fail to give heed—if there is no response, if there is no revolution, in God as in us, if there is no new bell tower, no temple of the future—then will the end message of the Endlösung remain a bleakness that rolls on and on and on.

The Christian revolutionary is the eschatological human

being, who sets his face, in faith, to the end-time. We have cited Ulrich Simon's judgment that without the Resurrection, the Holocaust is simply hell. He is right, in principle. But for the sufferers, as for the survivors and their descendants, the only way that hell can be defeated is through the hope of a future Resurrection, when God will be victorious over every satanic and evil power, including death itself. *No past event, however holy or divine, can ever redeem the terror of the present. Only a future event can do this.*

There is the assurance of the fully eschatological character of the Resurrection. Redemption comes, redemption is coming. "The creation waits with eager longing for the revealing of the sons of God. . . . the whole creation has been groaning in travail until now" (Rom. 8:19, 22). Our day remains, as it were, Holy Saturday, the strange in-between time, that day, that *shabbat,* when we stop and when we are stopped, when we face up to, and when we are faced by, the end-time. The veil of sadness that, until now, is spread upon all things and all men, upon utopian humanists as upon hopeless humanists, shall be taken up. That young Jewish prophet from the Galilee sleeps now. He sleeps with the other Jewish dead, with all the disconsolate and scattered ones of the murder camps, and with the unnumbered dead of the human and the nonhuman family. But Jesus of Nazareth shall be raised.[24] So too shall the small Hungarian children of Auschwitz. Once upon a time, they shall again play and they shall laugh. The little one of Terezín shall see another butterfly. We shall all sing and we shall all dance. And we shall love one another. "The wolf shall dwell with the lamb, and the leopard shall lie down with the kid, and the calf and the lion, and the fatling together. . . . They shall not hurt nor destroy in all my holy mountain; for the earth shall be full of the knowledge of the Lord as the waters cover the sea" (Isa. 11:6, 9). The last enemy, death, shall be *sentenced* to death (1 Cor. 15:26; Rev. 21:3, 4). There is no cause for despair. There is no need for anxiety. "He who keeps Israel will neither slumber nor sleep" (Ps. 121:4). "Do not be anxious" (Matt. 6:25). Everything will come right.

150

NOTES

Complete bibliographical details for works cited may be found in the Selected Bibliography. Translations, unless otherwise noted, are our own.

CHAPTER 1

1. To our knowledge, Elie Wiesel was the first to apply the phrase "kingdom of night" to the Holocaust; see his *Night*. This is his most explicitly confessional work, with the possible exception of the much later *A Jew Today*. An authoritative history of the Holocaust years is Lucy S. Dawidowicz, *The War against the Jews 1933–1945*. The title is not sufficiently discriminating: Dawidowicz is concerned with the destruction of Jews in Germany, Austria, Poland, the Baltic countries, and, to a very limited extent, western Russia; Czechoslovakia, Hungary, Rumania, Bulgaria, Yugoslavia, Greece, Italy, and western and northern Europe (areas with a prewar Jewish population of no less than 2.5 million) are only briefly considered in an appendix. For an informative survey of Hitlerism and Nazi Germany, with sections on the persecution of Jews, the SS and the ideological basis of its mentality and command structure, the concentration and death camps, and the mass executions of Russian war prisoners, see Helmut Krausnick et al., *Anatomy of the SS State*. For a thorough study of the deportation of Jews from Germany, with emphasis upon the kind of bureaucracy that reduces human beings to virtual robots, see Hermann G. Adler, *Der Verwaltete Mensch*. A volume put forth by a Christian scholar in East Germany is Heinrich Fink, ed., *Stärker als die Angst;* the most significant contribution to it is H. David Leuner, "Versagen und Bewährung der Christen in der Solidarität." See also Terence Des Pres, *The Survivor;* Saul Friedländer, *L'Antisémitisme Nazi;* Sebastian Haffner, *The Meaning of Hitler;* Nora Levin, *The Holocaust*. For a fine collection of testimonial literature from during and after the Holocaust, see Albert H. Friedlander, ed., *Out of the Whirlwind*.
2. Jules Isaac, *The Teaching of Contempt*.

3. Uri Zvi Greenberg, from "To the Mound of Corpses in the Snow," trans. A. C. Jacobs, in *Anthology of Modern Hebrew Poetry*, 2:259.
4. On the problematic character of the term "Holocaust," see Alice and Roy Eckardt, "Studying the Holocaust's Impact Today: Some Dilemmas of Language and Method," pp. 224–26.
5. So Gerhard Reitlinger argues in *The Final Solution*, p. 102. Raul Hilberg speaks of the fateful step across the "dividing line" that inaugurated the "killing phase," and he refers, in *The Destruction of the European Jews*, pp. 177ff., to two all-decisive orders by Hitler in 1941 that were to doom all European Jewry.
6. Of these, the Nazis succeeded in destroying about 6 million. It is not possible to furnish exact figures. The *Encyclopaedia Judaica* estimates 5,820,960.
7. Abel J. Herzberg illustrates this aspect of the truth in his essays on Bergen-Belsen in *Amor Fati*.
8. Abba Kovner, "A First Attempt to Tell"; Elie Wiesel, *Legends of Our Time*, p. 229; Cynthia Haft, *The Theme of Nazi Concentration Camps in French Literature*, p. 133.
9. Haft, *Theme of Concentration Camps*, p. 153.
10. *Yad Vashem* means "lasting memorial" (literally, "a monument and a name"; cf. Isa. 56:5).
11. See Léon Poliakov, *Auschwitz*, pp. 127–36.
12. In October 1943, the Germans razed what was left of the camp. They plowed the area and sowed it with fodder, hoping to hide Treblinka from the world. See Yuri Suhl, ed. and trans., *They Fought Back*, pp. 150–55; Wassilij Grossman, *Die Hölle von Treblinka*, pp. 45–48; Jean-François Steiner, *Treblinka*. A serious fault in Steiner's work (at one time a best-seller) is his failure to acknowledge his sources. He is also sensationalistic; see the critical remarks by Haft, *Theme of Concentration Camps*, pp. 190–91, and by Israel Gutman, "Remarks on the Literature of the Holocaust," p. 133.
13. "Tuchin."
14. The most comprehensive and authoritative single volume on this issue remains *Jewish Resistance during the Holocaust*; see also Yehuda Bauer, *They Chose Life*; K. Shabbetai, *As Sheep to the Slaughter*.
15. Raul Hilberg's *Destruction of the European Jews*, which is restricted to the Holocaust as such, is often singled out as an illustration of this outlook. Although Hilberg approaches the Endlösung as though from the standpoint of its perpetrators rather than of its victims, this is necessary for realizing his purpose. He is the foe of everything Nazi, and his brilliant work remains authoritative.
16. A. Roy Eckardt, *Christianity and the Children of Israel*. This volume is based on a doctoral dissertation supervised by Reinhold Niebuhr.
17. Jacob Robinson, assisted by Mrs. Philip Friedman, *The Holocaust and After*, p. 323.
18. Elie Wiesel, "Jewish Values in the Post-Holocaust Future," p. 283.
19. Immanuel Kant taught that the noumenal world forever eludes us, in contrast to the world of phenomena.
20. Haft, *Theme of Concentration Camps*, p. 11.

21. Lawrence L. Langer, *The Holocaust and the Literary Imagination*, p. xiii. The issue we raise is not quite the same as that of literary quality, although related to it. Cynthia Haft is entirely correct that the phenomenon of the concentration camps can penetrate the individual and collective consciousness of our time only through literature which manifests "the power of language . . . to contain and transmute all passions, all human experiences." As she observes, the mere fact of having been through a concentration camp, or of having learned what happened to others there, hardly bestows literary talent or creates a work of art (*Theme of Concentration Camps*, pp. 10–11, 189).

22. Cynthia Ozick, "The Uses of Legend: Elie Wiesel as Tsaddik," p. 19. Cf. Wilfred Owen, referring to World War I: "My subject is war, and the pity of war. The poetry is in the pity."

23. While Irving Greenberg does not go this far, he is yet taken by the baffling nature of the event, arguing that no final or definitive lessons can be learned from the Holocaust. "The event in itself is so radical a surd, it breaks so many limits and accepted norms, that its implications are more often paradoxical, dialectic, and baffling. Most attempts to give definitive or single meanings to Holocaust implications usually bespeak lack of knowledge of what happened or, what is worse, propaganda or use of the victims for selfish advantage" ("Lessons To Be Learned from the Holocaust"). In another place he speaks more positively respecting the Holocaust and its moral and spiritual lessons ("Cloud of Smoke, Pillar of Fire: Judaism, Christianity, and Modernity after the Holocaust").

24. Probably no other modern event has produced a comparable mass of writing. The single bibliography entitled *The Holocaust and After* (see n. 17 above) reflects the vast number of publications that bear in one or another way upon our present concerns. The annotated volume contains 6,637 items. However, it was published in 1973, the journal materials it lists are largely limited to Jewish periodicals, and the entries are restricted to literature in English (though much of this comprises translations from such other languages as Hebrew, Yiddish, Polish, and German). We estimate that at this writing the number of published items relating substantially to the Holocaust and its aftermath total at least thirty thousand.

CHAPTER 2

1. Langer, *Holocaust and the Literary Imagination*, p. 270.
2. Wiesel, "Jewish Values in the Post-Holocaust Future," p. 283.
3. Konrad Kellen, "*Seven Beauties:* Auschwitz—the Ultimate Joke?"
4. Nathan Rotenstreich, *Reflections on the Contemporary Jewish Tradition*, p. 13.
5. Golo Mann, as cited in *Newsweek*, 26 May 1975.
6. Abraham Zvie Bar-On, consultation, Jerusalem, 24 May 1976.
7. Harvey Cox, *Feast of Fools*, pp. 12, 13.

8. Hilel Klein, consultation, Jerusalem, 2 June 1976.
9. Jürgen Moltmann, consultation, Tübingen, 14 Aug. 1975; Alexander and Margarete Mitscherlich, *Die Unfähigkeit zu trauern, Grundlagen kollektiven Verhaltens;* Abba Kovner, "Threnody for a Movement."
10. Robinson and Friedman, *Holocaust and After,* p. 310.
11. Abel J. Herzberg, consultation, Amsterdam, 20 Jan. 1976; H. David Leuner, "Versagen und Bewährung—Die Welt und das Brandopfer der Juden," p. 5.
12. Alphons Silbermann, "Antisemitismus in der Bundesrepublik Deutschland." The study was commissioned by the German Research Society.
13. Such appears to be the judgment of the noted German public opinion analyst, Elisabeth Noelle-Neumann (as reported in *Deutschland Berichte* [Bonn-Holzlar] 12, no. 10 [Oct. 1976]:25-26).
14. Jürgen Neven-du Mont, *After Hitler.*
15. See, for example, Arthur R. Butz, *The Hoax of the Twentieth Century* (Richmond, Surrey: Historical Review Press), n.d., but probably 1976.
16. Langer, *Holocaust and the Literary Imagination,* pp. 248-49.
17. A. Roy Eckardt, *Your People, My People,* pp. 253, 254. In recent years the outlook of many of the young people who take part in Aktion Sühnezeichen/Friedensdienste has differed from that of their predecessors. It is now possible for German youth who are conscientious objectors to satisfy the requirement of alternate service through work in this group. Some of the participants in the program have no idea of voluntarily bearing "the sins of the fathers," despite the fact that the officially stated purposes of the movement have not been altered (Michael Krupp, consultation, Jerusalem, 22 Mar. 1976; consultation with AS/F volunteers in Jerusalem, 30 May 1976). From the beginning, Poland and Russia were designated as recipients of works of reconciliation, along with Israel.
18. Julius Cardinal Döpfner, as cited in the *Münchener Katholische Kirchen-Zeitung,* 6 Jan. 1975. Cardinal Döpfner died in 1976.
19. These lines appear as an epigraph in Jacob Presser, *The Destruction of the Dutch Jews.*

CHAPTER 3

1. Dorothea Dier, consultation, Summit, N.J., 14 Mar. 1975.
2. As cited in "Auschwitz."
3. Emil L. Fackenheim, as cited in the *Baltimore Jewish Times,* 10 June 1977, p. 40.
4. Cf. Vincent Canby: "As pop music is now being magnified to the point where we can barely hear it, the volume of screen violence is being raised close to the point where we no longer see it. . . . The same graphic scenes of violence that penetrate dull brains, make those brains duller, more impervious to shock, so that succeeding films must go even further. The volume of screen violence must continue to be raised" (*New York Times,* 17 Oct. 1976).

5. A special variation of the moral problem here is associated with the argument sometimes proffered that Hitler intended, ultimately, a "Final Solution" for the churches as well as for Jewry. Any reputed connection here is wholly misplaced. All Christians always had the "opportunity" to turn their backs on their faith. The Nazis themselves came largely out of the Christian community. There was no parallel with the Jews. A Jew who became a rabid anti-semite or sought to swear fealty to the Führer would meet the same fate as every other Jew.

6. In a discussion of global hunger, Joseph Holland includes the factor of discontinuity between that phenomenon and the Holocaust, but he also refers to a fundamental element of continuity in the two, namely, Christianity. "Before it was the gas ovens; today it is the slow and painful process of *starvation*. Despite the differences, the new holocaust shares one shattering fact with its predecessor. It is the powers, structures, and policies of the nations where Christianity is strongest which oversee the extermination" ("Hunger: Global Holocaust or Global Exodus?," p.17). The oil-rich Muslim Arab states must now be added to the Christian nations. For an analysis of the links among the Holocaust, modern technology and bureaucracy, demographic trends, and the future disposal of "surplus" populations, see Richard L. Rubenstein, *The Cunning of History*.

7. Saul S. Friedman, "Arab Complicity in the Holocaust," p. 9.

8. For an account of the Armenian massacres, see Howard Sachar, *The Emergence of the Middle East 1914–1924*, chap. 4; see also Marjorie Housepian, "The Unremembered Genocide." Housepian emphasizes that the event has been glossed over by historians.

9. Hermann G. Adler, consultation, London, 18 Feb. 1976.

10. Hans-Jochen Gamm, written communication, 23 Sept. 1975.

11. Klaus Scholder, consultations, Tübingen, 9 Aug., 27 Sept., 21 Dec. 1975.

12. Elie Wiesel, *A Beggar in Jerusalem*, p. 200.

13. There are moot questions here. Alternatives include 1939, the year World War II began, and 1942, for it was early in the latter year that the resolve to implement the Endlösung was officially made. The date 1941 is based upon the "killing phase" of the program against the Jews (see chap. 1, n. 5 above). Any advocated symbology faces the criticism that it is either arbitrary or contrived. One alternative is "B.A." and "A.A.," "Before Auschwitz" and "After Auschwitz." There are substantive and moral objections to singling out this one murder camp, despite its horribleness and dominance. Yet there is no doubt that this name has become the single most powerful symbol of the Holocaust.

14. "To the Fascists [the Nazis], the Jews are not a minority but the enemy race, the Negative Principle as such. The good fortune of the world is dependent upon their extermination" (M. Horkheimer and T. W. Adorno, *Dialektik der Aufklärung*, as cited in Manfred Franke, *Morderläufe 9./10. XI 1938*, p. 7). Among the more famous Nazi slogans was "Die Juden sind unser Unglück" ("The Jews are our disaster").

15. This phrasing was used by Dietrich Goldschmidt, consultation, Berlin, 19 Nov. 1975.

16. Zacharia Shuster, consultation, Paris, 29 Jan. 1976.
17. A. Roy Eckardt's "Is the Holocaust Unique?" was submitted to *Worldview* with the title "In What Senses Is the Holocaust Unique?"; in changing the title for publication, the editors showed a lack of familiarity with the contents of the essay, but in their error they also pointed up a fundamental conflict in the reading of events.
18. H. J. Zimmels, *The Echo of the Nazi Holocaust in Rabbinic Literature*, pp. xv–xxiii. The bare listing obviously requires amplification. Important specifics must include the assiduous utilizing of Jews as instruments of their own betrayal and destruction.
19. Abraham Zvie Bar-On, consultation, Jerusalem, 24 May 1976.
20. Just before his premature death, Robert Alden described the anti-Israeli tone within the United Nations. He saw the expressed anti-Jewishness as reflective of a seething hostility that had been brewing for many years. Before the packed chamber of the Security Council, Yakov Malik of the Soviet Union spoke of the Israelis as "murderers and international gangsters"—whereupon the room exploded into prolonged applause. The date of the meeting was four days after the Arabs launched the Yom Kippur War (*New York Times*, 11 Oct. 1973). It is one of the bizarre ironies of history that the headquarters of world antisemitism should come to be located in an American city containing the world's largest Jewish population.
21. James Parkes is disturbed by our associating the concept of the devil with antisemitism. "I am particularly distressed at the introduction of the devil now that Rosemary Ruether's book *Faith and Fratricide* has at last opened the way to a discussion of the Christian liturgy as the real root of antisemitism. If you read the New Testament in church as the 'Word of God' for two thousand years, I think it is enough explanation of that subconscious and instinctive hostility which is the 'abnormal' part of antisemitism." However, he has no objection to the phrasing "demonic forces"; his distress evidently centers in the suggestion of a "personal" devil (Parkes, written communication, 26 May 1976, slightly emended). In light of the traditional Christian stress upon the devil, in marked contrast to Jewish theology, it is noteworthy that, among others, the contemporary Jewish philosopher Emil L. Fackenheim is prepared to consider seriously the concept of the devil ("The Nazi Holocaust as a Persisting Trauma for the Non-Jewish Mind," pp. 375–76). John T. Pawlikowski argues that A. Roy Eckardt's effort to link the devil to antisemitism and the Holocaust wrongly calls human culpability into question and leaves human dignity intact (*The Challenge of the Holocaust for Christian Theology*, pp. 18–19). We seek to meet this criticism in the course of this chapter and succeeding ones.
22. The analysis at this point is aided by a consultation with Bernard Dupuy, Paris, 28 Jan. 1976.
23. David Polish, "The Tasks of Israel and Galut," p. 10; Eckardt, *Your People, My People*, p. 83.
24. Eckardt, *Your People, My People*, pp. 87–90. Those who equate Jews with the devil may have assured themselves that they are furnishing fresh, creative wisdom. In truth the equation erupts from a collective unconscious formed by

a centuries-long history. If the charge did not itself have devilish consequences, it could be dismissed as simply dull. More than a thousand years is a
long time for men in otherwise disparate places of the globe to mouth the
identical words. For additional discussion of the devil, see A. Roy Eckardt,
"The Devil and Yom Kippur," esp. pp. 70–74.

25. As reported in the *New York Times*, 16 Feb. 1974.
26. See chap. 2, n. 15.
27. They avow that the event never occurred, yet the rationale of that event is
the very thing that impels their efforts, the same rationale that impelled the
first Nazis. As one of these reincarnations of the Nazis has said, "All the
stories about Auschwitz aren't true, but I wish they were."
28. Arthur Hertzberg, "Response to Uriel Tal," p. 373.
29. Emil L. Fackenheim, "The Human Condition after Auschwitz: A Jewish
Testimony a Generation After," pp. 9, 10.
30. Levin, *Holocaust*, p. 91.
31. "It is true that, since Auschwitz, the calendar does not follow a new time
reckoning. Yet there has taken place in our mentality—rarely consciously, but
unavoidably unconsciously—something like a new way of measuring time. . . .
Although the mechanism of destruction had always existed, it was only its
perfection that made it into a category. The new, unprecedented element was
not the frightful cruelty of individual people, but the anonymous effortlessness
of desk work carried out conscientiously and without a flaw" (Günter Grass, as
cited and translated in Eva Fleischner, *Judaism in German Christian Theology since 1945*, pp. 20–21. Grass's piece originally appeared in the *Frankfurter
Allgemeine Zeitung*, 2 June 1970).
32. See John T. Pawlikowski, "The Dialogue Agenda," p. 2. For an interpretation quite different from ours, one that emphasizes independently causative
elements of specifically twentieth-century history, see Rubenstein, *Cunning
of History*. According to Rubenstein, the Holocaust must be placed "within
the context of the phenomenon of twentieth-century mass death. Never before have human beings been so expendable." The Holocaust is an expression *"of some of the most profound tendencies of Western civilization in the
twentieth century.* Given Britain's imperial commitments, Europe's Jews
were as much a superfluous population for Great Britain as they were for
Germany. . . . From a purely bureaucratic perspective, the extermination of
the Jews of Europe was the 'final solution' for the British as well as the
Germans" (pp. 12, 20). Rubenstein of course also takes seriously the elements
of historical uniqueness in the Holocaust.
33. Fackenheim, "Human Condition after Auschwitz," p. 7.
34. See A. Roy Eckardt, ed., *The Theologian at Work*, pp. 129–30, and *Der
Stellvertreter*, act 5, sc. 2, reproduced ibid., pp. 136–46.
35. Eliezer Berkovits, "The Hiding God of History, " in Yisrael Gutman and
Livia Rothkirchen, eds., *The Catastrophe of European Jewry*, p. 704.
36. Samuel Sandmel, "The New Movement," p. 13.
37. Elie Wiesel, *"Ani Maamin,"* pp. 89–103.
38. Wilm Sanders of Germany reports the following as a typical judgment of
"simple Catholic Christians": "The Jews are accursed. In the moment that

they crucified Christ, the Lord God repudiated them. And ask of him what they will, it is of no use—see what they have endured in the concentration camps. The Jews are accursed. The Lord God will refuse them a favorable hearing. They have no dwelling-place in the world. They crucified the Christ. And they refuse to be converted. They do not believe in Christ" (*Antisemitismus bei den Christen?*, pp. 7–8). A scholar in West Germany nevertheless contended to us that the vast majority of Christians in his country today remain unaware that the Holocaust had anything to do with religious influences (Rolf Rendtorff, consultation, Heidelberg, 30 Oct. 1975).

39. Relevant works include: Alan T. Davies, *Anti-Semitism and the Christian Mind;* Eckardt, *Your People, My People;* Malcolm Hay, *Thy Brother's Blood;* Friedrich Heer, *God's First Love;* Isaac, *Teaching of Contempt;* Charlotte Klein, *Theologie und Anti-Judaismus;* Pinchas E. Lapide, "Vom 'Gottesmorde' zum Völkermord"; Guenter Lewy, *The Catholic Church and Nazi Germany;* Franklin H. Littell, *The Crucifixion of the Jews;* Franklin H. Littell and Hubert G. Locke, eds., *The German Church Struggle and the Holocaust;* Reinhold Mayer, *Judentum und Christentum;* the following works of James Parkes: *Antisemitism; The Conflict of the Church and the Synagogue; A History of the Jewish People; The Jew in the Medieval Community; Judaism and Christianity;* Rudolf Pfisterer, *Im Schatten des Kreuzes;* Léon Poliakov, *The Aryan Myth;* Richard L. Rubenstein, *After Auschwitz;* Rosemary Radford Ruether, *Faith and Fratricide;* Frederick M. Schweitzer, *A History of the Jews since the First Century A.D.;* Uriel Tal, *Christians and Jews in Germany;* Joshua Trachtenberg, *The Devil and the Jews.*

40. Manès Sperber, the celebrated Jewish novelist and former psychiatrist, now living in France, said to us: "The seed of the Holocaust is Christianity, fertilized by other factors. The bankruptcy of Christian messianism is in my eyes" (consultation, Paris, 29 Jan. 1976).

41. Littell, *Crucifixion of the Jews,* pp. 2, 17.

42. Gregory G. Baum, *Christian Theology after Auschwitz,* pp. 8, 9, 11.

43. Gregory G. Baum, Introduction to Ruether, *Faith and Fratricide,* p. 8.

44. Paul van Buren, "The Status and Prospects for Theology," p. 3. Van Buren's article is based on a paper read before the annual meeting of the American Academy of Religion, Chicago, Nov. 1975.

45. Had Jesus been alive at the time of the Endlösung, he would not have been put to death for deliberately making an issue of himself (as seems to have been the case; see Luke 9:51), but instead with absolute fatefulness. He was one of those *Untermenschen.* On the Christological question, see Michael B. McGarry, *Christology after Auschwitz;* Eugene B. Borowitz, *Contemporary Christologies.*

46. Robert McAfee Brown, "The Holocaust: The Crisis of Indifference," pp. 18–19.

47. George Steiner, *In Bluebeard's Castle,* pp. 41, 44, 45. For a much earlier effort to link antisemitism with the attack upon God, but one that is somewhat paralleled by Steiner, see Eckardt, *Christianity and the Children of Israel,* chap. 2.

48. Saul Friedländer, "Some Aspects of the Historical Significance of the Holocaust."

49. Ismar Schorsch, "German Anti-Semitism in the Light of Post-War Historiography."

CHAPTER 4

1. Wiesel, *Legends of Our Time,* p. 6. But Wiesel contends that today it is harder to live with than without God. "Can you compare today the tragedy of the believer to that of the nonbeliever? The real tragedy, the real drama, is the drama of the believer" ("Talking and Writing and Keeping Silent," in Littell and Locke, eds. *German Church Struggle and the Holocaust,* p. 274).

2. William Jay Peck, "From Cain to the Death Camps: An Essay on Bonhoeffer and Judaism," pp. 159–60.

3. Fackenheim, "Nazi Holocaust," p. 376.

4. This rendering in the King James Version is the most familiar to religious people. Other versions present a quite different meaning, e.g., "Behold he will slay me; I have no hope" (Revised Standard Version).

5. Michael Wyschogrod protests that the Holocaust must not be permitted to mute or silence the basic Jewish message of a faithful, redeeming God. For him, the trouble with the emphasis upon not giving Hitler a posthumous victory is that "if I remain a Jew basically to frustrate Hitler's design, I place Hitler's evil design at the heart of Jewish faith. It does not belong there. Only the message that God is a redeeming God belongs there" ("Some Theological Reflections on the Holocaust," in Lucy Y. Steinitz and David M. Szonyi, eds., *Living after the Holocaust,* pp. 66–67).

6. Jakov Lind, *Counting My Steps,* p. 54.

7. Jakov Lind, "Resurrection," in *Soul of Wood and Other Stories,* p. 154.

8. Alexander Donat, "The Voice of the Ashes."

9. Rubenstein, *After Auschwitz,* pp. 46, 52–54.

10. Richard L. Rubenstein, "Some Perspectives on Religious Faith after Auschwitz," in Littell and Locke, eds., *German Church Struggle and the Holocaust,* pp. 261, 262.

11. Rubenstein, *After Auschwitz,* pp. 56, 58, 69.

12. Ibid., pp. x, 128, 223, 224–25. Rubenstein may be asked whether the Jewish people, having regained the land of Israel and national sovereignty, have not also become vulnerable again. Have they not reappropriated hope, and hence exposed themselves to the possibility of greater disappointment, even unto despair? See also Richard L. Rubenstein, "Jewish Theology and the Current World Situation."

13. Gregory Baum, *Man Becoming.* The quotations in this paragraph are taken from pp. 242–45 passim.

14. Ibid., pp. 248–49. Cf. this post-Holocaust interpretation of God by the Jewish philosopher Hans Jonas: God is a suffering, becoming, caring God, who is

159

not omnipotent. Omnipotence is "a self-contradictory, self-destructive, indeed senseless concept." For a time, God "has divested Himself of any power to interfere with the physical course of things" and "responds to the impact on His being of worldly events." A consequence is that we humans "literally hold in our faltering hands the future of the divine adventure and must not fail Him, even if we would fail ourselves" ("The Concept of God after Auschwitz," in Friedlander, ed., *Out of the Whirlwind*, pp. 465–76).

15. Franklin Sherman, "Speaking of God after Auschwitz."
16. Arthur J. Lelyveld, *Atheism Is Dead*, pp. 158–176, 177.
17. Ibid., pp. 172–83 passim.
18. Ibid., pp. 182–83, 184.
19. Viktor Frankl, *From Death Camp to Existentialism*, pp. 77, 105, 107.
20. Zvi Kolitz, "Yossel Rakover's Appeal to God," in Friedlander, ed., *Out of the Whirlwind*, p. 399. Cf. the Rebbe in a tale of Elie Wiesel: "There is joy as well as fury in the *hasid's* dancing. It's his way of proclaiming, 'You don't want me to dance; too bad, I'll dance anyhow. You've taken away every reason for singing, but I shall sing. I shall sing of the deceit that walks by day and the truth that walks by night, yes, and of the silence of dusk as well. You didn't expect my joy, but here it is; yes, my joy will rise up; it will submerge you' " (*The Gates of the Forest*, p. 196). Elsewhere the character Michael declaims: "I go up against Him. I shake my fist, I froth with rage, but it's still a way of telling Him that He's there, that He exists, that He's never the same twice, that denial itself is an offering to His grandeur" (Elie Wiesel, *The Town beyond the Wall*, p. 123).
21. A most powerful castigation of God on the ground of the Holocaust is Uri Zvi Greenberg, "To God in Europe," trans. Robert Friend, in *Anthology of Modern Hebrew Poetry*, 2:264–78.
22. Ulrich E. Simon, *A Theology of Auschwitz*, p. 82.
23. Eliezer Berkovits, "The Hiding God of History," in Gutman and Rothkirchen, eds., *Catastrophe of European Jewry*, pp. 694, 704; *Faith after the Holocaust*, pp. 99, 131. "God took a risk with man and he cannot divest himself of responsibility for man. If man is not to perish at the hand of man, . . . God must not withdraw his providence from his creation. . . . That man may be, God must absent himself; that man may not perish in the tragic absurdity of his own making, God must remain present. . . . He is present without being indubitably manifest; he is absent without being hopelessly inaccessible. Thus, many find him even in his 'absence'; many miss him even in his presence. Because of the necessity of his absence, there is the 'Hiding of the Face' and suffering of the innocent; because of the necessity of his presence, evil will not ultimately triumph; because of it, there is hope for man" (*Faith after the Holocaust*, p. 107).

We find it noteworthy that "The Hiding God of History," while it is the only explicitly theological study among a large number of contributions in *Catastrophe of European Jewry*, should nevertheless be placed at the end of the volume and form a kind of climax to the entire achievement. A full presentation of Berkovits's point of view is found in his *Faith after the Holocaust* and *With God in Hell*.

24. Wiesel, *Beggar in Jerusalem*, pp. 199–200.
25. Ibid., p. 30.
26. Ibid., p. 28.
27. Irving Greenberg, consultation, Southampton, England, 21 July 1977. The exact interpretation here is ours, but Greenberg has assured us that he is in essential agreement with the point, and we are indebted to him.
28. Yehuda Aschkenasy, consultation, Hilversum, Holland, 16 Jan. 1976. Nora Levin reminds us that incompleteness "is of a piece with the Jewish religious tradition"—a tradition that across the centuries has not only contended with God but even dared to entertain the idea that God can sin. Generally, Judaism has refrained from pursuing "the unknowable and the limitless," and it "does not insist on answers when there are none" ("Life over Death," pp. 22–23). There is a vital lesson here that Christian theologians might well take seriously. To seek an accounting from God must be consistent with the divine intent, for at stake is our dignity as free human beings whom he has created in his own image.
29. Reinhold Niebuhr, Frontispiece to Ursula M. Niebuhr, ed., *Justice and Mercy*.

CHAPTER 5

1. Friedrich Gruenagel, *Die Judenfrage*.
2. Ibid., pp. 7, 8, 16, 17, 19, 20. In fact, Gruenagel idealizes Cardinal Bea's contribution and correspondingly distorts the cardinal's actual point of view. See Augustin Cardinal Bea, *The Church and the Jewish People* and the critical commentary on that volume in Eckardt, *Your People, My People*, pp. 52–56. The latter study analyzes the historical fate of the Vatican schema *De Judaeis* (pp. 42–56; cf. pp. 189–93).
3. Gruenagel, *Judenfrage*, p. 23.
4. Ibid., pp. 23, 40–46. Space forbids attention to Gruenagel's defense in chap. 3 of Martin Luther's position on the Jews.
5. Rudolf Pfisterer, consultation, Schwäbisch-Hall, 24 Sept. 1975.
6. Franklin H. Littell, "Particularism and Universalism in Religious Perspective." Emil L. Fackenheim writes in similar vein: "If Nazi antisemitism was not *simply* anti-Christian but rather the nemesis of a bi-millennial disease within Christianity *itself*, transmuted . . . , [then] Auschwitz would be *the* central theological event of this century not only for the Jewish but also for the Christian faith" ("Nazi Holocaust," p. 373).
7. Rat der Evangelischen Kirche in Deutschland, *Christen und Juden*, pp. 25, 28–31.
8. Ibid., pp. 33–35.
9. So, for example, pp. 9, 15, 16, 17–24. Thus, we are reminded that the early church saw in Jesus' life, death, and Resurrection the realization of the divine promises for Israel and the nations. In consequence, the Christian community knew itself to be obliged to testify to Jews and gentiles of its faith, love, and

hope. The fact that a great deal of the exposition in *Christen und Juden* is couched in the form of historical-phenomenological analysis cannot hide the truth that Christian claims lie behind and motivate the presentation. Furthermore, the historical materials themselves are not always balanced. A grievous defect is that the authors fail to stress sufficiently that the enmity that developed and was perpetuated between the Jewish and Christian communities has been predominantly a matter of Christian culpability.

10. Ibid., pp. 17–18.
11. The Study Commission "Church and Judaism" that produced the statement included such noted figures as Otto Betz, Helmut Gollwitzer, Franz von Hammerstein, Martin Hengel, Heinz Kremers, Friedrich Wilhelm Marquardt, Reinhold Mayer, Peter-Christian von der Osten-Sacken, Rolf Rendtorff, and Martin Stöhr.

The conversionist problem is further exemplified in another church pronouncement stemming from an international consultation held in Oslo in August 1975. The predicament of the formulators of its report is revealed most vividly in these words of introduction by Paul D. Opsahl and Arne Sovik: "It is to be hoped that this report conveys to all readers the capacity to regard Jewish people with high honor, love, and a sense of eschatological wonder, as well as a clear witness to the name and honor of Jesus Christ, and the centrality of his crucifixion and resurrection" ("Christian Witness and the Jewish People: The Report of a Consultation Held under the Auspices of the Lutheran World Federation, Department of Studies," in World Council of Churches, *The Church and the Jewish People,* newsletter no. 4 [1975], pp. 10–18).
12. Klein, *Theologie und Anti-Judaismus;* Jürgen Moltmann, written communication, 3 Apr. 1975.
13. Jürgen Moltmann, *The Crucified God,* pp. 24, 33, 51, 68, 99, 125, 128, 133, 187, 190, 191, 193, 248, 297.
14. Ibid., p. 132.
15. Presenting a series of theses dealing with the emergence of Christianity from Judaism, David Flusser places this item first on the list: "Jesus was a Jew. He lived in accordance with the Jewish law, and died for it. He was 'born under the law' (Gal. 4:4) and did not wish to become a reformer of Judaism" (Thèses sur l'émergence du christianisme à partir du judaïsme," p.4). Among historical studies, a thoroughly documented work, written in a semipopular way, is Jules Isaac, *Jesus and Israel,* esp. pts. 1–3, on the wholly positive relation of Jesus of Nazareth to Judaism, Torah, and his own Jewish people. See also Ben Zion Bokser, *Judaism and the Christian Predicament,* esp. pp. 181–209; David Flusser, *Jesus,* esp. pp. 44–64; Joseph B. Tyson, *A Study of Early Christianity,* pp. 373–80.
16. Moltmann, *Crucified God,* pp. 114, 115.
17. Cf. ibid, pp. 128–35.
18. Haim Cohn, *The Trial and Death of Jesus,* pp. 53, 95–98, 101, 102, 105. The seven provisions of Jewish law are: 1) no Sanhedrin was permitted to try criminal cases outside the temple precincts, in any private home; 2) no criminal case could be conducted at night; 3) no one could be tried on criminal

charges or on the eve of a festival; 4) no one could be convicted on his own testimony or on the basis of his own confession; 5) a person could be convicted of a capital offense only on the testimony of two lawfully qualified eyewitnesses; 6) the eyewitnesses were required to have warned the accused of the criminality of his intended act and the legal penalties for it; 7) the meaning of "blasphemy" is the pronouncing of the name of God, and it is irrelevant what alleged "blasphemies" are uttered as long as the divine name is not expressed.

19. Moltmann, *Crucified God*, pp. 129, 156 n. 41.
20. Haim Cohn, "Reflections on the Trial and Death of Jesus," p. 17.
21. Moltmann, *Crucified God*, p. 128.
22. Ibid., p. 175.
23. Cf. Jules Isaac, *Genèse de l'antisémitisme; Teaching of Contempt.*
24. Greenberg, "Lessons to Be Learned."
25. Cf. Moltmann, *Crucified God*, pp. 40, 51.
26. Ibid., pp. 27, 39, 69, 140–41. See Klein, *Theologie und Anti-Judaismus*, chaps. 3, 4.
27. "According to this model, this habit-forming structure of theological thinking, Jewish attitudes and Jewish piety are by definition the example of the wrong attitude toward God. The Christian proposition in the teachings of Jesus, Paul, John and all the rest, is always described in its contrast to Jewish 'legalism,' 'casuistry,' 'particularism,' ideas of 'merit,' etc. This whole system of thinking, with its image of the Pharisees and of the political Messianism of the Jews, treats Jewish piety as the black background which makes Christian piety the more shining. In such a state of affairs, it is hard to engender respect for Judaism and the Jews. And the theological system requires the retention of such an understanding of Judaism, whether true or not. Even when the seriousness of Jewish piety is commended, it is done with faint praise: it may be admirable in its sincerity but just for that reason, it is more off the mark" (Krister Stendahl, "Judaism on Christianity: Christianity on Judaism," in Frank Ephraim Talmage, ed., *Disputation and Dialogue*, p. 335).
28. Cf. Moltmann, *Crucified God*, p. 147.
29. Ibid., p. 73.
30. Ibid., pp. 186, 176, 177, 272.
31. Ibid., pp. 134–35, 195.
32. Ibid., pp. 205, 102. See the reference in chap. 6, p. 121 above to Fackenheim's post-Holocaust call for a suspension of the ideal of Jewish martyrdom.
33. Moltmann, *Crucified God*, pp. 1, 52, 75, 153, 163, 263, 134, 100–102; emphases added.
34. Ibid., pp. 135, 134.
35. Ibid., p. 135.
36. Ibid., pp. 135, 194–95.
37. Ibid., p. 134.
38. Ibid., pp. 273ff.
39. Where does Judaism teach that "men must belong to this [Jewish] people through circumcision and obedience to the covenant in order to enter into his [God's] fellowship" (ibid., p. 276)?

40. Ibid., pp. 277–78.
41. Ibid., p. 3.
42. Ibid., pp. 51, 134.
43. As cited in Edward H. Flannery, *The Anguish of the Jews*, p. xi.
44. Schweitzer, *History of the Jews*, p. 222.
45. Moltmann, *Crucified God*, pp. 52, 185.
46. Ibid., p. 303.
47. Greenberg, "Lessons to Be Learned."
48. Moltmann, *Crucified God*, p. 5.
49. Ibid., pp. 148, 151.
50. This description is reproduced, with minor changes, from an account cited in Greenberg, "Lessons to Be Learned."
51. Jürgen Moltmann, *Kirche in der Kraft des Geistes*, pp. 156–57.
52. Ibid., pp. 157, 158, 159.
53. Ibid., p. 168.
54. Ibid., pp. 170–71.
55. Ibid., pp. 159–160, 164–65.
56. Ibid., p. 165.
57. Cf. A. Roy Eckardt, *Elder and Younger Brothers*, pp. 55–58. Our interpretation of Paul in 1967 is sustained by E. P. Sanders, who, in *Paul and Palestinian Judaism*, shows the impossibilty of trying to make Paul a support for Christian "acceptance" of Judaism. See also Sanders, "Given the Christian Claims . . . How Should Christians Think of Themselves and of the Jews in Light of the Continuation of the Jewish People?," in Josephine Knopp, ed., *International Theological Symposium on the Holocaust, October 15–17, 1978*, pp. 51–63.
58. Moltmann's triumphalism in the guise of opposition to triumphalism is subsequently embodied in a declaration that "the ecumenical movement will not . . . be complete without Israel." Alluding to the present organizational arrangement in the World Council of Churches of the working group called "Consultation on the Church and the Jewish People," Moltmann argues that it "would be a great step forward for the ecumenical movement if the churches' conversations with Israel were conducted in the framework of Faith and Order rather than in their 'Dialogue with other living Faiths and Ideologies' " (address on the occasion of the fiftieth anniversary of Faith and Order, Lausanne, Pentecost, 1977, as reported in *The Church and the Jewish People*, newsletter no. 2, p. 15). True dialogue means accepting the partner in his own self-understanding. The last thing that the Jewish community could tolerate would be identification as part of the Christian ecumenical movement, for this would mean being drawn into the Christian church. Moltmann's advocacy is a hidden form of the Christian "mission to the Jews." Doubtless he does not realize this.
59. Jürgen Moltmann, consultation, Tübingen, 29 Dec. 1975.
60. Ruether, *Faith and Fratricide*, p. 246; "Christian-Jewish Dialogue: New Interpretations," p. 4.
61. Cf. Moltmann, *Crucified God*, p. 7.
62. Moltmann is not alone in his predicament respecting the Jewish people and

Judaism. His problem is paralleled in the works of, among others, Hans Küng and Wolfhart Pannenberg. See, e.g., Küng, *Christsein*, pp. 166, 281–84, 328, 387, 542–44; Pannenberg, *Jesus—God and Man*, pp. 246, 247, 252, 253, 263. In a second English edition of the latter, published in 1977 (a translation of the fifth German edition), Pannenberg's strictures against "the Jewish law" and Judaism remain.

CHAPTER 6

1. Baum, *Christian Theology after Auschwitz*, p. 12. Baum defines "ideology" as "the deformation of truth for the sake of social interest."
2. Van Buren, "Status and Prospects for Theology."
3. Fackenheim, "Nazi Holocaust," p. 375.
4. Marie-Thérèse Hoch, *Encounter Today* 11, no. 4 (1976):165. Lamentably, *Encounter Today* ceased publication in 1980.
5. Rosemary Radford Ruether, *Liberation Theology*, pp. 136–37.
6. Will D. Campbell, "The World of the Redneck,"in Paul T. Jersild and Dale A. Johnson, eds., *Moral Issues and Christian Response*, p. 158.
7. Cf. Helmut Gollwitzer, "Christen Begegnen Juden Heute in Deutschland," in Helmut Gollwitzer and Eleonore Sterling, eds., *Das gespaltene Gottesvolk*, pp. 115–16. But how can the New Testament serve to correct antisemitism and anti-Judaism—as Gollwitzer claims for it—when the New Testament documents themselves are part of the problem?
8. Greenberg, "Cloud of Smoke," p. 23.
9. James Parkes, consultation, Iwerne Minster, 1 Mar. 1976; Heinz Kremers, "Das Judentum in Theologie und Religionsbüchern, aus christlicher Sicht," in *Stimmt Unser Bild vom Judentum?*, p. 44.
10. Cf. Arthur A. Cohen, "Messianism and Sabbatai Zevi," pp. 30–49, esp. p. 49; see also Joseph Klausner, "The Jewish and the Christian Messiah," in *The Messianic Idea in Israel*, pp. 519–31.
11. Cohn, *Trial and Death of Jesus*, p. 331, For a full discussion of this book, see Eckardt, *Your People, My People*, chap. 3.
12. Ulrich E. Simon, consultation, London, 20 Feb. 1976. See Eckardt, *Your People, My People*, pp. 8–13.
13. Ignaz Maybaum, *The Face of God after Auschwitz*, p. 11.
14. Eckardt, *Your People, My People*, p. 58.
15. Ibid., p. 226; Eckardt, *Elder and Younger Brothers*, pp. 157–58. For a fuller discussion of the missionary question, see the latter work, pp. 61–66, 73–74, 76–80, 86–88, 93–94, 152–58.
16. Mayer, *Judentum und Christentum*, p. 162; Rolf Rendtorff, "Juden sind keine potentiellen Christen," pp. 358–60; Kremers, "Judentum in Theologie und Religionsbüchern," p. 48.
17. N. Peter Levinsohn, address at the colloquium on "Antisemitism and Other Forms of Group Prejudice," University of Southampton, England, 20 July 1977.

18. Paul M. van Buren, *The Burden of Freedom*, pp. 14, 68, 74.
19. Emil L. Fackenheim, *God's Presence in History*, p. 87.
20. Manès Sperber speaks of the "victim of chosenness" that he had himself become on account of his father. Sperber continues: "Only a few non-Jews have ever understood that Jewish suffering has become our fate not in spite of chosenness, but, above all, because of it. By making a covenant with us, God has cast the divine brick of His grace at us. Ever since then we bear the crushing burden of chosenness like a curse. Yet we are supposed to praise it as though it were a blessing three times every day!" (as cited in a book review by Jakob J. Petuchowski, *Conservative Judaism* 31, nos. 1–2 [Fall-Winter 1976–77]:96).
21. Emil L. Fackenheim, unpublished paper prepared for the symposium on the Holocaust held at the Cathedral Church of Saint John the Divine, New York, 3–6 June 1974.
22. In the Jewish tradition there is a total of 613 commandments. See Fackenheim, *God's Presence in History*, p. 84 and passim; *Quest for Past and Future*, p. 20 and passim; cf. *Encounters between Judaism and Modern Philosophy*, pp. 166–167, and discussion of Jewish martyrdom, pp. 20–21, 73, 75–77; Eckardt, *Your People, My People*, pp. 228–31.
23. Eckardt, *Your People, My People*, p. 244. There is perhaps an analogue here to the Christian persuasion of love as the "fulfilling" of "the law." But the parallel assumes that the imperative "Thou shalt love" is transformed—through the power of love itself?—into a declarative "We do love." It seems clear that the way for human beings to live a fulfilled life is for them to love.
24. The renowned medieval philosopher Moses Maimonides ruled that any Jew "who is killed, though this may be for reasons other than conversion, but simply because he is a Jew, is called *Kaddosh*"—one who has sanctified God's name (as cited in Pesach Schindler, "The Holocaust and Kiddush Hashem in Hassidic Thought," p. 88). From the standpoint of Maimonides, those Jews who were killed in the Holocaust were martyrs. But cf. Richard L. Rubenstein: "One of Hitler's greatest victories was that he deprived the Jews of *all* opportunity to be martyrs. There can be no martyrdom without free choice" ("Some Perspectives on Religious Faith after Auschwitz," in Littell and Locke, eds., *German Church Struggle and the Holocaust*, p. 263).
25. Cf. Rubenstein, *After Auschwitz*, pp. 32–39.
26. Rabbi Pesach Schindler of Jerusalem emphasized to us that the command to live as Jews is immoral where sovereign power for the Jewish people is absent (consultation, Jerusalem, 18 June 1976). See Schindler's important essay, "Holocaust and Kiddush Hashem in Hassidic Thought."
27. Fackenheim, *God's Presence in History*, pp. 75–76.
28. The affirmation of sovereignty for the Jewish people is further considered in this chapter under the heading "Political Power and the People of God." In *Encounters Between Judaism and Modern Philosophy*, Fackenheim deals with the question of whether "pre-Messianic suffering, risked for the sake of a Messianic future" counts "against the assertion that God is merciful." He contends that in contrast to the Christian eschatological expectation, the Jewish expectation is "at least in part falsifiable by future history.... After

Auschwitz, it is a major question whether the Messianic faith is not *already* falsified—whether a Messiah who could come, and yet at Auschwitz did not come, has not become a religious impossibility" (pp. 20–21). Cf. Gregor in Wiesel's *Gates of the Forest:* "Whether or not the Messiah comes doesn't matter; we'll manage without him. It is because it is too late that we are required to hope" (p. 223).

29. Dov Marmur, consultation, London, 16 Feb. 1976.
30. For a consideration of the question of Jewish Christianity, see Eckardt, *Elder and Younger Brothers*, pp. 138–40, 155–57.
31. Ibid., pp. 159–60.
32. Heinz Kremers, written communication, 19 Nov. 1975.
33. Alan T. Davies, "Response to Irving Greenberg," in Fleischner, ed., *Auschwitz*, pp. 61–62.
34. Greenberg, "Cloud of Smoke," p. 24.
35. Ulrich E. Simon, consultation, London, 20 Feb. 1976. The "conquest of death by the One who acts for the many . . . enables us at last to say that the dead are not dead because they have been gassed and their bodies burnt in crematoria" (Simon, *Theology of Auschwitz*, pp. 109–10).
36. Pannenberg, *Jesus—God and Man*, pp. 67, 257, 258.
37. Van Buren, *Burden of Freedom*, pp. 90ff. Although van Buren nowhere uses the term "extra-bodily," he here argues that the Resurrection "was not, apparently, a case of resuscitation," and he speaks in behalf of a "strange variation on embodiment." For a later but similar exposition, see Paul M. van Buren, *Discerning the Way*, pp. 79, 82, 87, 190, 195, 196.
38. Ruether, *Liberation Theology*, pp. 62–63.
39. Pannenberg, *Jesus—God and Man*, pp. 75, 77.
40. On the basis of careful linguistic and translational analysis, Robert L. Lindsey argues the primacy of Luke (in, e.g., "A New Approach to the Synoptic Gospels"). Lindsey is supported by David Flusser (in, e.g., "The Crucified One and the Jews").
41. The theological and moral question of Jesus' Resurrection is more intensively analyzed in A. Roy Eckardt, "Toward a Critical Assessment of Christian Theology in the Aftermath of the Holocaust." In a critique of a preliminary commentary by Eckardt upon the Resurrection, John Carroll White identifies "the experience of a resurrection event" as "not nearly the obstacle to the reconstruction of Christian theology that A. Roy Eckardt makes it out to be." White confuses the issue, which is solely one of the reality or nonreality of the Resurrection event itself, and not one of "experience" (John Carroll White, "Resurrection, Pluralism, and Dialogue: A Response to A. Roy Eckardt," in Josephine Knopp, ed., *Proceedings of the Second Philadelphia Conference on the Holocaust*, pp. 140–48).
42. Thomas A. Idinopulos and Roy Bowen Ward, "Is Christology Inherently Anti-Semitic? A Critical Review of Rosemary Ruether's *Faith and Fratricide*," p. 209. Ruether clearly shows that human behavior cannot be separated from human beliefs. The former follows the latter, rather than the reverse. In arguing that political factors, instead of theological ones, were the real root of tensions between Christians and Jews, Idinopulos and Ward fail to see that the

original struggle was thoroughly religious. Social prejudices and political rivalries were ancillary to the church's main goal of establishing itself as the true—that is, God's—instrument of salvation. In their endeavor to undermine Ruether's understanding that "the anti-Judaic structure of Christian thought . . . has retarded Christian theological maturation," the two critics trivialize her challenge to a genuine Christian *metanoia*.

43. Alistair Kee, ed., *A Reader in Political Theology*, p. ix.

44. Here is the place where Jürgen Moltmann's emphasis upon the Godforsakenness of Jesus on the cross gains its force, in contrast to his erroneous effort to extract ultimate theological significance from Jesus' cry of abandonment.

45. Greenberg, "Cloud of Smoke," p. 54.

46. Rubenstein, "Some Perspectives on Religious Faith after Auschwitz," pp. 265, 266.

47. We are indebted to Irving Greenberg for this item concerning Eldridge Cleaver.

48. Pinchas Hacohen Peli, "The Future of Israel," p. 15.

49. Calvin Keene, "Prophecy and Modern Israel," pp. 1–3.

50. Uriel Tal, "Möglichkeiten einer jüdisch-christlichen Begegnung und Verständigung, Jüdische Sicht," p. 606. Cf. Reinhold Niebuhr: "patriotism transmutes individual unselfishness into national egoism" (*Moral Man and Immoral Society*, p. 91). Niebuhr understood sin as "the hidden pride that insinuates itself even into our most selfless endeavors. And this pride is particularly dangerous at the collective level" (June Bingham, "Carter, Castro, and Reinhold Niebuhr," p. 776).

51. See, among others, these works by Reinhold Niebuhr: *The Children of Light and the Children of Darkness; Christianity and Power Politics; Moral Man and Immoral Society; The Structure of Nations and Empires*.

52. Fadiey Lovsky, written communication, 1 Dec. 1975.

53. Niebuhr, *Children of Light*, p. xiii.

54. On the link between politics and forgiveness, our debt to Reinhold Niebuhr is as great as it is obvious. See esp. his essay "The Peace of God," in *Discerning the Signs of the Times*, pp. 174–94.

55. Greenberg, "Cloud of Smoke," p. 34.

CHAPTER 7

1. Greenberg, from "To the Mound of Corpses in the Snow," in *Anthology of Modern Hebrew Poetry*, 2:260–61.

2. Peck, "From Cain to the Death Camps," p. 162; Stefan Zeroniski, cited in David Rosenthal, "Thirty Years after the Liberation of Auschwitz and Bergen-Belsen," p. 9.

3. Manès Sperber, "Hurban or the Inconceivable Certainty," in . . . *than a Tear in the Sea*, pp. xi, xiii.

4. Paul Celan, as cited in Langer, *Holocaust and the Literary Imagination*, p. 9.

5. "Todesfuge" was composed on a train en route to the East and a forced labor camp. Celan's parents were murdered; he took his own life in Paris in 1970. See Paul Celan, *Selected Poems;* Paul Celan, *Nineteen Poems;* see also George Steiner, *Language and Silence;* Samuel Hux, "The Holocaust and the Survival of Tragedy."

6. David Wolf Silverman, "The Holocaust: A Living Force," p. 25.

7. From Uri Zvi Greenberg, "A Jew Stands at the Gates of Tears," in Joseph Leftwich, ed. and trans., *The Golden Peacock,* p. 199.

8. Yizhak Orpaz, "A Literature of Siege and Survival," p. 14. Most man-centered societies or cultures presuppose a transcendent frame of reference by way of justifying, implicitly, their humanism. The only exception to this, in principle, is a humanistic world view that seeks for a self-contained or perhaps self-evident justification of itself through a positing of strictly human needs and purposes as its ultimate norms. An illustration of a transcendent frame of reference for humanistic, political goals is found in David Polish's position respecting the contemporary state of Israel. After observing, with entire truth, that "a state is not a state if power is not its primary concern," Polish continues that the Jewish people must concern themselves with that, but also with more than that. The "more" is "the messianic component out of which the idea of the state emerged." Polish concludes that the very existence and viability of the Galut, the Dispersion, "prevent Israel from being like all the nations" (*Israel—Nation and People,* pp. 166, 174).

9. György Kemény, as cited in *Der Widerstandskämpfer* [Vienna] 23 (Spring 1975):6.

10. Orpaz, "Literature of Siege and Survival," p. 15; Aharon Megged, "Letter from Israel," p. 13.

11. Elie Wiesel, "Ominous Signs and Unspeakable Thoughts." The artist's sketch placed next to Wiesel's lament portrays a man wearing an Arab head-dress blowing out the candles of a menorah, whose seven flames are human skulls.

12. Rudolf Pfisterer, written communication, 14 Oct. 1975.

13. "Conversation with Elie Wiesel," p. 5.

14. From an address by Moshe Dayan at Lehigh University, 13 Feb. 1977.

15. Louis Halle sustains political realism in international politics, a position for which Reinhold Niebuhr and Hans J. Morgenthau also have been eloquent spokesmen. Halle shows how the high degree of instability that characterized relations between the United States and the Soviet Union at the end of the 1950s was subsequently overcome "not by disarmament, but by its opposite." Peace has been made possible by the increase and technical improvement of nuclear weaponry, together with effective espionage satellites, all of which foster mutual deterrence. Accordingly, those who automatically equate disarmament with morality are urged to think twice ("Applying Morality to Foreign Policy," in Kenneth W. Thompson, ed., *Foreign Policy and Morality,* pp. 30–32).

16. See, for example, Robert M. Lawrence and Joel Larus, eds., *Nuclear Proliferation,* esp. Avigdor Haselkorn, "Israel: From an Option to a Bomb in the Basement?," pp. 149–82.

17. See Mikhail Agursky, "Russian Neo-Nazism: A Growing Threat."
18. Cf. Moltmann, *Crucified God*, pp. 251–52.
19. Bertrand Joseph, written communication, Strasbourg, 27 Oct. 1975.
20. Rubenstein, *Cunning of History*, p. 93.
21. Finn Henning Lauridsen, consultation, Copenhagen, 31 July 1975.
22. We do not, alas, know his name. The statement was reported to us in a conversation with Avraham Soetendorp, The Hague, 22 Jan. 1976.
23. Robert McAfee Brown, *Theology in a New Key: Responding to Liberation Themes*, p. 187.
24. Jesus' coming Resurrection will be distinctive for Christians because his is the history through which they were brought into the covenant with Israel—just as the future resurrection of Abraham and Moses will have peculiar significance for the eschatological community of Jews, as, secondarily, for Christians. For the Christian of the end-time, what joy will surpass that of meeting the transfigured Jesus, face-to-face?

SELECTED
BIBLIOGRAPHY

Adam, Uwe Dietrich. *Judenpolitik im Dritten Reich.* Düsseldorf: Droste Verlag, 1972.

Adler, Hermann G. *Der Verwaltete Mensch: Studien zur Deportation der Juden aus Deutschland.* Tübingen: J. C. B. Mohr, 1975.

Agursky, Mikhail. "Russian Neo-Nazism: A Growing Threat." *Midstream* 22, no. 2 (Feb. 1976):35–42.

Alexander, Edward. "Abba Kovner: Poet of Holocaust and Rebirth." *Midstream* 23, no. 8 (Oct. 1977):50–59.

Annals of the American Academy of Political and Social Science 450 (July 1980). Special number on "Reflections on the Holocaust: Historical, Philosophical, and Educational Dimensions."

Anthology of Modern Hebrew Poetry. Vol. 2. Selected by S. Y. Penueli and A. Ukhmani. Jerusalem: Institute for the Translation of Hebrew Literature and Israel Universities Press, 1966.

Aron, Robert. *Lettre ouverte à l'église de France.* Paris: Albin Michel, 1975.

"Auschwitz." *Encyclopaedia Judaica,* vol. 3, pp. 854–55.

Bar-On, Abraham Zvie. "The Holocaust: Who Is to Blame?" Unpublished preparatory paper for International Scholars Conference on the Holocaust, New York, 3–6 Mar. 1975.

Bastiaans, Jan. "The KZ-Syndrome: A Thirty Year Study of the Effects on Victims of Nazi Concentration Camps." *Revista Medico-Chirurgicală* [Belgrade] 68, no. 3 (July–Sept. 1974):573–78.

————. *Psychosomatische Gevolgen van Onderdrukking en Verzet.* Amsterdam: N. V. Noord-Hollandsche Uitgevers Maatschappij, 1957.

————. "Vom Menschen im KZ und vom KZ in Menschen: Ein Beitrag zur Behandlung des KZ-Syndroms und dessen Spätfolgen." In *Essays über Nazi-*

171

verbrechen: Simon Wiesenthal Gewidmet, pp. 177–201. Amsterdam: Wiesenthal Fonds, 1973.

Bauer, Yehuda. *The Holocaust in Historical Perspective.* Seattle: University of Washington Press, 1978.

———. *They Chose Life: Jewish Resistance in the Holocaust.* New York: Institute of Human Relations, American Jewish Committee; Jerusalem: Institute of Contemporary Jewry, Hebrew University, 1973.

Baum, Gregory G. *Christian Theology after Auschwitz.* London: Council of Christians and Jews, 1976.

———. *Man Becoming: God in Secular Experience.* New York: Herder and Herder, 1971.

———. "Theology after Auschwitz: A Conference Report." *The Ecumenist* 12, no. 5 (July–Aug. 1974):65–80.

Baumgärtel, Friedrich. *Wider die Kirchenkampf-Legenden.* Neuendettelsau: Freimund-Verlag, 1976.

Bea, Augustin Cardinal. *The Church and the Jewish People.* London: Geoffrey Chapman, 1966.

Berenbaum, Michael J. "Elie Wiesel and Contemporary Jewish Theology." *Conservative Judaism* 30, no. 3 (Spring 1976):19–39.

———. *The Vision of the Void: Theological Reflections on the Works of Elie Wiesel.* Middletown, Conn.: Wesleyan University Press, 1979.

Berkovits, Eliezer. *Faith after the Holocaust.* New York: Ktav Publishing House, 1973.

———. *With God in Hell: Judaism in the Ghettos and Death Camps.* New York and London: Sanhedrin Press, 1979.

Bethge, Eberhard. *Bonhoeffer: Exile and Martyr.* Edited by John W. De Gruchy. New York: Seabury Press, 1975.

———. *Dietrich Bonhoeffer.* New York: Harper and Row, 1970.

Bingham, June. "Carter, Castro, and Reinhold Niebuhr." *Christian Century* 94, no. 28 (14 Sept. 1977):775–76.

Bishop, Claire Huchet. *How Catholics Look at Jews: Inquiries into Italian, Spanish, and French Teaching Materials.* New York: Paulist Press, 1974.

Blumenkranz, Bernhard. "L'Holocauste dans l'enseignement public en France." *Archives Juives* 11, no. 2 (1975):127–34.

Bokser, Ben Zion. *Judaism and the Christian Predicament.* New York: Alfred A. Knopf, 1967.

Boon, Rudolf. *Outmoeting Met Israël: Het Volk van de Torah.* Kampen: Uitge-versmaats-chappij J. H. Kok, 1974.

Bor, Josef. *Theresienstädter Requiem.* Berlin: Buchverlag der Morgen, 1975.

Borowitz, Eugene B. *Contemporary Christologies: A Jewish Response.* New York and Ramsey: Paulist Press, 1980.

Bracher, Karl Dietrich. *The German Dilemma: The Throes of Political Emancipation.* Translated by Richard Barry. London: Weidenfeld and Nicolson, 1974.

Brandon, S. G. F. *The Trial of Jesus of Nazareth.* London: B. T. Botsford, 1968.

Brenner, Reeve Robert. *The Faith and Doubt of Holocaust Survivors.* New York: Free Press, 1980.

Brown, Robert McAfee. "From the Death Camps to Israel." *Christianity and Crisis* 40, no. 2 (18 Feb. 1980):18, 27–31.

———. "The Holocaust: The Crisis of Indifference." *Conservative Judaism* 31, no. 1–2 (Fall–Winter 1976–77):16–20.

———. *Theology in a New Key: Responding to Liberation Themes.* Philadelphia: Westminster Press, 1978.

Busi, Frederick. "The Impact of Fascism: The Jew in Twentieth Century French Thinking." *Patterns of Prejudice* 8, no. 1 (Jan.–Feb. 1974):9–16.

Cargas, Harry James. *Harry James Cargas in Conversation with Elie Wiesel.* New York: Paulist Press, 1976.

Celan, Paul. *Nineteen Poems.* Translated by Michael Hamburger. Oxford: Carcanet Press, 1972.

———. *Selected Poems.* Translated by Michael Hamburger and Christopher Middleton. Harmondsworth: Penguin Books, 1972.

Cohen, Arthur A. "Messianism and Sabbatai Zevi." *Midstream* 20, no. 8 (Oct. 1974):30–49.

———. *The Tremendum: A Theological Interpretation of the Holocaust.* New York: Crossroad, 1981.

Cohn, Haim. "Reflections on the Trial and Death of Jesus." *Israel Law Review* 2, no. 3 (July 1967):279–332.

———. *The Trial and Death of Jesus.* New York: Harper and Row, 1971.

Concilium [Mainz] 10, no. 10 (Oct. 1974). Special number on "Christians and Jews."

"Conversation with Elie Wiesel." *Women's American ORT Reporter* [New York], Mar.–Apr. 1970.

173

Cox, Harvey. *Feast of Fools: A Theological Essay on Festivity and Fantasy.* Cambridge, Mass.: Harvard University Press, 1969.

Croner, Helga, ed. *Stepping Stones to Further Jewish-Christian Relations: An Unabridged Collection of Christian Documents.* New Malden, Surrey: Stimulus Books, 1977.

——— and Klenicki, Leon, eds. *Issues in the Jewish-Christian Dialogue: Jewish Perspectives on Covenant, Mission, and Witness.* New York and Ramsey: Paulist Press, 1979.

Davies, Alan T. *Anti-Semitism and the Christian Mind: The Crisis of Conscience after Auschwitz.* New York: Herder and Herder, 1969.

———. "Anti-Zionism, Anti-Semitism, and the Christian Mind." *Christian Century* 87, no. 33 (19 Aug. 1970):987–89.

———, ed. *Antisemitism and the Foundations of Christianity,* New York, Ramsey, and Toronto: Paulist Press, 1979.

Dawidowicz, Lucy S. *The War against the Jews, 1933–1945.* New York: Holt, Rinehart and Winston, 1975.

De Graaf, Theo. "Pathological Patterns of Identification in Families of Survivors of the Holocaust." *Israel Annals of Psychiatry and Related Disciplines* 13, no. 4 (Dec. 1975):335–63.

Delbo, Charlotte. *None of Us Will Return.* Translated by John Githens. Boston: Beacon Press, 1978.

Des Pres, Terence. *The Survivor: An Anatomy of Life in the Death Camps.* New York: Oxford University Press, 1976.

Dicks, Henry V. *Licensed Mass Murder: A Socio-Psychological Study of Some SS Killers.* Columbus Centre Series, Studies in the Dynamics of Persecution and Extermination. London: Sussex University Press, 1972.

Diem, Hermann. *Ja Oder Nein: 50 Jahre Theologe in Kirche und Staat.* Stuttgart: Kreuz Verlag, 1974.

Donat, Alexander. "A Letter to My Grandson." *Midstream* 16, no. 6 (June–July 1970):41–45.

———. "The Voice of the Ashes." Unpublished preparatory paper for International Scholars Conference on the Holocaust, New York, 3–6 Mar. 1975.

Dubois, Marcel-Jacques. "Theological Implications of the State of Israel: The Catholic View." *Encyclopaedia Judaica Year Book 1974,* pp. 167–73. Jerusalem: Keter Publishing House, 1974.

Dupuy, Bernard. "Un théologien juif de l'Holocauste, Emil Fackenheim." *Foi et Vie* 73, no. 4 (Sept. 1974):11–21.

174

"The Echo of *Mein Kampf* in Arab Antisemitism." *Patterns of Prejudice* [London] 9, no. 2 (Mar.–Apr. 1975):15–16, 25.

Eckardt, A. Roy. "Christian Responses to the Endlösung." *Religion in Life* 47, no. 1 (Spring 1978):33–45.

———. *Christianity and the Children of Israel*. New York: King's Crown Press, 1948.

———. "Christians and Jews: Along a Theological Frontier." *Encounter* 40, no. 2 (Spring 1979):89–127.

———. "Contemporary Christian Theology and a Protestant Witness for the Shoah." *Shoah* 2, no. 1 (Spring–Summer 1980):10–13.

———. "Covenant-Resurrection-Holocaust." In Knopp, ed., *Proceedings of the Second Philadelphia Conference on the Holocaust*, pp. 39–47.

———. "Death in the Judaic and Christian Traditions." *Death in American Experience*, pp. 123–48. Edited by Arien Mack. New York: Schocken Books, 1973.

———. "The Devil and Yom Kippur." *Midstream* 20, no. 7 (Aug.–Sept. 1974):67–75.

———. *Elder and Younger Brothers: The Encounter of Jews and Christians*. New York: Charles Scribner's Sons, 1967; Schocken Books, 1973.

———. "Is the Holocaust Unique?" *Worldview* 17, no. 9 (Sept. 1974):31–36.

———. "Jürgen Moltmann, the Jewish People, and the Holocaust." *Journal of the American Academy of Religion* 44, no. 4 (Dec. 1976):675–91.

———. "The Recantation of the Covenant?" in Rosenfeld and Greenberg, eds., *Confronting the Holocaust*, pp. 159–68.

———. "Recent Literature on Christian-Jewish Relations." *Jewish Book Annual* 38 (1980–81):47–61.

———. "The Shadow of the Death Camps." *Theology Today* 34, no. 3 (Oct. 1977):285–90.

———. "Theological Implications of the State of Israel: The Protestant View." *Encyclopaedia Judaica Year Book 1974*, pp. 158–66. Jerusalem: Keter Publishing House, 1974.

———. "Toward a Critical Assessment of Christian Theology in the Aftermath of the Holocaust." Unpublished preparatory paper for "Thinking About the Holocaust: An International Scholars' Conference Devoted to Historiographical and Theological Questions," Bloomington, Ind., 3–5 Nov. 1980.

———. "Toward a Secular Theology of Israel." *Religion in Life* 48, no. 4 (Winter 1979):462–73.

175

———. *Your People, My People: The Meeting of Jews and Christians.* New York: Quadrangle, New York Times Book Co., 1974.

———, ed. *The Theologian at Work.* New York: Harper and Row, 1968.

Eckardt, Alice L. "The Holocaust: Christian and Jewish Responses." *Journal of the American Academy of Religion* 42, no. 3 (Sept. 1974):453–69.

———. "In Consideration of Christian Yom Hashoah Liturgies." *Shoah* 1, no. 4 (1979):1–4.

———, and Eckardt, A. Roy. "The Achievements and Trials of Interfaith." *Judaism* 27, no. 3 (Summer 1978):318–23.

———. "Christentum and Judentum: Die theologische und moralische Problematik der Vernichtung des europäischen Judentums." *Evangelische Theologie* 36, no. 5 (Sept.–Oct. 1976):406–26. English version "The Theological and Moral Implications of the Holocaust." *Christian Attitudes on Jews and Judaism* 52 (Feb. 1977):1–7, 53 (Apr. 1977):7–12.

———. *Encounter with Israel: A Challenge to Conscience.* New York: Association Press, 1970.

———. "German Thinkers View the Holocaust." *Christian Century* 93, no. 9 (17 Mar. 1976):249–52.

———. "The Holocaust and the Enigma of Uniqueness: A Philosophical Effort at Practical Clarification." *Annals of the American Academy of Political and Social Science* 450 (July 1980):165–78.

———. "Studying the Holocaust's Impact Today: Some Dilemmas of Language and Method." *Judaism* 27, no. 2 (Spring 1978):222–32.

Eckert, W. P. "The Final Solution and the Response of the Catholic Church." Unpublished paper for International Conference on the Church Struggle and the Holocaust, Hamburg, 8–11 June 1975.

———, ed. *Jüdisches Volk-gelobtes Land: Die Biblischen Landesverheissungen als Problem des jüdischen Selbstverständnisses und der christlichen Theologie.* Munich: Chr. Kaiser Verlag, 1970.

———; Levinson, N. P.; Stöhr, M., eds. *Antijudaismus im Neuen Testament? Exegetische und systematische Beiträge.* Munich: Chr. Kaiser Verlag, 1967.

Eitinger, Leo. *Concentration Camp Survivors in Norway and Israel.* Translated by Peggy Houge. The Hague: Martinus Nijhoff, 1972.

———, and Strøm, Axel. *Mortality and Morbidity after Excessive Stress.* New York: Humanities Press, 1973.

Elyashiv, Vera. "Germans, Jews, Israelis: The Indissoluble Complicity." *Jewish Quarterly* 21, nos. 1–2 (1973):31–41.

Engelmann, Bernt. *Deutschland ohne Juden: Eine Bilanz.* Munich: Franz Schneekluth Verlag, 1970.

Epstein, Helen. "The Heirs of the Holocaust." *New York Times Magazine,* 19 June 1977, pp. 12–15, 74–77.

Evangelische Theologie 34, no. 3 (May–June 1974). Special number on "Toward Christian-Jewish Dialogue."

Ezrahi, Sidra. "Holocaust Literature in European Languages." *Encyclopaedia Judaica Year Book 1973,* pp. 106–19. Jerusalem: Keter Publishing House, 1973.

Fackenheim, Emil L. "Concerning Authentic and Unauthentic Responses to the Holocaust." Unpublished preparatory paper for International Scholars Conference on the Holocaust, New York, 3–6 Mar. 1975.

———. *Encounters between Judaism and Modern Philosophy: A Preface to Future Jewish Thought.* New York: Basic Books, 1973.

———. *From Bergen-Belsen to Jerusalem: Contemporary Implications of the Holocaust.* Jerusalem: Institute of Contemporary Jewry, Hebrew University, 1975.

———. *God's Presence in History: Jewish Affirmations and Philosophical Reflections.* New York: New York University Press, 1970.

———. "The Holocaust and the State of Israel: Their Relation." *Encyclopaedia Judaica Year Book 1974,* pp. 152–57. Jerusalem: Keter Publishing House, 1974.

———. "The Human Condition after Auschwitz: A Jewish Testimony a Generation After." *Congress Bi-Weekly* 39, no. 7 (28 Apr. 1972):6–10; no. 8 (19 May 1972):5–8.

———. *The Jewish Return into History: Reflections in the Age of Auschwitz and a New Jerusalem.* New York: Schocken Books, 1978.

———. "The Nazi Holocaust as a Persisting Trauma for the Non-Jewish Mind." *Journal of the History of Ideas* 36, no. 2 (Apr.–May 1975):369–76.

———. "The People Israel Lives." *Christian Century* 87, no. 18 (6 May 1970):563–68.

———. *Quest for Past and Future.* Boston: Beacon Press, 1970.

Farber, Klaus, and Kremers, Heinz, eds. *Juden: Ein Beitrag zur Behandlung der Vorurteilsproblematik im Unterricht.* Dortmund: W. Crüwell Verlag, 1974.

Fink, Heinrich, ed. *Stärker als die Angst: Den sechs Millionen, die keinen Retter fanden.* Berlin: Union Verlag, 1968.

Fisher, Eugene. *Faith without Prejudice.* New York, Ramsey, and Toronto: Paulist Press, 1977.

Flannery, Edward. *The Anguish of the Jews: Twenty-three Centuries of Anti-Semitism.* New York: Macmillan Co., 1965.

Fleischner, Eva, ed. *Auschwitz: Beginning of a New Era? Reflections on the Holocaust.* New York: Ktav Publishing House, 1977.

———. *Judaism in German Christian Theology since 1945: Christianity and Israel Considered in Terms of Mission.* Metuchen, N. J.: Scarecrow Press, 1975.

Flinker, Moshe. *Young Moshe's Diary: The Spiritual Torment of a Jewish Boy in Nazi Europe.* Jerusalem: Yad Vashem; New York: Board of Jewish Education, 1971.

Flusser, David. "The Crucified One and the Jews." *Immanuel* [Jerusalem], no. 7 (Spring 1977), pp. 25–37.

———. *Jesus.* Translated by Ronald Walls. New York: Herder and Herder, 1969.

———. "Theses sur l'émergence du christianisme à partir du judaïsme." *Vav* 8, no. 11 (Mar. 1975):4–16.

Forster, Arnold, and Epstein, Benjamin R. *The New Anti-Semitism.* New York: McGraw-Hill, 1974.

Frank, Anne. *The Diary of a Young Girl.* New York: Doubleday, 1952.

———. *The Works of Anne Frank.* Introduction by Ann Birstein and Alfred Kazin. New York: Doubleday, 1959.

Franke, Manfred. *Morderläufe 9./10. XI 1938.* Darmstadt: Luchterhand Verlag, 1973.

Frankl, Viktor. *From Death Camp to Existentialism: A Psychiatrist's Path to a New Therapy.* Boston: Beacon Press, 1959.

Friedlander, Albert H. "Kafka's Ape: A Meditation on Religious Dialogue." *European Judaism* 10, no. 1 (Winter 1975–76):30–36.

———, ed. *Out of the Whirlwind: A Reader of Holocaust Literature.* New York: Schocken Books, 1976.

Friedlander, Henry. "Historians on the Holocaust: An Analysis." Unpublished preparatory paper for International Scholars Conference on the Holocaust, New York, 3–6 Mar. 1975.

Friedländer, Saul. *L'Antisémitisme Nazi: Histoire d'une psychose collective.* Paris: Seuil, 1971.

———. "Some Aspects of the Historical Significance of the Holocaust." *Jerusalem Quarterly,* 1 (Fall 1976):36–59.

Friedman, Saul S. "Arab Complicity in the Holocaust." *Jewish Frontier* 42, no. 4 (Apr. 1975):9–17.

————. "Universal Anti-Semitism." *Jewish Frontier* 43, no. 7 (Aug.–Sept. 1976):14–18.

Gershon, Karen, ed. and trans. *Postscript: A Collective Account of the Lives of Jews in West Germany since the Second World War.* London: Victor Gollancz, 1969.

————, ed. *We Came as Children: A Collective Autobiography.* New York: Harcourt, Brace and World, 1966.

Gerssen, Samuel. *Het Grote Schisma: Israël in de theologie van dr. K. H. Miskotte.* Kampen: Uitgeversmaatschappij, J. H. Kok, 1975.

Giniewski, Paul. *L'antisionisme.* Brussels: Éditions de la Librairie Encyclopedique, 1973.

Glatstein, Jacob; Knox, Israel; and Margoshes, Samuel, eds. *Anthology of Holocaust Literature.* Philadelphia: Jewish Publication Society of America, 1973.

Goldschmidt, Dietrich, and Kraus, Hans-Joachim, eds. *Der Ungekündigte Bund: Neue Begegnung von Juden und christlicher Gemeinde. Im Auftrag der Arbeitsgemeinschaft Juden und Christen beim Deutschen Evangelischen Kirchentag.* Stuttgart: Kreuz-Verlag, 1962.

Gollwitzer, Helmut, and Sterling, Eleonore, eds. *Das Gespaltene Gottesvolk: Im Auftrag der Arbeitsgemeinschaft Juden und Christen beim Deutschen Evangelischen Kirchentag.* Stuttgart: Kreuz-Verlag, 1966.

Greenberg, Irving. "Cloud of Smoke, Pillar of Fire: Judaism, Christianity, and Modernity after the Holocaust." In Fleischner, ed., *Auschwitz,* pp. 7–55.

————. "Lessons To Be Learned from the Holocaust." Unpublished paper at International Conference on the Church Struggle and the Holocaust, Hamburg, 8–11 June 1975.

————. "New Revelations and New Patterns in the Relationship of Judaism and Christianity." *Journal of Ecumenical Studies* 16, no. 2 (Spring 1979):249–67.

Greenberg, Uri Zvi. "A Jew Stands at the Gates of Tears." In Leftwich, ed., *The Golden Peacock,* pp. 193–99.

————. "To God in Europe." Translated by Robert Friend; "To the Mound of Corpses in the Snow," translated by A. C. Jacobs. In *Anthology of Modern Hebrew Poetry,* vol. 2, pp. 264–78, 259–61.

Grossmann, Wassilij. *Die Hölle von Treblinka.* Moskau: Verlag für Fremdsprachige Literatur, 1946.

Gruenagel, Friedrich. *Die Judenfrage, Die geschichtliche Verantwortung der Kirchen und Israels.* Stuttgart: Calwer Verlag, 1970.

Gutman, Israel. "Remarks on the Literature of the Holocaust." *In the Dispersion* [Jerusalem], no. 7 (1967).

—— and Rothkirchen, Livia, eds. *The Catastrophe of European Jewry: Antecedents—History—Reflections.* Jerusalem: Yad Vashem, 1976.

Gutteridge, Richard. *Open Thy Mouth for the Dumb!: The German Evangelical Church and the Jews 1879–1950.* Oxford: Basil Blackwell, 1976.

Haffner, Sebastian. *The Meaning of Hitler.* Translated by Ewald Osers. New York: Macmillan Publishing Co., 1979.

Haft, Cynthia. *The Theme of Nazi Concentration Camps in French Literature.* The Hague and Paris: Mouton, 1973.

Hallie, Philip P. *Lest Innocent Blood Be Shed: The Story of the Village of Le Chambon and How Goodness Happened There.* New York: Harper and Row, 1979.

Harkabi, Yehoshafat. *Arab Attitudes to Israel.* Jerusalem: Israel Universities Press, 1971.

Hay, Malcolm. *Thy Brother's Blood: The Roots of Christian Anti-Semitism.* New York: Hart Publishing Co., 1975.

Heer, Friedrich. "The Catholic Church and the Jews Today." *Midstream* 17, no. 5 (May 1971):20–31.

——. *God's First Love: Christians and Jews over Two Thousand Years.* Translated by Geoffrey Skelton. New York: Weybright and Talley, 1970.

Heering, H. J. *Franz Rosenzweig: Joods Denker in de 20e EEUW.* The Hague: Martinus Nijhoff, 1974.

Heimler, Eugene. *A Link in the Chain.* London: Bodley Head, 1962.

——. *Night of the Mist.* New York: Vanguard Press, 1960.

Helmreich, Ernst Christian. *The German Churches under Hitler: Background, Struggle, and Epilogue.* Detroit, Mich.: Wayne State University Press, 1978.

Herberg, Will. *Faith Enacted as History: Essays in Biblical Theology.* Edited by Bernhard W. Anderson. Philadelphia: Westminster Press, 1976.

Herman, Simon N. *Israelis and Jews: The Continuity of an Identity.* New York: Random House, 1970.

Hertzberg, Arthur. *Anti-Semitism and Jewish Uniqueness: Ancient and Contemporary.* Syracuse: Syracuse University, 1975.

——. "Response to Uriel Tal." *Union Seminary Quarterly Review* 26, no. 4 (Summer 1971).

Herzberg, Abel J. *Amor Fati: Zeven opstellen over Bergen-Belsen.* Amsterdam: Moussault's Uitgeverij, 1950.

——. *Brieven aan mijn kleinzoon: De geschiedenis van een joodse emigrantenfamilie.* Amsterdam: Em. Querido's Uitgeverij B.V., 1975.

Heyman, Éva. *The Diary of Éva Heyman.* Introduction and notes by Moshe M. Kohn. Jerusalem: Yad Vashem, 1974.

Hilberg, Raul. *The Destruction of the European Jews.* Rev. ed. Chicago: Quadrangle Books, 1967.

———. ed. *Documents of Destruction: Germany and Jewry 1933–1945.* Chicago: Quadrangle Books, 1971.

Hochhuth, Rolf. *The Representative.* Translated by Robert David MacDonald. London: Methuen and Co., 1963.

Holland, Joseph. "Hunger: Global Holocaust or Global Exodus?" *The Ecumenist* 13, no. 2 (Jan.–Feb. 1975):17–21.

Holocaust. Jerusalem: Keter Publishing House, 1974.

The Holocaust. Jerusalem: Yad Vashem, 1975.

"The Holocaust: Our Generation Looks Back." *Response* 25 (Spring 1975).

Holocaust and Rebirth: A Symposium. Jerusalem: Yad Vashem, 1974.

Hoppe, Klaus D. "The Aftermath of Nazi Persecution Reflected in Recent Psychiatric Literature." In *Psychic Traumatization: Aftereffects in Individuals and Communities,* edited by Henry Krystal and William G. Niederland. Boston: Little, Brown, 1971.

Housepian, Marjorie. "The Unremembered Genocide." *Commentary* 42, no. 3 (Sept. 1966):55–61.

Houtart, François, and Lemercinier, Geneviève. *Les Juifs dans la catéchèse: Étude sur la transmission des codes religieux.* Louvain: Université Catholique de Louvain, 1972.

Hux, Samuel. "The Holocaust and the Survival of Tragedy." *Worldview* 20, no. 10 (Oct. 1970):4–10.

Idinopulos, Thomas A., and Ward, Roy Bowen. "Is Christology Inherently Anti-Semitic? A Critical Review of Rosemary Ruether's *Faith and Fratricide.*" *Journal of the American Academy of Religion* 45, no. 2 (June 1977):193–214.

Interpreting the Holocaust for Future Generations: Proceedings of a Symposium. New York: Memorial Foundation for Jewish Culture, 1974.

Isaac, Jules. *Genèse de l'antisémitisme.* Paris: Calmann-Lévy, 1956.

———. *Jesus and Israel.* Edited by Claire Huchet Bishop. Translated by Sally Gran. New York: Holt, Rinehart and Winston, 1971.

———. *The Teaching of Contempt: Christian Roots of Anti-Semitism.* Translated by Helen Weaver. New York: Holt, Rinehart and Winston, 1964.

Israel, Gérard. *Heureux comme Dieu en France . . . 1940–1944.* Paris: Éditions Robert Leffont, 1975.

Jaffe, Ruth. "The Sense of Guilt within Holocaust Survivors." *Jewish Social Studies* 32, no. 4 (Oct. 1970):307–14.

Jansen, John Frederick. *The Resurrection of Jesus Christ in New Testament Theology.* Philadelphia: Westminster Press, 1980.

Jersild, Paul T., and Johnson, Dale A., eds. *Moral Issues and Christian Response.* 2d ed. New York: Holt, Rinehart and Winston, 1976.

"Jesu Verhältnis zum Judentum. Das Judentumsbild im christlichen Religionsunterricht." *Freiburger Rundbrief* 26, nos. 97/100 (1974):21–30.

Jewish Resistance during the Holocaust: Proceedings of the Conference on Manifestations of Jewish Resistance. [Jerusalem, 7–11 Apr. 1968]. Supervised by Meir Grubsztein. Jerusalem: Yad Vashem, 1971.

Les Juifs dans la catéchèse: Étude des manuels de catéchèse. Louvain: Centre de Recherches socie-religieuses, 1969.

Kallenbach, Hans, and Schemel, Willi, eds. *Judentum im christlichen Religionsunterricht.* Frankfurt: Verlag Evangelischer Presseverband für Hessen und Nassau, 1972.

Kalow, Gert. *Hitler—des deutsche Trauma.* Munich: Piper, 1974.

Kee, Alistair, ed. *A Reader in Political Theology.* Philadelphia: Westminster Press, 1974.

Keene, Calvin. "Prophecy and Modern Israel." *The Link* 10, no. 3 (Summer 1977):1–3.

Kellen, Konrad. "*Seven Beauties:* Auschwitz—the Ultimate Joke?" *Midstream* 22, no. 8 (Oct. 1976):59–66.

Kestenberg, Judith S. "Psychoanalytic Contributions to the Problem of Children of Survivors of the Nazi Persecution." *Israel Annals of Psychiatry and Related Disciplines* 10, no. 4 (Dec. 1972):311–25.

Klausner, Joseph. *The Messianic Idea in Israel.* Translated by W. F. Stinespring. New York: Macmillan, 1955.

Klein, Charlotte. *Theologie und Anti-Judaismus: Eine Studie zur deutschen theologischen Literatur der Gegenwart.* Munich: Chr. Kaiser Verlag, 1975.

Klein, Hilel. "Families of Holocaust Survivors in the Kibbutz: Psychological Studies." In *Psychic Traumatization: Aftereffects in Individuals and Communities,* edited by Henry Krystal and William G. Niederland, pp. 67–92. Boston: Little, Brown, 1971.

———. "Holocaust Survivors in Kibbutzim: Readaptation and Reintegration." *Israel Annals of Psychiatry and Related Disciplines* 10, no. 1 (Mar. 1972):78–91.

——— and Last, Uriel. "Cognitive and Emotional Aspects of the Attitudes of

American and Israeli Jewish Youth towards the Victims of the Holocaust." *Israel Annals of Psychiatry and Related Disciplines* 12, no. 2 (June 1974):111–31.

—— and Reinharz, Shulamit. "Adaptation in the Kibbutz of Holocaust Survivors and Their Families." In *Mental Health and Rapid Social Change*, edited by Louis Miller, pp. 302–19. Jerusalem: Jerusalem Academic Press, 1972.

Knopp, Josephine. *The Trial of Judaism in Contemporary Jewish Writing.* Urbana: University of Illinois Press, 1975.

——, ed. *International Theological Symposium on the Holocaust, October 15–17, 1978.* Philadelphia: National Institute on the Holocaust, 1979.

——, ed. *Proceedings of the Second Philadelphia Conference on the Holocaust* [16–18 Feb. 1977]. Philadelphia: Temple University, 1977.

Kogon, Eugen. *Der SS-Staat: Das System der deutschen Konzentrationslager.* Munich: Kindler Verlag, 1974.

Kohn, Hans. *The Mind of Germany: The Education of a Nation.* New York: Harper Torchbooks, 1965.

Kolinsky, Martin, and Kolinsky, Eva. "The Treatment of the Holocaust in West German Textbooks." In *Yad Vashem Studies on the European Jewish Catastrophe and Resistance,* edited by Livia Rothkirchen, vol. 10, pp. 149–216. Jerusalem: Yad Vashem, 1974.

Kolitz, Zvi. "Yossel Rakover's Appeal to God." In Friedlander, ed., *Out of the Whirlwind,* pp. 390–99.

Korey, William. *The Soviet Cage: Anti-Semitism in Russia.* New York: Viking Press, 1973.

Korman, Gerd, ed. *Hunter and Hunted: Human History of the Holocaust.* New York: Viking Press, 1973.

Kovner, Abba. "A First Attempt to Tell"; "The Miracle in the Midst of Destruction"; "Threnody for a Movement." Unpublished preparatory papers for International Scholars Conference on the Holocaust, New York, 3–6 Mar. 1975.

—— and Sachs, Nelly. *Selected Poems.* Harmondsworth: Penguin Books, 1971.

Krausnick, Helmut; Buchheim, Hans; Broszat, Martin; and Jacobsen, Hans-Adolf. *Anatomy of the SS State.* Translated by Richard Barry, Marian Jackson, and Dorothy Long. London: Collins, 1968.

Kremers, Heinz, ed. *Juden und Christen Lesen Dieselbe Bibel.* Duisburg: Walter Braun Verlag, 1973.

——. *Judenmission heute? Von der Judenmission zur brüderlichen Solidarität und zum ökumenischen Dialog.* Neukirchen-Vluyn: Neukirchener Verlag, 1979.

———. *Das Verhältnis der Kirche zu Israel.* Düsseldorf: Pressseverband der Evangelischen Kirche im Rheinland, 1965.

Kulka, Erich. *Die Massenvernichtung der Juden Wird Geleugnet: Eine Studie über die beunruhigenden Perspektiven der Vergangenheit.* Jerusalem: Yad Vashem, 1975.

Küng, Hans. *Christsein.* Munich: R. Piper Verlag, 1974.

Langbein, Hermann. *Hommes et Femmes à Auschwitz.* Translated by Denise Meumer. Paris: Fayard, 1975.

———. "Überblick über neonazistische Literatur." *Zeit Geschichte* [Salzburg] 9–10 (1975): 236–42.

Langer, Lawrence L. *From Death to Atrocity.* Boston: Beacon Press, 1978.

———. *The Holocaust and the Literary Imagination.* New Haven, Conn.: Yale University Press, 1975.

Lapide, Pinchas E. "Jesu Judesein: Christliches Unbehagen." *Tribüne* [Frankfurt-am-Main] 14, no. 55 (1975): 6356–66.

———. *Juden und Christen.* Cologne: Benziger Verlag, 1976.

———. "Vom 'Gottesmord' zum Völkermord." *Tribüne* [Frankfurt-am-Main] 14, no. 53 (1975): 6134–50.

Lauran, Annie. *La casquette d'Hitler ou le temps de l'oubli.* Paris: Éditions Francais Réunis, 1974.

Lawrence, Robert M., and Larus, Joel, eds. *Nuclear Proliferation: Phase II.* Lawrence, Kans.: University Press of Kansas, 1974.

Leftwich, Joseph, ed. and trans. *The Golden Peacock: A Worldwide Treasury of Yiddish Poetry.* New York and London: Thomas Yoseloff, 1961.

Lelyveld, Arthur J. *Atheism Is Dead: A Jewish Response to Radical Theology.* Cleveland and New York: World Publishing Co., 1968.

Lendvai, Paul. *Anti-Semitism without Jews: Communist Eastern Europe.* New York: Doubleday, 1971.

Lessing, Abba. "Jewish Impotence and Power." *Midstream* 22, no. 8 (Oct. 1976):52–58.

Leuner, H. David. "Das Rätsel des Antisemitismus in kommunistischen Ländern." *Dokumentation: Ein Informationsdienst.* Frankfurt-am-Main: Haus der Evangelischen Publizistik, 18 Sept. 1972.

———. "Versagen und Bewährung—Die Welt und das Brandopfer der Juden." *Israel-Forum* 17, no. 2 (1975):2–9.

———. *Zwischen Israel und den Völkern: Vorträge eines Judenchristen.* Edited by Peter von der Osten-Sacken. Berlin: Institut Kirche und Judentum, 1978.

Levin, Nora. *The Holocaust: The Destruction of European Jewry 1933–1945*. New York: Schocken Books,1973.

———. "Life over Death." *Congress Bi-Weekly* 40, no. 8 (18 May 1973): 22–23.

Levine, Herbert H. "Munich Thirty Years Later: Trying to Erase the Shadow." *Present Tense* 2, no. 3 (Spring 1975):31–35.

Lewy, Guenter. *The Catholic Church and Nazi Germany*. New York: McGraw-Hill, 1964.

Lind, Jakov. *Counting My Steps: An Autobiography*. London: Jonathan Cape, 1970.

———. *Soul of Wood and Other Stories*. Translated by Ralph Manheim. New York: Fawcett Crest Books, 1966.

Lindsey, Robert L. "A New Approach to the Synoptic Gospels." *Christian News from Israel* [Jerusalem] 22, no. 2 (1971):56–63.

Littell, Franklin H. "Christendom, Holocaust, and Israel: The Importance for Christians of Recent Major Events in Jewish History." *Journal of Ecumenical Studies* 10, no. 3 (Summer 1973):483–97.

———. *The Crucifixion of the Jews: The Failure of Christians to Understand the Jewish Experience*. New York: Harper and Row, 1975.

———. "Particularism and Universalism in Religious Perspective." Unpublished lecture at Beth Tzedec Congregation, Toronto, 11 May 1972.

——— and Locke, Hubert G., eds. *The German Church Struggle and the Holocaust*. Detroit, Mich.: Wayne State University Press, 1974.

Lorenz, Friedebert, ed. *Juden und Deutsche: Ihr Weg zum Frieden. Vortrag gehalten anlässlich des 13. Evangelischen Kirchentags Hannover 1967*. Stuttgart: Kreuz-Verlag, 1967.

Lovsky, Fadiey. *La Déchirure de l'absence: Essai sur les rapports de l'église du Christ et du peuple d'Israël*. Paris: Calmann-Lévy, 1971.

McEvoy, Donald W., ed. *Christians Confront the Holocaust: A Collection of Sermons*. New York: National Conference of Christians and Jews, 1980.

McGarry, Michael B. *Christology after Auschwitz*. New York: Paulist Press, 1977.

Ma'oz, Moshe. *The Image of the Jew in Official Arab Literature and Communications Media*. Jerusalem: Shazar Library, Institute of Contemporary Jewry, 1976.

Marquardt, Friedrich-Wilhelm. *Die Bedeutung der biblischen Landesverheissungen für die Christen. Theologische Existenz heute, no. 116*. Munich: Chr. Kaiser Verlag, 1964.

——. *Die Juden und ihr Land.* Hamburg: Siebenstern Taschenbuch Verlag, 1975.

Matussek, Paul, et alia. *Internment in Concentration Camps and Its Consequences.* Translated by Derek and Inge Jordan. Berlin: Springer-Verlag, 1975.

Maybaum, Ignaz. *The Face of God after Auschwitz.* Amsterdam: Polak and Van Gennep, 1965.

Mayer, Reinhold. *Judentum und Christentum.* Aschaffenburg: Paul Pattloch Verlag, 1973.

Megged, Aharon. "Letter from Israel." *Jewish Quarterly* [London] 22, no. 4 (Winter 1975).

Merk, Hans Günther. "Rechtsradikalismus in der Bundesrepublik Deutschland." *Tribüne* [Frankfurt-am-Main] 14, no. 56 (1975):6496–500.

Mitscherlich, Alexander, and Mitscherlich, Margarete. *Die Unfähigkeit zu trauern: Grundlagen kollektiven Verhaltens.* Munich: R. Piper Verlag, 1967.

Moltmann, Jürgen. *The Crucified God.* Translated by R. A. Wilson and John Bowden. New York: Harper and Row, 1974.

——. *Kirche in der Kraft des Geistes.* Munich: Chr. Kaiser Verlag, 1975.

Morley, John F. *Vatican Diplomacy and the Jews during the Holocaust 1939–1943.* New York: Ktav Publishing House, 1980.

Morse, Arthur D. *While Six Million Died.* New York: Hart Publishing Co., 1975.

Neher, André. *L'Exil de la parole: Du silence biblique au silence d'Auschwitz.* Paris: Éditions du Seuil, 1970.

Neven-du Mont, Jürgen. *After Hitler: Report from a West German City.* Translated by Ralph Manheim. Harmondsworth: Penguin Books, 1970.

Niebuhr, Reinhold. *The Children of Light and the Children of Darkness: A Vindication of Democracy and a Critique of its Traditional Defense.* New York: Scribner Lyceum Editions, 1960.

——. *Christianity and Power Politics.* Hamden, Conn.: Archon Books, 1969.

——. *Discerning the Signs of the Times.* New York: Charles Scribner's Sons, 1946.

——. *Moral Man and Immoral Society: A Study in Ethics and Politics.* New York: Charles Scribner's Sons, 1941.

——. *The Structure of Nations and Empires: A Study of the Recurring Patterns and Problems of the Political Order in Relation to the Unique Problems of the Nuclear Age.* New York: Charles Scribner's Sons, 1959.

Niebuhr, Ursula M., ed. *Justice and Mercy.* New York: Harper and Row, 1974.

O'Collins, Gerald. *What Are They Saying about the Resurrection?* New York, Ramsey, and Toronto: Paulist Press, 1978.

Opsahl, Paul D., and Tanenbaum, Marc H., eds. *Speaking of God Today: Jews and Lutherans in Conversation.* Philadelphia: Fortress Press, 1974.

Orpaz, Yizhak. "A Literature of Siege and Survival." *Jewish Quarterly* [London] 22, no. 4 (Winter 1975).

Osten-Sacken, Peter von der. "Anti-Judaism in Christian Theology." *Christian Attitudes on Jews and Judaism* 55 (Aug. 1977):1–6.

————, ed. *Treue zur Thora: Beiträge zur Mitte des christlich-jüdischen Ge-sprächs. Festschrift für Günther Harder zum 75. Geburtstag.* Berlin: Institut Kirche und Judentum, 1977.

————, ed. *Zionismus: Befreiungsbewegung des jüdischen Volkes.* Berlin: Institut Kirche und Judentum bei der Kirchlichen Hochschule Berlin, 1977.

Ozick, Cynthia. "The Uses of Legend: Elie Wiesel as Tsaddik." *Congress Bi-Weekly* 36, no. 9 (9 June 1969):16–20.

Pannenberg, Wolfhart. *Jesus—God and Man.* Translated by Lewis L. Wilkins and Duane A. Friebe. Philadelphia: Westminster Press, 1968.

————. "Zukunft und Einheit der Menschheit." *Evangelische Theologie* [Munich] 32, no. 4 (July–Aug. 1972):384–402.

Parkes, James. *Antisemitism.* London: Vallentine, Mitchell, 1963.

————. *The Conflict of the Church and the Synagogue: A Study in the Origins of Antisemitism.* Cleveland: World Publishing Co., 1961.

————. *A History of the Jewish People.* Harmondsworth: Penguin Books, 1964.

————. *The Jew in the Medieval Community: A Study of His Political and Economic Situation.* 2d ed. New York: Hermon Press, 1976.

————. *Judaism and Christianity.* Chicago: University of Chicago Press, 1948.

————. *Prelude to Dialogue: Jewish-Christian Relationships.* London: Vallentine, Mitchell, 1969.

————. *Whose Land? A History of the Peoples of Palestine.* New York: Taplinger Publishing Co., 1971.

Pawlikowski, John T. *Catechetics and Prejudice: How Catholic Teaching Materials View Jews, Protestants, and Racial Minorities.* New York: Paulist Press, 1973.

————. *The Challenge of the Holocaust for Christian Theology.* New York: Anti-Defamation League of B'nai B'rith, 1978.

————. "The Contemporary Jewish-Christian Theological Dialogue Agenda." *Journal of Ecumenical Studies* 11, no. 4 (Fall 1974):599–616.

187

———. "The Dialogue Agenda." *ADL Bulletin* 31, no. 9 (Nov. 1974).

———. *What Are They Saying about Christian-Jewish Relations?* New York: Paulist Press, 1980.

Peck, William Jay. "From Cain to the Death Camps: An Essay on Bonhoeffer and Judaism." *Union Seminary Quarterly Review* 28, no. 2 (Winter 1973):158–76.

Peli, Pinchas Hacohen. "The Future of Israel." *Proceedings of the Rabbinical Assembly 74th Annual Convention* [5–9 May 1974] pp. 8–19.

Pennie, David A., ed. *A Bibliography of the Printed Works of James Parkes.* Compiled with bibliographical notes by Sidney Sugarman and Diana Bailey. Southampton: University of Southampton, 1977.

Pfisterer, Rudolf. "Alter Feind in neuem Kleid: Erwägungen über den Anti-semitismus." *Tribüne* [Frankfurt-am-Main] 12, no. 48 (1973):5462–88.

———. "Antizionismus und Antisemitismus." *Tribüne* [Frankfurt-am-Main] 8, no. 32 (1969): 3407–18.

———. *Im Schatten des Kreuzes.* Hamburg-Bergstedt: Herbert Reich Evang. Verlag, 1966.

———. "Judaism in the Preaching and Teaching of the Church." *Lutheran World* [Geneva] 11, no. 3 (July 1964):311–25.

———. "Rechtsradikale in Frankreich." *Tribüne* [Frankfurt-am-Main] 14, no. 56 (1975):6490–93.

———. *Von A-Bis Z: Quellen zu Fragen um Juden und Christen.* Schriftenmissions-Verlag Gladbeck, 1971.

———. "Wiederum Schweigen?" *Tribüne* [Frankfurt-am-Main] 14, no. 53 (1975): 6116–33.

Poliakov, Léon. *The Aryan Myth: A History of Racist and Nationalist Ideas in Europe.* London: Heinemann Educational Books and Sussex University Press, 1974.

———. *Auschwitz.* Paris: Rene Julliard, 1964.

———. "The Catholic Church and the Jews: The Vatican's New Guidelines." *Midstream* 22, no. 8 (Oct. 1976):29–35.

———. *De l'antisionisme à l'antisémitisme.* Paris: Calmann-Lévy, 1969.

Polish, David. *Israel—Nation and People.* New York: Ktav Publishing House, 1975.

———. "The Tasks of Israel and Galut." *Judaism* 28, no. 1 (Winter 1969):3–16.

Postal, Bernard, and Abramson, Samuel H. *The Traveler's Guide to Jewish Landmarks of Europe.* New York: Fleet Press, 1971.

Presser, Jacob. *The Destruction of the Dutch Jews.* Translated by Arnold Pomerans. New York: E. P. Dutton, 1969.

Rabi, Wladimir. "La théologie juive après Auschwitz." *Dispersion et Unité* [Jerusalem] 12 (1972):186–204.

Rabinowitz, Dorothy. *New Lives: Survivors of the Holocaust Living in America.* New York: Alfred A. Knopf, 1976.

Rash, Yohoshua. "French, Foreigners, and Jews." *Patterns of Prejudice* [London] 10, no. 1 (Jan.–Feb. 1976):6–13.

Rat der Evangelischen Kirche in Deutschland. *Christen und Juden: Eine Studie des Rates der Evangelischen Kirche in Deutschland.* Gütersloh: Gütersloher Verlagshaus Gerd Möhn, 1975.

Reitlinger, Gerhard. *The Final Solution: The Attempt to Exterminate the Jews of Europe 1939–1945.* New York: A. S. Barnes, 1961.

Rencontre: Chrétiens et Juifs [Paris] 10, no. 46 (1976). Special issue on "Après l'Holocauste."

Rendtorff, Rolf, ed. *Arbeitsbuch Christen und Juden.* Gütersloh: Gütersloher Verlagshaus Gerd Möhn, 1979.

———. "Ende oder Erfüllung der Geschichte? Das Problem des jüdischen Nationalstaats." *Evangelische Kommentare* [Stuttgart] 6, no. 5 (May 1973):273–75.

———. *Israel und sein Land: Theologische Überlegungen zu einem politischen Problem.* Munich: Chr. Kaiser Verlag, 1975.

———. "Juden sind keine potentiellen Christen." *Evangelische Kommentare* [Stuttgart] 5, no. 6 (June 1972):358–60.

———. "Die neutestamentliche Wissenschaft und die Juden: Zur Diskussion zwischen David Flusser und Ulrich Wilckens." *Evangelische Theologie* [Munich] 36, no. 2 (Mar.–Apr. 1976):191–200.

———. "Der Staat Israel und die Christen." *Zeitwende* [Gütersloh] 45, no. 3 (May 1974):183–96.

Reznikoff, Charles. *Holocaust.* Los Angeles: Black Sparrow Press, 1975.

Robinson, Jacob. *Psychoanalysis in a Vacuum: Bruno Bettelheim and the Holocaust.* New York: Yad Vashem-Yivo Documentary Projects, 1970.

Robinson, Jacob, assisted by Mrs. Philip Friedman. *The Holocaust and After: Sources and Literature in English.* Yad Vashem Martyrs' and Heroes' Memorial Authority, Jerusalem, and Yivo Institute for Jewish Research, New York, Joint Documentary Projects; Bibliographical Series, no. 12. Jerusalem: Israel Universities Press, 1973.

Rosenbaum, Irving J. *The Holocaust and Halakhah.* New York: Ktav Publishing House, 1976.

Rosenfeld, Alvin H. *A Double Dying: Reflections on Holocaust Literature.* Bloomington, Ind. and London: Indiana University Press, 1980.

—— and Greenberg, Irving, eds. *Confronting the Holocaust: The Impact of Elie Wiesel.* Bloomington, Ind. and London: Indiana University Press, 1978.

Rosenthal, David. "Thirty Years after the Liberation of Auschwitz and Bergen-Belsen." *Jewish Frontier* 42, no. 3 (Mar. 1975):4–10.

Rosenzweig, Franz. *The Star of Redemption.* Translated by William W. Hallo. New York: Holt, Rinehart and Winston, 1970.

Roskies, Diane K. *Teaching the Holocaust to Children: A Review and Bibliography.* New York: Ktav Publishing House, 1975.

Rotenstreich, Nathan. *Reflections on the Contemporary Jewish Condition.* Jerusalem: Institute of Contemporary Jewry, Hebrew University, 1975.

Roth, John K. *A Consuming Fire: Encounters with Elie Wiesel and the Holocaust.* Atlanta, Ga.: John Knox Press, 1979.

Rottenberg, Isaac C. "Fulfillment Theology and the Future of Christian-Jewish Relations." *Christian Century* 97, no. 3 (23 Jan. 1980):66–69.

——. "Should There Be a Christian Witness to the Jews?" *Christian Century* 94, no. 13 (13 Apr. 1977):352–56.

Rubenstein, Richard L. *After Auschwitz: Radical Theology and Contemporary Judaism.* Indianapolis, Ind.: Bobbs-Merrill Co., 1966.

——. "Auschwitz and Covenant Theology." *Christian Century* 86, no. 21 (21 May 1969):716–18.

——. *The Cunning of History: Mass Death and the American Future.* New York: Harper and Row, 1975.

——. "Jewish Theology and the Current World Situation." *Conservative Judaism* 28, no. 4 (Summer 1974):3–25.

——. "Job and Auschwitz." *Union Seminary Quarterly Review* 25, no. 4 (Summer 1970):421–37.

Ruether, Rosemary Radford. "Christian-Jewish Dialogue: New Interpretations." *ADL Bulletin* 30, no. 5 (May 1973):3–4.

——. *Faith and Fratricide: The Theological Roots of Anti-Semitism.* New York: Seabury Press, 1974.

——. "The Future of Christian Theology about Judaism." *Christian Attitudes on Jews and Judaism* [London] 49 (Aug. 1976):1–5.

——. "An Invitation to Jewish-Christian Dialogue: In What Sense Can We Say That Jesus Was 'The Christ'?" *The Ecumenist* 10, no. 2 (Jan.–Feb. 1972):17–24.

————. *Liberation Theology: Human Hope Confronts Christian History and American Power.* New York: Paulist Press, 1972.

Ryan, Michael. *The Contemporary Explosion of Theology.* Metuchen, N.J.: Scarecrow Press, 1975.

————. "Some Protestant Theological Reflections on Jews and Judaism since 1945: Towards a Definition of Theological Anti-Semitism." Unpublished paper at Annual Scholars' Conference on the Church Struggle and the Holocaust, New York, 17–20 Mar. 1974.

Rylaarsdam, J. Coert. "Jewish-Christian Relationship: The Two Covenants and the Dilemmas of Christology." *Journal of Ecumenical Studies* 9, no. 2 (Spring 1972):249–70.

Sachar, Howard. *The Emergence of the Middle East 1914–1924.* New York: Alfred A. Knopf, 1971.

Sachs, Nelly. *O the Chimneys: Selected Poems.* New York: Farrar, Straus and Giroux, 1967.

Sanders, E. P. *Paul and Palestinian Judaism: A Comparison of Patterns of Religion.* Philadelphia: Fortress Press, 1977.

Sanders, Wilm. *Antisemitismus bei den Christen? Gedanken zur christlichen Judenfeindschaft am Beispiel der Oberammergau Passionsspiele.* Leutesdorf-am-Rhein: Johannes-Verlag, 1970.

Sandmel, Samuel. *Anti-Semitism in the New Testament?* Philadelphia: Fortress Press, 1978.

————. "The New Movement." *Common Ground* [London] 23, no. 2 (Summer 1969).

Schenk, Rosemarie; Schenk, Otto; Nessler, Eva; and Nessler, Udo. ... *Und gruben Brunnen in der Wüste: Junge Deutsche ziehen Bilanz ihrer 8 Aufbaujahre zwischen Jerusalem und Beer Sheva.* Darmstadt: Eduard Roether Verlag, 1975.

Schindler, Pesach. "Faith after Auschwitz in Light of the Paradox of Tikkun in Hassidic Documents." *Sidic* [Rome] 7, no. 3 (1974):24–30.

————. "The Holocaust and Kiddush Hashem in Hasidic Thought." *Tradition* 13, no. 4 and 14, no. 1 (Spring-Summer 1973):88–104.

Schmid, Herbert. "Holokaust, Theologie, und Religionsunterricht." *Judaica* [Zurich] 35 (1979):5–11.

Schneider, Gertrude. "Survival and Guilt Feelings of Jewish Concentration Camp Victims." *Jewish Social Studies* 37, no. 1 (Jan. 1975):74–83.

Schorsch, Ismar. "German Anti-Semitism in the Light of Post-War Historiography." Unpublished preparatory paper for International Scholars Conference on the Holocaust, New York, 3–6 Mar. 1975.

191

————. "Historical Reflections on the Holocaust." *Conservative Judaism* 31, nos. 1–2 (Fall–Winter 1976–77):26–33.

Schulz, Gerhard. *Faschismus-Nationalsozialismus: Versionen und theoretische Kontroversen.* Frankfurt-am-Main: Verlag Ullstein, 1974.

Schweitzer, Frederick M. *A History of the Jews since the First Century A.D.* New York: Macmillan, 1971.

Seiden, Morton Irving. *The Paradox of Hate: A Study in Ritual Murder.* New York and London: Thomas Yoseloff, 1967.

Senesh, Hannah. *Hannah Senesh: Her Life and Diary.* Translated by Marta Cohn. New York: Schocken Books, 1973.

Sereny, Gitta. *Into That Darkness: From Mercy Killing to Mass Murder.* New York: McGraw-Hill, 1975.

Shabbetai, K. *As Sheep to the Slaughter: The Myth of Cowardice.* New York and Tel Aviv: World Association of the Bergen-Belsen Survivors Associations, 1963.

Sherman, Franklin. "Speaking of God after Auschwitz." *Worldview* 17, no. 9 (Sept. 1974):26–30.

Sherwin, Byron L., and Ament, Susan G. *Encountering the Holocaust: An Interdisciplinary Survey.* Chicago: Impact Press, 1979.

Sidic [Rome] 7, no. 2 (1974), special number on the Holocaust; 8, no. 3 (1975), special number on Jewish-Christian relations, 1965–75.

Silbermann, Alphons. "Antisemitismus in der Bundesrepublik." Offprint from *Bild der Wissenschaft,* June 1976, pp. 68–74.

Silverman, David Wolf. "The Holocaust: A Living Force." *Conservative Judaism* 31, no. 1–2 (Fall–Winter 1976–77):21–25.

Simon, Ulrich E. *A Theology of Auschwitz.* London: Victor Gollancz, 1967; SPCK, 1978.

Sloyan, Gerard S. *Is Christ the End of the Law?* Philadelphia: Westminster Press, 1978.

Sontag, Frederick. *The God of Evil: An Argument from the Existence of the Devil.* New York: Harper and Row, 1970.

Sosnowski, Kiryl. *The Tragedy of Children under Nazi Rule.* Warsaw: Western Agency Press, 1962.

Sperber, Mànes. . . . *than a Tear in the Sea.* Translated by Constantine Fitzgibbon. New York and Tel Aviv: Bergen-Belsen Memorial Press, 1967.

————. *Die Wasserträger Gottes.* Vienna: Europaverlag, 1974.

Steiner, George. *In Bluebeard's Castle: Some Notes Towards the Re-definition of Culture.* New Haven: Yale University Press, 1979.

———. *Language and Silence: Essays on Language, Literature, and the Inhuman.* London: Penguin Books, 1969.

Steiner, Jean-François. *Treblinka.* Translated by Helen Weaver. London: Weidenfeld and Nicholson, 1967.

Steinitz, Lucy Y., and Szonyi, David M., eds. *Living after the Holocaust: Reflections by the Post-War Generation in America.* New York: Bloch Publishing Co., 1976.

Stiegnitz, Peter. "Angst und Antisemitismus: Sozialpsychologie der Judenfeindschaft in Deutschland und Österreich." *Tribüne* [Frankfurt-am-Main] 14, no. 55 (1975):6368–74.

Stierlin, Helm. *Adolf Hitler: Familienperspektiven.* Frankfurt-am-Main: Suhrkamp, 1975.

Stimmt unser Bild vom Judentum? Fazit aus 20 Jahren christlich-jüdischen Dialogs. Papers given before a conference at the Evangelical Academy, Bad Boll, 7–9 Nov. 1975.

Stöhr, Martin; Maier, Johann; Kremers, Heinz; Konrad, J. F.; and Lapide, Pinchas E. *Judentum im christlichen Religionsunterricht.* Frankfurt: Verlag Evangelischer Presseverband für Hessen und Nassau, 1972.

Strober, Gerald S. *Portrait of the Elder Brother: Jews and Christians in Protestant Teaching Materials.* New York: American Jewish Committee-National Conference of Christians and Jews, 1972.

Stroh, Hans. "Die gegenseitige Befragung: Zum Stand des jüdisch-christlichen Gesprächs." *Zeitwende* [Gütersloh] 45, no. 3 (May 1974):196–99.

———. "Gibt es Verständigung zwischen Juden und Christen?" *Zeitschrift für Theologie und Kirche* [Tübingen] 71, no. 2 (June 1974):227–38.

Suhl, Yuri, ed. and trans. *They Fought Back: The Story of the Jewish Resistance in Nazi Europe.* London: MacGibbon and Kee, 1968.

Tal, Uriel. *Christians and Jews in Germany: Religion, Politics, and Ideology in the Second Reich, 1870–1914.* Translated by Noah J. Jacobs. Ithaca, N.Y.: Cornell University Press, 1975.

———. "Möglichkeiten einer jüdisch-christlichen Begegnung und Verständigung, Jüdische Sicht." *Concilium* [Mainz] 10, no. 10 (Oct. 1974):605–9.

———. "On the Study of the Holocaust and Genocide." In *Yad Vashem Studies,* edited by Livia Rothkirchen, vol. 13, pp. 7–52. Jerusalem: Yad Vashem Martyrs' and Heroes' Remembrance Authority, 1979.

———. "Zur neuen Einstellung der Kirche zum Judentum." *Freiburger Rundbrief* 24, nos. 89–92 (Dec. 1972):150–60.

Talmage, Frank Ephraim, ed. *Disputation and Dialogue: Readings in the Jewish-Christian Encounter.* New York: Ktav Publishing House, 1975.

Thoma, Clemens. *A Christian Theology of Judaism.* Translated and edited by Helga Croner. New York and Ramsey: Paulist Press, 1980.

————. *Kirche aus Juden und Heiden: Biblische Informationen über das Verhältnis der Kirche zum Judentum.* Vienna: Herder and Co., 1970.

Thompson, Kenneth W., ed. *Foreign Policy and Morality: Framework for a Moral Audit.* New York: Council on Religion and International Affairs, 1979.

Toland, John. *Adolf Hitler.* Garden City, N.Y.: Doubleday and Co., 1976.

Trachtenberg, Joshua. *The Devil and the Jews: The Medieval Conception of the Jews and Its Relation to Modern Antisemitism.* Cleveland, Ohio: Meridian Books, 1961.

"Tuchin." *Encyclopaedia Judaica,* vol. 15, pp. 1420–21.

Tyson, Joseph B. *A Study of Early Christianity.* New York: Macmillan, 1973.

Van Buren, Paul M. "Affirmation of the Jewish People: A Condition of Theological Coherence." *Journal of the American Academy of Religion* 45, no. 3, Supplement (Sept. 1977):1075–100.

————. *The Burden of Freedom: Americans and the God of Israel.* New York: Seabury Press, 1976.

————. *Discerning the Way: A Theology of the Jewish-Christian Reality.* New York: Seabury Press, 1980.

————. "The Status and Prospects for Theology." *CCI Notebook* 24 (Nov. 1975).

Vermes, Geza. *Jesus the Jew: A Historian's Reading of the Gospels.* London: Collins, 1973.

Vogt, Judith. "Old Images in Soviet Anti-Zionist Cartoons." *Soviet Jewish Affairs* [London] 5, no. 1 (1975):20–38.

Volavkora, Hana, ed. *Children's Drawings and Poems—Terezín 1942–1944.* Prague: State Jewish Museum, 1959.

Wardi, Charlotte. *Le juif dans le roman français.* Paris: Nizet, 1973.

Wellers, Georges. *L'Étoile jaune à l'heure de Vichy: De Drancy à Auschwitz.* Paris: Fayard, 1973.

Wiesel, Elie. *"Ani Maamin": A Song Lost and Found Again.* Translated by Marion Wiesel. New York: Random House, 1973.

————. *A Beggar in Jerusalem.* Translated by Lily Edelman and the author. New York: Random House, 1970.

————. *The Gates of the Forest.* Translated by Frances Frenaye. New York: Holt, Rinehart and Winston, 1966.

194

————. *A Jew Today*. Translated by Marion Wiesel. New York: Random House, 1978.

————. "Jewish Values in the Post-Holocaust Future." *Judaism* 16, no. 3 (Summer 1967):281–84.

————. *Legends of Our Time*. Translated by Stephen Donadio. New York: Avon Books, 1968.

————. *Night*. Translated by Stella Rodway. New York: Hill and Wang, 1960.

————. "Ominous Signs and Unspeakable Thoughts." *New York Times*, 28 Dec. 1974.

————. *The Town beyond the Wall*. Translated by Stephen Becker. New York: Avon Books, 1964.

———— *The Trial of God*. Translated by Marion Wiesel. New York: Random House, 1979.

Wiesenthal, Simon. *The Sunflower*. New York: Schocken Books, 1976.

Willis, Robert E. "Auschwitz and the Nurturing of Conscience." *Religion in Life* 44, no. 4 (Winter 1975):432–47.

————. "Christian Theology after Auschwitz." *Journal of Ecumenical Studies* 12, no. 4 (Fall 1975):493–519.

World Council of Churches. *The Church and the Jewish People*. Newsletter no. 4 (1975). Newsletter no. 2 (1977). Geneva: World Council of Churches, Consultation on the Church and the Jewish People.

Wormser-Migot, Olga. *L'Ère des camps*. Paris: Union Générale d'Éditions, 1973.

Wundheiler, Luitgard N. "Paul Celan, Poet of the Holocaust." *Worldview* 19, no. 12 (Dec. 1976):24–26.

Wyschogrod, Michael. "Faith and the Holocaust." *Judaism* 20, no. 3 (Summer 1971):268–94.

Yahil, Leni. "The Holocaust in Jewish Historiography." *Yad Vashem Studies*, edited by Livia Rothkirchen, vol. 7, pp. 57–73. Jerusalem: Yad Vashem, 1968.

Zeitwende [Gütersloh] 46, no. 6 (Nov. 1975). Special number on Paul Celan.

Zerner, Ruth. "Dietrich Bonhoeffer and the Jews: Thoughts and Actions, 1933–1945." *Jewish Social Studies* 37, nos. 3–4 (Summer–Fall 1975):235–50.

Zimmels, H. J. *The Echo of the Nazi Holocaust in Rabbinic Literature*. New York: Ktav Publishing House, 1977.

Zucker, Wolfgang. "Thirty Years after the Holocaust: A Midrash for the Church." *Lutheran Forum* 9, no. 3 (Sept. 1975).

INDEX

Abraham, 60, 77, 94, 97, 112, 118, 123, 170 n. 24
Absolutism, Christian, 95–99, 105, 108, 114, 127; political, 136–37
Adler, Hermann G., 44, 151 n. 1
Adorno, T. W., 142
Aichinger, Ilse, 143
Aktion Suhnezeichen/Friedens-dienste, 37, 154 n. 17
Amichai, Yehuda, 142
Amnestia, concept of, 27
Anarchism, 136–37
Ani Ma-amin, liturgy of, 74
Anthropotheism, 148
Anti-Israelism, 50
Anti-Judaism, 105, 107, 108, 163 n. 27
Antisemitism, 23, 29, 30, 48–50, 55, 61, 84, 133, 147; blame on Jews for, 64, 85; Christian, 22, 44, 50, 60–62, 64, 71, 84, 86, 105, 107, 112, 114, 128, 129, 157 n. 38, 162 n. 11; and Christian liturgy, 156 n. 21; condemnation of, 84; freedom from, 109; and Germans today, 29, 35; and Holocaust, 48–57, 106; religion of, 54; and Resurrection, 130; roots of, 84; uniqueness of, 48–57 passim, 95. *See also under* Devil; Guilt; New Testament; Passion story; West Germany
Anti-Zionism, 50, 86
Apocalyptic, Christian, 107
"Apprehension," ambiguity of, 26
Arab Christians, 84

Arabs, 136, 144; and propaganda, 50; rights of, 142
Arab states, 155 n. 6; and state of Israel, 145–47 passim
Arendt, Hannah, 41–42
Argentine, the, 147
Armenians, 44, 155 n. 8
Aronsfeld, Caesar C., 29
Aryans, 44, 56
Aschkenasy, Yehuda, 80
Atheism, and Christians, 94; and Jews, 94
Auschwitz, 21, 41, 98, 99, 133–34, 140, 141, 142, 148; as symbol, 155 n. 13

Baal Shem Tov, 40
Barabbas, 117
Bastiaans, Jan, 19
Baum, Gregory, 62, 71–72, 73, 74, 111; on ideology, 165 n. 1
Bea, Augustin Cardinal, 84, 161 n. 2
Belzec, 140
Bergen-Belsen, 68, 100
Berkovits, Eliezer, 76–77, 79, 142, 160 n. 23
B.F.S., usage of, 45
Biblical world view, 127
Birkenau, 140
Black power, 134
Blacks, 113
"Blasphemer," Jesus as, 88, 90–91
Blasphemy, 98–99, 101–2, 116; meaning of, 162 n. 18; and theology, 133
Bloch, Ernst, 94

Blumhardt, Christoph, 97
Body-soul dualism, 131
Borowski, Tadeusz, 141
Brown, Robert McAfee, 62, 149
Buchenwald, 100

Cambodia, Cambodians, 54
Cammerer, Joseph S., 143
Campbell, Will D., 113
Camus, Albert, 70
Celan, Paul, 141, 169 n. 5
Children, 34, 143; in Holocaust, 25–
  26, 31, 43, 103–4, 115, 122, 138,
  141, 143, 150. *See also under* Kingdom of day
Christ, 98; faith in, 89; and freedom,
  93; as "hidden," 101; rejection of,
  107; as Savior, 86; second advent
  of, 106–7; suffering of, 100, 101.
  See also Jesus, Messiah
Christian faith, 87, 99, 103, 118; as
  ally of Jews, 148; and crucifixion of
  Jesus, 104; and Jewishness, 125–
  26; need for regeneration of, 102;
  and new revelations, 127; and salvation, 126–27. *See also* Christ;
  Christianity; Church; Jesus; *and
  see under* Relativization; Triumphalism
Christianity, 67, 92, 93; credibility of,
  61; cynic's definition of, 135; fate of,
  108; and history, 127; impact of Holocaust on, 108–9; and Jews and Judaism, 22, 65, 73, 106–7, 147, 148; man
  in, 136; and New Testament, 117;
  and other faiths, 126. *See also* Christian faith; Christians; Church; *and
  see under* Holocaust; Ideology; Jewishness; Justice; Nazism; Supersessionism; Triumphalism
Christian Jewishness, 125–26, 130–31
Christian-Jewish relations, 83, 105,
  111; and fatefulness of Resurrection, 129
Christian Judaism, 102
Christian responses to Holocaust, typology of, 82–83

Christians: as adopted by God, 126;
  Eastern Orthodox, 114; and Jewishness, 132, 148; and Jews and Judaism, 84, 85, 111, 164 n. 62; need for
  behavioral change among, 114–15;
  Protestant, 114; Roman Catholic,
  114; and state of Israel, 86, 105, 140;
  in Third World, 114. *See also* Christian faith; Christianity; Church; *and
  see under* Devil; Freedom; Germans; Historicalness; Holocaust;
  Jews; Liberation; *Metanoia;* People
  of God
Christian teachings on Jews: moral
  consequences of, 112; norms for
  judging, 112. *See also under* Holocaust; Jews; Judaism; Revolution;
  Triumphalism
Christology, 62, 87
Chrysostom, John, 50, 109
Church, 62, 98, 120; and divine promises, 161 n. 9; foundation of, 86, 118;
  and Holocaust, 112; and hope, 107,
  140, 147–49; imperfection of, 95;
  and Israel, 96, 105, 107; and Jewishness, 128; and Jews, 101, 134; mission of, 161 n. 9; paganization of,
  105; past of, 82; plight of, 87; and
  revolution, 109–10; sins of, 85–86,
  148; and truth, 111. *See also* Christianity; Christians; *and see under*
  Election; Germans; Ideology; Liberation; Salvation; Triumphalism
Church Fathers, 92
Cleaver, Eldridge, 134
Cohn, Haim, 90, 91, 116–17, 162 n.
  18
Commandment, meanings of, 123–24
Command to live, 123–25; and element of demand, 124, 166 n. 24
Communists, 54, 134
Conscience, 36, 38, 86, 98
Covenant, the, 61, 66, 77–80; of demand, 79–80, 120–22, 135; obliga-
  tions of, 73–74; of promise, 96, 126;
  rethinking of, 80–81; and state of
  Israel, 142; and suffering, 166 n.

Covenant (*cont.*)
20; theology of, 69; transformation
of, 78–80; as voluntary, 79–80. *See
also under* God; Israel; People of
God; Responsibility; Sinai
Cox, Harvey, 31
Creation, biblical understanding of,
131; and nonbeing, 52
Crisis, concept of, 65; Holocaust as,
65
Cross, the, 73, 99–104, 120; and dev-
ilishness, 99–100; and God, 101;
Godforsakenness and, 120, 123; and
Judaism, 129; smashing of, 134;
theology of, 97. *See also under* Cru-
cifixion
Crucifixion: of God, 95; and Jews, 87,
88, 96, 116–18, 129; as robbed of
redemptiveness, 101. *See also*
Cross; *and see under* Jesus;
Romans
Crusades, 57
Cynicism, 143

Darmstadt, 44
Davies, Alan T., 127
Dead, respect for, 98
Death, 19, 22, 28, 31, 57–58, 59, 71,
72, 75, 99, 100, 141, 150; conquest
of, 150, 167 n. 35; and Nazism, 56;
by stoning, 91
Deicide, 88
Democracy, and political power, 136–
37
Demonic, the, 48, 51, 55, 57, 101,
113, 135, 149, 156 n. 21
Denmark, 149
Deutsche Christen, Die, 91
Devil, 46, 57, 58, 80, 83–84, 101, 125,
136, 156 nn. 21, 24; agents of, 65; and
antisemitism, 50–57; and Christians,
54; concept of, 52–53; and God, 53,
58, 59, 123; and Jews, 52, 54, 55, 156
n. 24; and religion, 54
Dialogue: meaning of, 164 n. 58; and
mission, 87
Donat, Alexander, 68

Döpfner, Julius Cardinal, 39
Dresden, 34
Dutch Christians, 118–19

Eastern Europe, 147
East Germany, 38
Eckardt, A. Roy, and Resurrection,
167 n. 41
Ecumenical movement, Jews and,
164 n. 58
Eichmann, Adolf, 41, 56
Election, and church, 107; idea of,
84, 123. *See also under* Israel
Elijah, 60
Endlösung. See Final Solution; Holo-
caust
Eretz Yisrael, 135
Eschatology, 78, 109–10; and Chris-
tian revolutionary, 149–50. *See also
under* Hope
Evangelische Kirche in Deutschland
(EKD). *See* Protestant Church in
Germany
Evil, 41–42, 52–53, 62, 66, 71, 74, 80,
101, 140; absolute, 104. *See also
under* God; Man; Responsibility
Exodus, 45, 57, 140

Fackenheim, Emil L., 41–42, 55–56,
95, 112, 121, 123–25, 128, 146, 161
n. 6; 166 n. 28; on devil, 156 n. 21
Faith, 75, 76–77; and despair, 143–
44; and history, 112, 142; and Holocaust, 65, 67–71; against life, 68–
71. *See also under* Christian faith;
God; Jews; Political domain; Truth
Fate, 49, 75, 132. *See also under*
God; Responsibility
Final Solution, 18–22, 26, 140;
churches as potential targets of, 155
n. 5; and dating procedures, 45, 155
n. 13, 157 n. 31; and logic of antisemitism, 29. *See also* Holocaust
Flannery, Edward H., 99–100
Flusser, David, 162 n. 15, 167 n. 40
Forgiveness. *See under* God; Jesus;
Political domain

Frankl, Viktor, 74–75
Freedom, and Christians, 109–10; of God, 89, 121
Friedländer, Saul, 64
Friedman, Saul, 43
F.S., usage of, 45
Fundamentalism, 93; and historical-ness, 132; and Resurrection, 131, 132

Geistliche Endlösung, eine, 85
Genocide, 30, 44, 45, 46, 48, 61, 62, 71, 119, 145
Gentiles, 96, 102, 107; American, 113; and covenant, 119; and Jesus, 126. See also under Idolatry
German biblical scholarship, 129
"German Nazis," usage of phrase, 33
Germans, Germany, 21, 29–44 passim, 68–69, 82, 116, 147; and biblical scholarship, 92; Christians in, 69, 85, 86–87, 157 n. 38; and church, 86–87; and guilt, 32–33, 34, 36–37
God, 21, 46, 51, 52, 60, 61, 63, 65, 72, 80, 85, 97; absence/presence of, 160 n. 23; accounting from, 161 n. 28; as beyond reproach, 67; castigation of, 160 n. 20; compassion of, 80; concept of, 52; of covenant, 70; culpability of, 76–77; death of, 70, 98; deliverance of, 142–43; as de-manding, 66–67, 73; and evil, 58–59, 72, 73–74; faith in, 67, 76–77; faithfulness of, 97, 107, 112, 118–19, 122; fate of, 58; forgiveness of, 80, 94; grace of, 92–93, 96; guilt of, 59, 76; and history, 71, 76, 127; his-tory of, 65, 82, 98; and Holocaust, 57–60, 76–77; as human, 100; and human dignity, 76–77; image of, 76, 77, 137, 161 n. 28; Jewish doc-trine of, 136; and Jews, 48, 61, 69, 84, 101, 115, 125–26, 143, 150; judgment of, 78, 137; kingdom of, 110; love of, 60, 124; man's forgive-ness of, 77; mercy of, 138, 166 n.

28; and Messiah, 116; and murder, 67; name of, 91, 106, 133; and om-nipotence, 72, 73, 159 n. 14; and omniscience, 72; opposition to tra-ditional view of, 71–72; penitence of, 59–60, 79, 120, 122; proofs of, 51; providence of, 71; and punish-ment, 69–70; as redemptive, 72, 159 n. 5; and responsibility, 46–60 passim; revolt against, 85; and sad-ism, 69, 75; salvation of, 60, 125; si-lence of, 76; sin of, 106; and state of Israel, 142; and suffering, 66, 71, 76–77; suffering of, 72–73, 74, 106, 159 n. 14; sympathy of, 73–74; trial of, 58–60, 67, 122–23; trust in, 61, 72, 76; truth of, 87, 138; unforgiv-ability of, 76–77; victory of, 150; weeping of, 74; will of, 66–67, 69–70, 71, 80–81, 89, 120, 122, 129, 135. See also under Devil; Free-dom; Israel; Justice; Laughter; Man; Morality; People of God; Revelation
Godforsakenness, 95, 101, 103; and Holocaust, 127. See also under Cross; Jesus
Goebbels, Joseph, 56
Goes, Albrecht, 40
Gollwitzer, Helmut, 165 n. 7
"Gospel" and "law," 90–97 passim, 109
Gospels, 92, 131
Great Britain, and Jews, 157 n. 32
Greek thinking, 128, 130–31, 132
Greenberg, Irving, 79, 92, 101, 115, 127, 133–34, 138, 153 n. 23, 161 n. 27
Greenberg, Uri Zvi, 18, 139
Gross-Wannsee, conference at, 18
Grüber, Heinrich, 69, 70
Gruenagel, Friedrich, 83–86, 161 nn. 2, 4
Guilt, 27–40 passim, 51; and antisem-itism, 112–14; collective, 33, 35, 36–37; ontology of, 113. See also under Germans; God; Vicariousness

Guilt feelings, dissociation from, 112–14
Gypsies, 44

Haft, Cynthia, 20, 24, 153 n. 21
Haggadah, 60
Halakah, 91
Halle, Louis, 146, 169 n. 15
Hamburg Holocaust Conference, 29, 97
Hammerstein, Franz von, 37
Hasidim, Polish, 59
Heidelberg, 36
Heilsgeschichte, heilsgeschichtliche. *See* Salvation history
Heine, Heinrich, 84
Hell, 103, 127; and Holocaust, 128, 150
Heresy, 126
Hertzberg, Arthur, 55
Herzberg, Abel J., 33
"Hiding of the Face," 66, 160 n. 23
Hilberg, Raul, 152 n. 15
Hiroshima, 54
Historical criticism, 90
Historical events: discontinuity of, 44; faith and, 112; kinship of, 43–44
Historicalness: Christians and, 127–33; and Resurrection, 130–33. *See also under* Fundamentalism; Jewishness
Historiography, on Christian contribution to Holocaust, 112–13
History: fatefulness of, 122; and Holocaust, 82; in Jewish thought, 125, 127; nonrepeatability of, 46; theology of, 46–60 passim. *See also under* Christianity; Faith; God; Philosophy; Theology
Hitler, Adolf, 18–19, 28, 32, 56, 64, 67, 69, 70, 74, 100, 146–47, 152 n. 5, 155 n. 5; posthumous victory, 123, 124, 146, 159 n. 5
Hochhuth, Rolf, 58
Holland, Joseph, 155 n. 6
Holocaust: annihilation of, 79; attempt at Christianization of, 98–99; causes of, 64; Christian contribution to, 23, 49, 57, 60–65, 99–100, 102, 106, 112–13, 114, 133, 134, 139, 158 n. 40; as Christian event, 17, 62, 85–86, 140; and Christian teaching, 23, 111–12, 133; complicity in, 20, 33; components of, 145; concept of, 18–22; and demand for power, 134; denial of, 36, 55, 157 n. 27; denial of theological significance in, 127; dilemmas in studying, 22–26; as eschatological deed, 57; as fate, 49, 57; and impact on German theology, 88; Israeli commemoration of, 30; and Jesus, 158 n. 45; and Jewish dogma, 82; and Jewish theology, 70; and Jewish uniqueness, 49; and Jews, 17; and language, 141–42; liberation from complicity in, 110; as mystery, 66; as nonevent, 67, 82, 83–86; obscuring of, 41–42; as partial event, 82–83, 86–110; and the past, 49; as "perpetuating event," 85; pornography of, 28; problematic character of term, 152 n. 4; and psychiatric disorders, 31; repetition of, 123, 144–47, 149; resistance to, 21–22, 74, 141–42; and Resurrection, 130; as revolutionary event, 83, 140; significance of, 127; and surplus populations, 155 n, 6, 157 n. 32; survivors of, 20, 23, 24, 30, 31, 32, 41, 42; as theological event, 161 n. 6; transfiguration of, 109–10; as "trial," 58–60; typology of Christian responses to, 82–83; understanding of, 17–18, 153 n. 23; writing on, 153 n. 24. *See also* Final Solution; *see also under* Antisemitism; Christianity; Crisis; Faith; God; "Law"; Messiah; *Metanoia;* Mission to Jews; Political power; Responsibility; Revolution; Sin; state of Israel; Theology; Uniqueness
Holy Saturday, 150
Holy Spirit, 99, 109
Holy Week/Unholy Week, 115

Hope: authentic, 141; and Christian faith, 103, 107; and eschatology, 140, 149–50; for Israel, 97; and Jesus, 126; Jewish, 107, 159 n. 12; misguiding, 141. *See also under* Church; Kingdom of day; Man; Messianic hope; People of God; Resurrection; Theology

Hopelessness, 150. *See also under* Kingdom of night

Human dignity, 134. *See also under* God; Power

Humanism, and transcendence, 169 n. 8

Humanness, of evildoers, 113; and history, 127; meaning of, 35, 36; and responsibility, 51

Human rights, as nonabsolute, 135

Hunger, and Holocaust, 155 n. 6

Id, 28

Idealism, 140; and behavior, 118

Ideology, 102, 133; Christianity and, 50, 108–9, 111, 121, 130; concept of, 44. *See also under* Nazism

Idinopulos, Thomas A., 133, 167 n. 42

Idolatry, idols, 83, 94, 126, 148; of gentiles, 126; and theology, 133. *See also under* Jesus

Imperialism, Christian. *See* Supersessionism, Christian

"Inability to mourn," 32

Individual, alleged sovereignty of, 36–37

Inquisition, 57

Institute for Sociological Research (Cologne), 35

Intolerance, 126, 148

Isaac, 60, 77, 118

Isaac, Jules, 17, 162 n. 15

Islam, 45

Israel, 45, 69, 95, 96, 118, 121, 123, 126, 140; Christian solidarity with, 105; covenant with, 66, 116; deliverance of, 142; demands upon, 106; election of, 53, 70, 78, 79, 84, 97, 118; and God, 143, 150, 161 n. 9; as

hope of church, 107; Paul and, 107; purifying of, 67. *See also under* Church; Messianic hope; People of God; Suffering

Israelis, 84–85, 156 n. 20; rights of, 149

Israel, state of, 30, 37, 106, 111, 135, 159 n. 12, 169 n. 8; and future Holocaust, 145–47; and Holocaust, 142, 143; Jews of, 114; meaning of, 135; as resistance, 142; threat to, 144; West German policy to, 38–39. *See also under* Covenant; God

Jacob, 60, 118

Jerusalem, 77, 81, 104, 114

Jesus, 17, 120; condemnation of, 90; crucifixion of, 35, 45, 84, 87, 88–89, 99–104, 116–18, 123, 127; and forgiveness, 89, 90, 93; and Godforsakenness, 103–4, 142, 168 n. 44; and idolatry, 126; Jewishness of, 64, 89–90, 94, 102–3; and Judaism, 89, 116–17, 162 n. 15; and "the law," 88–92, 96; and Pharisees, 89–90; rejection of, 88; as second Abraham, 126; trial of, 88–89, 90, 116–17, 162, 162 n. 18. *See also under* Gentiles; Jews; Messiah; Resurrection

Jewish Christianity, 102, 125, 167 n. 30

Jewish historicalness, 125; and Christians, 126

Jewish law, 90; and Jesus, 116

Jewishness: and historicalness, 125, 130–33; and Resurrection, 128–29. *See also under* Christian faith; Christians

Jewish theology, and Holocaust, 70

Jews, Jewish people, 46, 70, 86, 87, 95, 101; accusations against, 85, 115–18; and blame for antisemitism, 63–64, 84–85; calling of, 106; and the Christ, 63, 106–7; and conscience, 28; crimes against, 83; of death camps, 101; demands upon, 106, 120–22, 166 nn. 20, 22; deportations of, 151 n. 1; of Europe, 19,

Jews (*cont.*)
20, 30, 33, 44, 70–71, 86, 134, 152
n. 5, 157 n. 32; extinction of, 67,
69; and faith, 67, 96; forsakenness
of, 102; freedom of, 71; future of,
108; gaining of power by, 135; as
incarnation of Torah, 124; and Jesus, 88–89, 108, 115–18; justice for,
132; and "the law," 84; and legalism, 91–92; mission to, 85, 86–87,
96, 118; mission to, and Holocaust,
85; persecution of, 47–48, 51, 55,
61, 62, 98, 114, 117; and powerlessness, 125, 134; and readiness to
suffer, 120; and responsibility, 73;
in Soviet Union, 145, 147; and suffering, 19–20, 28, 33, 42, 44, 59, 63,
67, 69–70, 77, 78, 79, 100, 106, 120,
121–22, 166 n. 20; threat to, 147;
uniqueness of, and Holocaust, 49;
in United States, 113; as victims,
52. *See also under* Christianity;
Crucifixion; Devil; Election; God;
Holocaust; Judaism; Martyrdom;
Particularism
Job, Book of, 123
John, Gospel of, 54, 93; defamation of
Jews in, 117
John XXIII, pope, 84, 119
Jonas, Hans, 159 n. 14
Judaism, 63, 67, 84, 92–95, 95–96, 97,
98, 106, 127; integrity of, 86; and
justice, 94; misrepresentation of,
93. *See also under* Christianity;
God; History; Holocaust; Jesus;
Jews; Messiah; Paul; Perfection
Judaizers, 125
Judenfeindschaft. See Antisemitism
Judenmission. See Mission to Jews
Justice, 137, 149; and Christianity,
94; and compromise, 137; of God,
123; and international affairs, 137.
See also under Jews; Judaism

Kant, Immanuel, 152 n. 19
Kee, Alistair, 133
Keene, Calvin, 135–36

Kemény, György, 144
Keynes, John Maynard, 147
Kiddush ha-Haim, 80
Kiddush ha-Shem, 80. *See also* Sanc-
tification of Name of God
Kingdom of day: and children, 141;
and hope, 140; and humanization,
141; and political power, 141; resis-
tance and, 145
Kingdom of night: and goodness, 140;
and hopelessness, 140; reappear-
ance of, 144–47. *See also under*
Torah
Klein, Charlotte, 88
Klein, Hilel, 31
Kolitz, Zvi, 75
Kovner, Abba, 19–20, 32, 149
Kremers, Heinz, 115–16, 119, 127
Kreyssig, Lothar, 37
Küng, Hans, 164 n. 62

Langer, Lawrence L., 25, 27, 28
Laughter, 78; of God, 146
Lauridsen, Finn Henning, 149
"Law, the," and Holocaust, 91–92.
See also under Jesus; Jews; Pan-
nenberg
"Law" and "gospel," 90–97 passim,
109
Lelyveld, Arthur J., 73–74
Levin, Nora, 161 n. 28
Levinsohn, H. Peter, 120
Liberation: of Christians, 83, 108–10;
and church, 95; from complicity in
Holocaust, 110; meaning of, 83. *See
also under* Torah
Life, and death, 72; meaning of, 76,
80–81; meaning of, and suffering,
74–75; sanctification of, 80; sanc-
tity of Jewish, 124. *See also under*
Faith; Love
Lind, Jakov, 68
Lindsey, Robert L., 167 n. 40
Littell, Franklin H., 61–62, 85–86
Love, 150; and fulfilled life, 166 n.
23. *See also under* God
Lovsky, Fadiey, 136

Luke, Gospel of, 167 n. 40; and Resurrection, 131–32
Lutheran thought, 93
Lutheran World Federation, and problem of mission, 162 n. 11
Luther, Martin, 93, 109, 138

Maimonides, Moses, 166 n. 24
Malik, Yakov, 156 n. 20
Man: biblical view of, 131; forgiveness of God by, 76–77; hope for, 160 n. 23; innocence of, 76, 160 n. 23; as partner of God, 73–74; redemption of, 73; and responsibility, 75; as responsible for evil, 58; as superior to God, 75. See also under Christianity
Manicheanism, 128
Mann, Golo, 30
Marie-Thérèse de Sion, 113
Mark, Gospel of, 131
Martyrdom, martyrs, 21, 77; Jewish, 120, 121, 124–25, 163 n. 32, 166 n. 24
Marx, Karl, 44
Matthew, Gospel of, 147–48
Maybaum, Ignaz, 118
Mayer, Reinhold, 119
Meaning of life, 66, 76, 80–81, 126; and power, 136; and suffering, 74–75
Megged, Aharon, 144
Messiah, 62, 68, 74; Christ and, 107; false, 91; and Holocaust, 116; Jesus and, 62, 91, 109–10, 116; Jewish teaching of, 116. See also under God
Messianic hope, 105, 166 n. 28; and body, 131; and Israel, 169 n. 8
Messianism, 63, 91; false, 109–10
Metanoia: and Christians, 109, 112, 140, 167 n. 42; Holocaust as, 65, 83, 109
Middle East conflict, West Germany and, 39
Mission to Jews, 85, 86–87, 96, 118, 164 n. 58, 165 n. 15; and Holocaust, 85, 119; opposition to, 118–19; and pacifism, 135
Mitscherlich, Alexander and Margarete, 32
Moltmann, Jürgen, 29, 32, 87–110, 120, 127, 168 n. 44; and hopelessness, 102, 109–10; and ideology, 92, 94; influence of Holocaust on, 88; triumphalism in, 164 n. 58
Morality: and deeds, 38–39; and divine norms, 70; double standard in, 135–36; and God, 122; and government, 38–39; Jewish and Christian, 112; of nations, 39; as one with theology, 79–80. See also under Political power; Responsibility
Morgenthau, Hans J., 169 n. 15
Moses, 170 n. 24
Muhammad, 45

Nachman of Bratzlav, 78
Nagasaki, 54
Nash, Arnold, 138
National Socialism. See Nazism, Nazis
Nazism, Nazis, 17–24 passim, 28, 30, 32, 35, 36, 41–42, 44, 47, 57, 64, 65, 66, 69, 84, 91, 94, 99, 119, 134, 145, 148, 151 n. 1, 152 nn. 6, 12, 155 nn. 5, 14; and Christianity, 63, 114; and devil, 81; dualistic system of, 44; ideology of, 44; meaning of, 56; reincarnations of, 157 n. 27; resistance to, 36, 68–69; and war effort, 56
Neo-Nazism, 35
Neven-du Mont, Jürgen, 36
New Testament, 90, 92; and antisemitism, 114, 117, 156 n. 21, 165 n. 7; contemporary scholarship of, 89–91; and historical truth, 117; speciousness in, 116–17; theology of, 88; and Word of God, 114. See also under Christianity
Niebuhr, Reinhold, 35, 39, 49, 81, 101–2, 168 n. 54, 169 n. 15; on democracy, 137; on political power, 136; on sin, 168 n. 50

Noumenal truth, 24, 26, 152 n. 19
Nuclear deterrent, 146–47
Nuclear weapons, 146; and peace, 146, 169 n. 15

Objectivity, problem of, 22–24
Orpaz, Yizhak, 143
Ozick, Cynthia, 25

Pacifism, 136
Paganism, pagans, 58, 63, 64, 85–86, 126
Pannenberg, Wolfhart, 129–30; and Christian predicament, 130, 164 n. 62; and Judaism, 129; "the law" in, 129, 164 n. 62; and Resurrection, 129, 131, 132–33
Parkes, James, 92, 112, 115; on devil, 156 n. 21
Particularism: and Jews, 98; and universalism, 42–43, 52, 127
Passion story, and antisemitism, 115–16
Past, alienation from, 31; freedom from, 82; slavery to, 109
Pathology, Christian, 113–14
Pauck, Wilhelm, 93
Paul, Apostle, 84, 93, 97, 107, 109, 126, 128, 149; on Judaism, 164 n. 57; and Resurrection, 131
Pawlikowski, John, 62; on Eckardt and devil, 156 n. 21
Peck, William Jay, 67, 139
Peli, Pinchas, 135
Penitence, 32. See also under God
People of God, 58, 59, 66–67, 70, 86, 123; and Christians, 140; and hope, 140, 140–47; Israel as, 121; and political power, 133–38; and suffering, 67, 69. See also under Suffering
Perfection: and Judaism, 63, 64; of world, 73
Perfectionism, 121, 136, 140
Pfisterer, Rudolf, 85
Pfrondorf, West Germany, 34
Pharisees, and Jesus, 89–90
"Phenomenal," usage of term, 26

Philosophy: of history, 45–57 passim; task of, 58
Polish, David, 52, 169 n. 8
Political domain: and compromise, 138; and faith, 137–38; and forgiveness, 138, 168 n. 54; indispensableness of, 112; and religion, 135. See also under Kingdom of day; Theology
Political power: and Holocaust, 134; and human dignity, 134; and international justice, 137; morality of, 133–38, 142; need for, 142; temptations of, 136. See also Democracy; Kingdom of day; People of God; Niebuhr; Theology
Pontius Pilate, 89
Post-Christian era, 147
Post-concentration-camp syndrome, 32
Post-Holocaust theology, 80–81, 98–99, 104, 108; and "blasphemy," 122
Pre-Holocaust theology, 104, 108
Prejudice, and historical analysis, 117
Protestant Church in Germany, 119; Council of, 86–87
Protestantism, 93
Providence, 71; forms of, 74

"Race of the dead," 19
Racism, 46, 56, 84–85; American, 113
Rakover, Yossel, 75
"Realized eschatology," repudiation of, 109
Redemption, 73, 95, 131, 150; future, 95; lack of, 95, 101; of world, 95. See also under God; Man
Red Sea, 123
Reductionism, 125–26
Reformed Church of Holland, General Synod of, 118
Relativization, of Christian faith, 109, 126, 148; need for, 97
Religion: pluralism in, 147; and secularity, 80. See also under Devil; Political domain
Rendtorff, Rolf, 119, 157 n. 38

Responsibility, 143; ambiguity in term, 33–34; to covenant, 74; for evil, 76, 136; and fate, 46; and German people, 36–37; for Holocaust, 65; Jewish, 73; moral, 27–40 passim, 58–59, 75, 134, 160 n. 23; and shame, 37; and sin, 137–38. *See also under* God; Humanness; Man

Resurrection, 68; future, 150, 170 n. 24; hope of, 95

Resurrection of Jesus, 45, 62, 87, 93, 100, 102, 125–33, 150, 167 nn. 37, 41; centrality of, 128; controversy over, 125–33; and Crucifixion, 128; demythologizing of, 131; as future, 102, 150, 170 n. 24; and Holocaust, 128, 130; and hostility to Jews and Judaism, 130. *See also under* Fundamentalism; Historicalness; Jewishness; Pannenberg; Paul

Revelation, 57, 79–80

Revolution, in Christian theology and behavior, 114, 115–50; moral-theological, 111. *See also under* Church

"Righteous of the Nations," 143

Robinson, Jacob, 23

Romans, 116–17, 129; and Crucifixion, 87, 88

Roosevelt, Franklin D., 33

Rosenzweig, Franz, 105, 107, 126

Rotenstreich, Nathan, 29

Rubenstein, Richard L., 68–71, 134, 155 n. 6, 157 n. 32, 159 n. 12, 166 n. 24

Ruether, Rosemary, 109–10, 113, 131, 133, 156 n. 21, 167 n. 42

Russians, as partisans, 21; as prisoners of war, 42; and propaganda, 50

Sadducees, 90

Salvation, 127; and church, 167 n. 42. *See also under* God

Salvation history, 45, 119

Sanctification of Name of God, 106, 121, 125, 166 n. 24

Sanders, E. P., 164 n. 57

Sanders, Wilm, 157 n. 38

Sanhedrin, 89, 90

Schmidt, Helmut, 30, 38–39

Schindler, Pesach, 166 n. 26

Scholder, Klaus, 44

Schorsch, Ismar, 64

Secularity. *See under* Religion; Theology

Secularization, 147

Sermon on the Mount, 89

Shapiro, Israel, 67

Sherman, Franklin, 72–73

Silverman, David Wolf, 142

Simon, Ulrich E., 76, 117, 128, 150, 167 n. 35

Sin, 44, 48, 58, 67, 97, 136, 137, 168 n. 50; and Holocaust, 44, 136; of Jews, 84; solidarity in, 114. *See also under* Church; God; Responsibility

Sinai, 45, 57, 63, 77, 123, 140; covenant of, 127

Soetendorp, Avraham, 170 n. 22

Sonderbehandlung, 145

Soviet Union, 146, 156 n. 20; Jews in, 145, 147; and United States, 169 n. 15

Sperber, Manès, 141, 158 n. 40, 166 n. 20

Steiner, George, 63, 64

Steiner, Jean-François, 152 n. 12

Stendahl, Krister, 93, 163 n. 27

Strasbourg, 148

Suffering, 41, 59, 60, 77–78, 101, 104; continuity and discontinuity in, 41–43; of innocent, 160 n. 23; of Israel, 95; and sympathy, 42–43. *See also under* God; Jews; Life; Meaning of life; Theology

"Suffering servant syndrome," 120, 122

Superego, 28

Supersessionism, Christian, 61–62, 115, 118, 119, 120; definition of, 118; condemnation of, 105

Survivors of Holocaust, 20, 23, 24, 30, 31, 32, 41, 42–43

Swastika, and cross, 99–100

Syrian army, 146

Talmud, 77
"Teaching of contempt," 17
Terezín, 140, 150
Theodicy, 66, 72
Theologizing of politics, contra theology of politics, 135
Theology: in Germany, 92–93; and history, 92; of history, 46–60 passim; and Holocaust, 111–12; of Holocaust, 57–60, 66; of hope, 109–10; humanization of, 110; need for reconstruction of, 120; of politics, 39, 133, 134–35; of politics, meaning of term, 133; possibility of, 95; and secularity, 122; of suffering, 80; of victimization, 125. See also under Covenant; Cross; Morality; Post-Holocaust theology; Pre-Holocaust theology; Revolution; Supersessionism
Theresienstadt. See Terezín
Third World, Christians in, 114
Time, sense of, 31
Torah, 45, 77, 78, 89, 96, 105; as embodied in Jewish people, 124; and kingdom of night, 78–80; as liberation, 93
Treblinka, 19, 21, 67, 140, 142, 152 n. 12
Trinity, 127
Triumphalism, Christian, 83, 95–99, 105, 106–10, 119, 127, 130, 131, 132–33, 148; Christian, end of, 105; in guise of antitriumphalism, 96–99; opposition to, 73; "postponed," 107–8
Truth, 96, 102, 112, 118, 126; and faith, 87; and goodness, 24, 122–23. See also under Church; God
Tuchin (Tuczyn), 21

Ukraine, Ukrainians, 21
Unbewältigte Vergangenheit, eine, 32, 83
Unforgivability. See under God
Uniqueness, of Christ-event, 96; of Holocaust, 22, 41–65, 66, 79; types

of, 43–45. See also under Antisemitism
United Nations, as center of antisemitism, 50, 156 n. 20
United States, 146; and immigration of Jews, 33; and Soviet Union, 169 n. 15
Universalism, Christian, 97. See also under Particularism
Untermensch, Untermenschen, 19, 22
Utopianism, 143, 150

Van Buren, Paul M., 62, 111–12, 121, 130–31, 167 n. 37
Vatican Council II, 84, 161 n. 2
Vicariousness, and guilt, 37
Vietnam, Vietnamese, 42–43
Vilna Ghetto, 19–20, 140

Ward, Roy Bowen, 133, 167 n. 42
Warsaw Ghetto, 21, 141
Weintraub, Sholom, 68
West Germany, 27–40 passim; antisemitism in, 35; neo-Nazism in, 35. See also under Israel, state of
White, John Carroll, 167 n. 41
Wiedergutmachung, 38
Wiesel, Elie, 17, 20, 28, 45, 60, 66, 77, 78, 81, 98, 144–45, 146, 151 n. 1, 160 n. 20; and question of God, 159 n. 1
World, dedivinizing of, 94; unredeemedness of, 116
World Council of Churches, Consultation on Church and Jewish People, 114, 164 n. 58
World War I, 64
World War II, 34
Wyschogrod, Michael, 159 n. 5

Yad Vashem, 21, 29, 40, 143; meaning of phrase, 152 n. 10
Yom Kippur War, 144, 156 n. 20

Zeffirelli, Franco, 116
Zeroniski, Stefan, 139
Zimmels, H. J., 47

Singly and together, A. Roy Eckardt and Alice L. Eckardt have lectured and published extensively in Holocaust studies and on the subject of relations between Christians and Jews. A. Roy Eckardt has been a Ford fellow at Harvard University, Lilly fellow at the University of Cambridge, and editor-in-chief of the *Journal of the American Academy of Religion*. The present volume results from his appointment as a Rockefeller Foundation humanities fellow at the University of Tübingen and the Hebrew University. Alice L. Eckardt teaches in Holocaust studies and Christian-Jewish relations, and has served as chairperson of the Israel Study Group. The Eckardts currently are members of the Department of Religion Studies at Lehigh University. Among their important earlier books are A. Roy Eckardt, *Elder and Younger Brothers* (1967) and *Your People, My People* (1974); Alice L. Eckardt and A. Roy Eckardt, *Encounter with Israel* (1970).

The manuscript was edited by Sherwyn T. Carr. The book was designed by Mary Primeau. The typeface for the text is Caledonia, based on a design by W. A. Dwiggins in 1938. The display face is Caledonia.

The text is printed on 60 lb. Worthington Natural text paper and the book is bound in Holliston Mills' Roxite cloth over binder's boards.

Manufactured in the United States of America.

WESTMAR COLLEGE LIBRARY